Confederate Slave Impressment in the Upper South

Civil War America

*Gary W. Gallagher, Peter S. Carmichael, Caroline E. Janney,
and Aaron Sheehan-Dean, editors*

CONFEDERATE SLAVE IMPRESSMENT
in the Upper South

JAIME AMANDA MARTINEZ

The University of North Carolina Press
CHAPEL HILL

© 2013 The University of North Carolina Press
All rights reserved
Set in Miller by codeMantra
Manufactured in the United States of America

The paper in this book meets the guidelines for permanence and durability of the Committee on Production Guidelines for Book Longevity of the Council on Library Resources. The University of North Carolina Press has been a member of the Green Press Initiative since 2003.

Library of Congress Cataloging-in-Publication Data
Martinez, Jaime Amanda.
Confederate slave impressment in the
upper South / Jaime Amanda Martinez.
  pages cm. — (Civil War America)
Includes bibliographical references and index.
ISBN 978-1-4696-1074-0 (cloth : alk. paper)
ISBN 978-1-4696-2648-2 (pbk.: alk. paper)
1. Slavery—Confederate States of America. 2. United States—History—Civil War, 1861–1865—African Americans. 3. War and society—Confederate States of America. 4. Confederate States of America—Race relations. I. Title.
E453.M263 2013
973.7′415—dc23
2013021361

THIS BOOK WAS DIGITALLY PRINTED.

for my mom, with love and gratitude

Contents

INTRODUCTION / Cornerstones and Construction Workers, 1
Slave Labor and the Confederate War Effort

1 / Hundreds Have Been Called, 18
Slave Impressment at the Local and State Levels, 1861–1863

2 / Throwing Up Breastworks, 45
Slave Laborers under the Engineer Bureau

3 / Provisions Are Needed Worse Than Fortifications, 71
Slave Impressment and Confederate Agriculture

4 / To Equalize the Burden, 98
Slave Impressment and the Expanding Confederate State, 1863–1864

5 / The President's Mishap, 132
From Engineer Laborers to Potential Confederate Soldiers, 1864–1865

EPILOGUE / Black Confederates?, 159
Slave Impressment and Confederate Memory

APPENDIX / Tables, 165
Notes, 187
Bibliography, 213
Acknowledgments, 226
Index, 229

Figures, Maps, and Tables

FIGURES

1.1. Slaves building fortifications, January 31, 1863, 22
2.1. Layout of ditch from Mahan's *Treatise on Field Fortification*, 1846, 48
2.2. Slaves building fortifications, April 18, 1863, 49
2.3. Chaffin's Bluff fortifications, 54
2.4. Slaves in Engineer Hospital, June–December 1862, 61
3.1. Confederate fortifications at Drewry's Bluff, December 13, 1862, 74
3.2. Wilmington coastline and Fort Fisher, April 2, 1864, 80
4.1. Map of Richmond fortifications, 1863, 104
4.2. Albemarle County impressment quotas, 119
4.3. Map of Wilmington fortifications, including U.S. plan of attack, 1865, 124
5.1. Plan and sections of Fort Fisher, 1865, 140
5.2. Petersburg fortifications, 151

MAPS

1. Primary points of fortification, 8
2. Virginia counties, 1860, 36
3. North Carolina counties, 1860, 42
4. Responses to January 1864 call in Virginia, 113

TABLES

1.1. First Call for Slaves to Work on Fortifications in Virginia, October 1862, 165

1.2. Second Call for Slaves to Work on Fortifications in Virginia, November 1862, 166

1.3. Third Call for Slaves to Work on Fortifications in Virginia, January 1863, 167

1.4. Call for Slaves to Work on Fortifications in North Carolina, March 1863, 168

3.1. Fourth Call for Slaves to Work on Fortifications in Virginia, March 1863, 169

3.2. French's Report of Virginia Slaves Impressed Prior to March 1863, 170

3.3. Calls for Slaves to Work on Fortifications in North Carolina (Estimated), March–April 1863, 171

4.1. Fifth Call for Slaves to Work on Fortifications in Virginia, August 1863, 172

4.2. Calls for Slaves to Work on Fortifications in North Carolina (Estimated), August–October 1863, 173

4.3. Sixth Call for Slaves to Work on Fortifications in Virginia, January 1864, 174

5.1. Virginia Slaves Impressed by Enrolling Office, September 1864, 176

5.2. Slaves Impressed for Fortifications at Weldon, North Carolina, October and December 1864, 178

5.3. Seventh Call for Slaves to Work on Fortifications in Virginia, December 1864, 180

5.4. Eighth Call for Slaves to Work on Fortifications in Virginia, March 1865, 182

5.5. Auditor's Statement of Black Men, 18–45, Fit for Service in Virginia, March 1865, 184

Confederate Slave Impressment
in the Upper South

INTRODUCTION

Cornerstones and Construction Workers

Slave Labor and the Confederate War Effort

"We have nothing to fear from any action of our slaves in this crisis," intoned the editor of the *Richmond Whig* in February 1864. Instead, he proposed, Confederate fiscal and impressment policies had steadily undermined the institution of slavery, the Confederacy's "sheet anchor" in its struggle for independence. While inflation had devalued slave property and government seizure of grains and livestock made it difficult to feed large slave populations, the paper focused much of its ire on government requisitions for slave labor. By impressing slaves, he suggested, the Confederate and state governments had forced each slaveholder to calculate "the value of his slaves, and in some instances [he] is ready to discard them as burdensome to him. Slavery will nowhere exist where it proves unprofitable."[1]

This bombast masked a well-known reality: slaves were running away from their owners, often in large numbers, especially in Virginia. Rather than slaveholders calculating the costs and benefits of slavery with an eye toward discarding the institution, slaves themselves were making daily decisions about how and under what circumstances to resist and perhaps even escape. The purpose of this particular editorial, however, was not to explore the process of wartime emancipation but rather to excoriate the practice of slave impressment by both state and national officials. From the perspective of at least some slaveholders, the government they had founded to protect their interests had become the primary threat.

Through impressment, white Virginians and North Carolinians temporarily surrendered control over portions of their slave populations to state authorities, military officials, and finally the national government in order to prosecute their war for Confederate independence. In one of the most ironic developments of the war, Confederate citizens who had emphatically rejected the United States government's attempts to interfere with the institution of slavery came, reluctantly, to accept that interference from their new government. In part, this acceptance reflected their confidence that no Confederate officials secretly harbored abolitionist tendencies, although, as the *Richmond Whig* noted, their actions did ultimately hasten emancipation. But the dire necessity of war encouraged voters, elected officials, and state governments to give the Confederate government more latitude to enact policies regarding slavery than the U.S. government had boasted. This latitude was not unlimited, however, and slaveholders would raise numerous objections to the practice of slave impressment.

Slaveholders, fearing that the government's seizure of slaves for military work would leave them without sufficient laborers, objected to slave impressment for both practical and ideological reasons. Many questioned the right of state and national officials to impress all forms of property, not just slaves. Yet despite any furor over slave impressment, winning the war was the primary aim of most white North Carolinians and Virginians, and thousands of slaveholders in both states quietly—no doubt begrudgingly—acquiesced in recurring requisitions for slave labor, thus demonstrating their continuing support of the Confederate war. More important, the high level of cooperation between local, state, and national government officials that slave impressment required suggests that the existence of powerful governors, state legislatures, and county court officers strengthened, rather than undermined, the Confederate nation. By 1864, in fact, the governors of Virginia and North Carolina responded to complaints from their constituents not by obstructing Confederate requisitions for slave labor but instead by supporting a more intrusive national impressment plan. These observations fly in the face of much popular and historical orthodoxy about the nature and success of Confederate governance.

Academic and popular histories have long suggested that the Confederacy collapsed due to some internal failure. Many, taking their cue from President Jefferson Davis's suggestion that the Confederacy "died of a theory"—that theory being states' rights—have emphasized the ways that state governments resisted central authority and thus undermined the war effort.² In some iterations of this argument, Governor Zebulon Baird Vance of North Carolina has come under particularly harsh criticism, although recent biographies by Gordon McKinney and Joe Mobley have correctly emphasized the many actions Vance took in support of the Confederate war and government.³ This included working to make slave impressment a success. Other scholars have emphasized class conflict, offering more sophisticated versions of the popular refrain that the Confederate experience was "a rich man's war but a poor man's fight." In his most recent study, for example, Paul Escott indicts the slaveholding elite for placing the well-being of their plantations above the success of their new country and further indicates that the broad mass of the nonslaveholding population lost faith in the Confederacy when poverty became a greater threat than the U.S. armies.⁴

The states' rights and class conflict theses both begin with the assumption that residents of the Confederacy lacked a unified sense of national purpose. Some, like Escott, suggest that the planter class was ultimately motivated by self-interest rather than by national identity and therefore deserted the Confederacy when maintaining national identity would have required more economic sacrifices than they were willing to make.⁵ More often, historians have asserted that those outside the circles of political and economic power in the slaveholding South were the residents least likely to hold strong attachments to the Confederacy. William W. Freehling, for example, places great emphasis on the populations of the border states, as well as on slaves and Unionists within the Confederacy, suggesting that the new nation could have won its independence if all these parties had supported it.⁶ The most recent contribution to this school of argument is Stephanie McCurry's *Confederate Reckoning*. McCurry proposes that resistance on the part of white women—by definition a disenfranchised population—both challenged and reshaped the Confederate government but did not ultimately bear sole responsibility for its defeat. She also argues that resistance to impressment on the part of both slaves and planters doomed the policy at all stages of its development, irrevocably harming the Confederate war effort.⁷

McCurry is not the first historian to pronounce impressment policy a dismal failure.⁸ While her work contains more details about the process of impressment than do earlier treatments of the subject, she ultimately repeats many of their assumptions, taking the complaints of planters and lamentations of government officials at face value. It is hardly surprising that slaveholders and slaves would object to impressment, or that government officials and newspaper editors would thunder against that resistance. What is surprising is that slave impressment was often successful. That success was never perfect, but it was probably more complete than many scholars of the Confederacy have suggested. In Virginia, for example, state-directed requisitions between 1862 and 1865 garnered nearly 29,300 laborers out of the 35,000 called for two-month terms of service on the fortifications. In addition, hundreds of slaves served under ad hoc requisitions during the first year of the war, especially in the southeastern portion of the state, while several thousand were impressed by the Conscript Bureau in the fall of 1864.

Examining the step-by-step process of slave impressment in Virginia and North Carolina—its progress from localized ad hoc requisitions by individual commanders, to statewide requisitions for thousands of workers under state law, to a cooperative venture between state and national legislators, and finally to a fully nationalized call for 20,000 laborers in the fall of 1864—demonstrates that while planters and slaves regularly resisted impressment, they could not prevent it from happening and often could not completely avoid participation. If self-interested slaveholders did not entirely derail slave impressment, perhaps blaming them for Confederate defeat more generally may be unrealistic. After all, even the heavily fortified town of Wilmington eventually surrendered to a large and well-trained Union army. When they worked together, Confederate and state government officials had the power to overcome planter resistance, putting vast numbers of slaves to work for the Confederate war effort.

An unpopular program that state governments enacted for the benefit of the nation, slave impressment demonstrated the efficacy of federalism in the Confederate state. From the very beginning of its existence, the Confederacy placed great powers in the hands of local and state governments. The preamble to the Confederate constitution insisted that the new nation remained a collection of strong states, each "acting in its sovereign and independent character, in order to form a permanent federal government." While "sovereign and independent," though, the states did not have unlimited powers. Ultimately, Confederate framers recognized that the central government would need to exercise some control, and so Article IV insisted that "this Constitution, and the laws of the Confederate States made in pursuance thereof, and all treaties made, or which shall be made, under the authority of the Confederate States, shall be the supreme law of the land." The mere fact that the members of the Confederate provisional Congress chose to model their new state after the 1787 Constitution—rather than on the Articles of Confederation—indicates that they envisioned a stronger central government than their preamble suggested.[9]

The exact nature of the relationship between state and national governments, however, was something at which the constitution only hinted. In reality, the federal nature of the Confederate state was always in flux and firmly connected to the difficulties of fighting a long and complex war for independence. In general, states took the lead on most questions, but policies and actions became more centralized over time. This was certainly the case with slave impressment. The officers seeking slave laborers early in the war came from both state and national engineering departments, but eventually most fortifications came under national control. In a similar vein, some states passed comprehensive slave impressment legislation before the Confederate Congress did so. After 1863, with a few exceptions, the legislative and practical steps associated with impressing slave laborers became increasingly centralized. This process did not move in a single direction, however, and the governors retained significant powers—powers they used, for the most part, to increase the capacity of the Confederate armies to protect their new country. Local, state, and national leaders had to sort out their relationship on a daily basis, and enforcing slave impressment on a reluctant population was one of the ways they proceeded to do so.

In terms of both the sheer number of slaves and the proportion of the state's slave population put to work for the Confederate War Department, Virginia was the state with the most successful combination of impressment and government hiring. The city of Lynchburg, for example, sent approximately 350 slaves to meet state requisitions for labor over the course of the war. More significant, nearly 500 of the city's slaves worked for the Confederate Medical Department or other military employers, while another 300 were hired by private employers serving the needs of the Confederate army, including the Virginia and Tennessee Railroad. Although far from perfect, Virginia's successes at marshaling slave labor for the war effort turned the Old Dominion's impressment legislation into a model for other states and the national government. While effective, slave impressment was still unpopular, and the increasing reluctance of local officials in Virginia to comply with labor requisitions during the last two years of the war demonstrates a fairly common pattern in other states with slave impressment laws, most notably Mississippi.

In other ways, North Carolina's experience with slave impressment was more typical. The smaller proportion of its adult male slave population usually involved—10 percent—was more common in the other states than was Virginia's 20 or 25 percent, although North Carolina had unusually high rates of compliance because its pro-impressment governor used armed militia officers, rather than county courts, to enforce each requisition. But once the Conscript Bureau assumed responsibility for slave impressment in the late summer of 1864, North Carolina and most of the other states encountered the same basic process for enforcing requisitions, one that largely bypassed state and local elected officials. Only in Virginia did the governor remain actively involved in slave impressment even after this point. In most aspects of slave impressment, then, North Carolina provides scholars with a reliable model for almost all the Confederate states, while Virginia serves as an illuminating aberration. While it would be wonderful to see additional state studies in the future, starting with Virginia and North Carolina lays a crucial foundation. Widely recognized as two states of great importance to the Confederate war effort— contemporary observers and scholars alike noting their large free and slave populations, heavy production of crucial grain crops, and successful industrial operations—it is perhaps fair to say that if slave impressment had not worked in Virginia and North Carolina, its success in the other states would have been of little value. Indeed, the early and imperfect successes of state-directed slave impressment in these two states probably helped ease the path toward national legislation.

The success of slave impressment in Virginia prompted another set of national laws with more lasting implications—the U.S. Congress's Confiscation Acts and, eventually, emancipation. Major General John Bankhead Magruder's heavy use of slave labor to build fortifications southeast of Richmond helped slow the Union Army of the Potomac's advance toward the Confederate capital in the spring and summer of 1862. As Glenn David Brasher demonstrates in *The Peninsula Campaign and the Necessity of Emancipation*, many Union soldiers and commanders were frustrated that the Confederate army had such a large and effective pool of labor and wished to turn Virginia's black population into an asset for the Union. Slaves who escaped from Confederate fortifications, meanwhile, provided valuable information to Union officers. When the Army of the Potomac failed to capture Richmond, President Lincoln and many military and government officials came to the conclusion that emancipation was a military necessity—a conclusion impelled largely by the efficacy of local slave impressments in southeastern Virginia.[10]

Understanding the full story of slave impressment in Virginia and North Carolina also reiterates the importance of slavery to the Upper South. Over the decades, some scholars have suggested that the Upper South's slower progress toward secession reflected a weaker commitment to the preservation of slavery.[11] Even the Fire-eaters of the Lower South feared this might be the case. Yet the history of slave impressment in these two states tells a very different story. Planters' intransigence when confronted with labor requisitions, their insistence that each slave was crucial to agricultural production, and the wide variety of industrial operations employing slaves in support of the war effort all demonstrated the continuing salience of slavery in the Upper South's economy.

As with many aspects of the Confederate war effort, states took the first steps by enacting clear policies on slave impressment. The Virginia General Assembly did not approve its first official legislation to impress slave labor until October 3, 1862, but slaves were already an integral component of the engineer labor pool from the very beginning of the war. Indeed, a bewildering array of officials borrowed, hired, and impressed slaves to perform manual labor for the armies, particularly in coastal and tidewater areas. The inability of the local labor supply to meet this demand was one factor leading to the General Assembly's legislative action. The North Carolina state legislature enacted its own impressment legislation a few months later. The series of impressment laws that followed in both states, and eventually from the Confederate Congress, would attempt to draw labor from an ever-widening geographic area as well as, in some cases, to improve the conditions under which those slaves worked. Slave impressment would not have been possible without the cooperation of civilian officials at every level of government throughout the Confederacy.

The vast majority of impressed slaves served their terms of employment with the Engineer Bureau, digging defensive trenches outside key cities and along important transportation routes. In its early days, the Engineer Bureau relied heavily on state engineer forces and individual Confederate commands. Virginia state engineers began designing and erecting fortifications in the southeastern portion of the state at Gloucester Point, Yorktown, and Williamsburg in April 1861. Virginia engineers also began constructing defensive lines around Richmond before November 1861, when the Engineer Bureau assumed responsibility for all fortifications.[12] Key points of fortification along the James River included Mulberry Point, Drewry's Bluff, and Chaffin's Bluff. Slaves dug ditches and built walls outside Petersburg, Lynchburg, Danville, and Saltville and along the railroad lines connecting these cities with Richmond. In North Carolina, the most significant installations were those guarding the approach to Wilmington, including Fort Fisher, Fort Caswell, Fort Pender, and Fort Anderson. Slaves also regularly worked to protect railroad depots like Weldon, Tarboro, Goldsboro, and Greensboro, as well as the Cape Fear River near the Fayetteville arsenal.

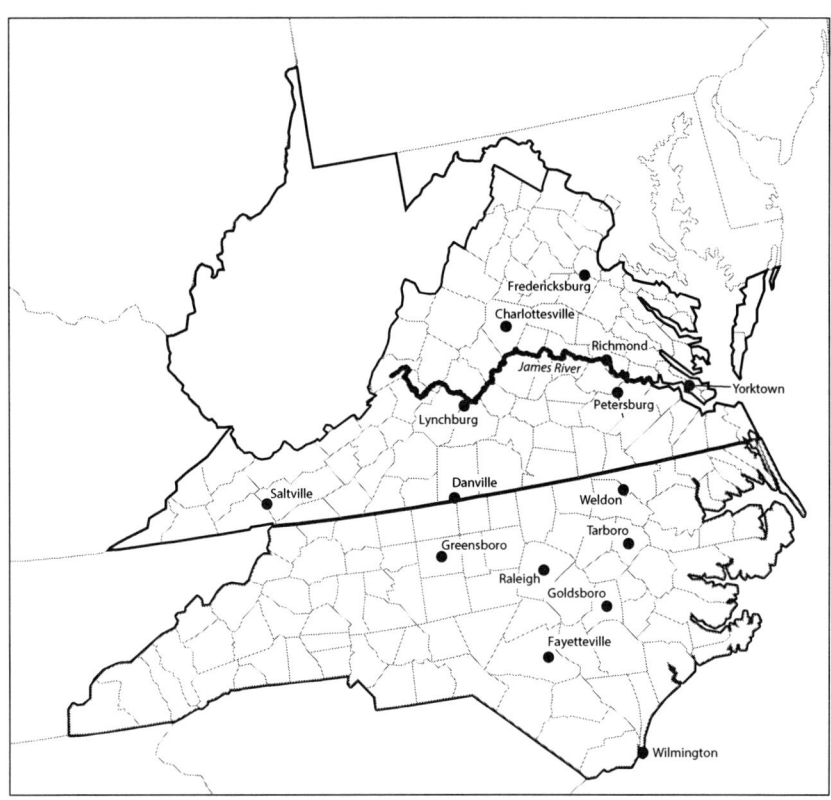

Map 1. Primary points of fortification

Many government officials at the local, state, and national levels participated in slave impressment. In Virginia, county court officers assembled the slaves targeted for impressment and appointed overseers to accompany them on the fortifications; county sheriffs and their assistants delivered the slaves to engineer officers and collected receipts for their owners. In North Carolina, local militia officers fulfilled this responsibility. Legislators at the state and national level demonstrated at least some support for slave impressment by enacting it into law. Virginia governors John Letcher and William "Extra Billy" Smith and North Carolina governor Zebulon Baird Vance issued and enforced numerous requisitions for slaves to work on Confederate fortifications. The Confederate secretaries of war, especially James A. Seddon, facilitated communications between the governors, Confederate army officers, and President Davis.

This approach to slave impressment was designed to centralize control over each state's slave labor force, to resolve any legal or constitutional objections to slave impressment, and to create a consistent and efficient system for delivering laborers to the fortifications. Impressment laws needed to grant each governor, and eventually the president, adequate authority to impress slaves for Confederate service while still protecting the property rights of southern slaveholders. Virginia's October 1862 slave impressment law was much more stringent than its North Carolina counterpart, passed in December 1862. The Virginia law guaranteed that no more than 10,000 slaves would be impressed for Confederate service at any one time and that slaves would serve a maximum of two months under each impressment quota. The Virginia General Assembly also stipulated a clear chain of authority for slave impressment that granted much of the impressment power to state officials rather than to Confederate officers. Those in North Carolina's General Assembly, while intending to give their governor primary authority over slave impressments, failed to place any limitations on Confederate officers' ability to impress slaves without the governor's approval.

North Carolina and Virginia were two of seven Confederate states that passed slave impressment laws in late 1862 and early 1863. The state legislatures of Florida, Louisiana, Mississippi, and Alabama also enacted comprehensive slave impressment legislation during this period, while Georgia's legislature allowed a few labor requisitions on a case-by-case basis. Each state law established different procedures, and the remaining states failed to pass any laws on the subject.[13] For this reason, national legislation needed to resolve discrepancies in how slave impressment would proceed in each state. The Confederate Congress tackled slave impressment as one portion of a general impressment bill passed in March 1863, but this law specifically respected state acts on the subject of slave impressment. Later amendments to the Confederate legislation were intended to create uniformity and cement central authority over impressment. They often adopted Virginia's provisions as the most effective at collecting slaves while also respecting slaveholders' property rights.

Viewed through the lens of slave impressment, it becomes clear that the strong state and local governments in North Carolina and Virginia contributed immeasurably to the Confederate war effort rather than undermined it. Local elected governments played a more active role in Virginia than they did in North Carolina. The county courts in Virginia debated, apportioned, and enforced every statewide quota issued prior to the summer of 1864, although they became increasingly reluctant as the burdens of the war mounted. In contrast, the North Carolina county courts only rarely involved themselves in slave impressment. In both states, however, the governors provided vital support to the Confederate army's requisitions of slave labor, often in the face of opposition from the slaves' owners and state legislatures.

Slaveholders objecting to slave impressment most commonly argued that taking slaves to work on fortifications reduced the number available for labor at home, making it harder for them to meet the heightened needs of wartime production. Thus, it is necessary to explore the impact of slave impressment, both real and imagined, on agriculture in Virginia and North Carolina. Because slaves were crucial to food production for both the Confederate armies and civilians in each state, the governors proved far more likely to interpose their power between the national government and the slaveholders of their states to protect agriculture than for any other reason. It is fair to describe their actions in these cases not as denying laborers necessary to the Confederate war effort but rather as declining to redistribute laborers already forced to work on behalf of Confederate victory. Even so, the governors only rarely interfered with requisitions from Confederate officials, and they usually acted to reduce impressment quotas rather than to rescind them entirely.

Growing opposition from slaveholders and local leaders, however, prompted the centralization of slave impressment that began in February 1864, which mirrored the growing strength of the Confederate government as a whole. Control over slave impressment passed into the hands of the Confederate Bureau of Conscription, bypassing local and state governments. Impressed slaves would be organized into Negro Labor Battalions that the government could assign to any location and any type of work without the consent of their owners. Congress also created the Confederate Board of Slave Claims, which met in the summer of 1864 to determine compensation for slaves who died as a result of government service. Legislators hoped that establishing a process to better compensate slaveholders for their losses would preempt at least some slaveholders' objections to the national impressment plan.

The Conscript Bureau put the new procedures into action in October 1864, when it began collecting 20,000 slaves from across the Confederacy who would work for the traditional sixty days; in November, the bureau impressed an additional 2,000 Virginia slaves for a twelve-month term of service. In North Carolina, Governor Vance gladly relinquished responsibility for slave impressment to the Confederate government. While Governor Smith of Virginia continued to play an active role in each requisition, he also welcomed the more centralized procedure under the direction of the Conscript Bureau. Both men chose to support the centralization of slave impressment as a response to the petitions and complaints they received from their constituents, believing that a more regulated and centrally organized process would solve many of the political problems those letters presented. If slave impressment is a reliable model, then, the growing strength of the Confederate government during the last eighteen months of the war was the direct—if unintended—consequence of its citizens' pleas for assistance.

Both the problems and the potential benefits of slave impressment became more pronounced during the last six months of the war. Planters continued to protest slave impressment at every available opportunity, reflecting the dearth of laborers and resources throughout the Confederacy. But by late 1864, the governors' patience for such complaints was wearing thin. A new Virginia law passed in March 1865 at Governor Smith's request prescribed harsh penalties for both slaveholders and local officials who resisted slave impressment; these newer, stricter plans for requisitioning slave laborers exemplified the state government's strong commitment to the Confederate war effort, even in the face of opposition from many voters. Governor Smith, President Davis, and General Robert E. Lee saw the potential application of the new Negro Labor Battalions to the percolating debate over enlisting slaves as soldiers and thus wanted to ensure a continued supply of laborers. Both state and national governments expected any changes they made to either the legal theory or the actual practice of slave impressment in early 1865 to have a long-term impact on the Confederacy's prospects for victory.

Wartime labor requisitions often targeted several thousand slaves at a time, so an enormous number of people participated in the process of slave impressment in some fashion. Among top officials and the most active participants, individual personalities and relationships shaped each requisition's enforcement. Most actors in the process of slave impressment, unfortunately, remained anonymous or at least voiceless. Compliance rates suggest that for every slaveholder who wrote a letter protesting impressment, for example, there were several others who sent their slaves without public complaint, and probably one who refused to obey the summons but did not openly seek to justify his resistance. Most of the men who enforced slave impressment quotas—county court officers and sheriffs in Virginia, militia members and officers in North Carolina, and Confederate impressment agents and enrolling officers—went unnamed in official correspondence. As a group, their participation may not suggest much about their support for or interest in slave impressment. Most were simply following orders. The speed and accuracy with which they executed those orders, though, provides some insight into their opinions on impressment, especially among the county court officials in Virginia.

Of course, the names and opinions of the laborers were almost always excluded from government records. Some of their voices came through the testimony their masters and overseers offered before the Confederate Board of Slave Claims in 1864. A few ex-slaves spoke of impressment in statements to U.S. Army personnel, in Southern Claims Commission cases, in state pension applications, or in Works Progress Administration (WPA) interviews, but most of those descriptions were perfunctory, with little opportunity for the men to share their personal experiences or thoughts on impressment. Internal correspondence between engineer officers regarding slaves' work on the fortifications was similarly devoid of detail; statements like "hands digging along river" or "hands cutting timber" were the only type of records most left. Major General William H. C. Whiting, commanding the Wilmington fortifications, was the only person to offer descriptive comments, often complaining to state and national officials that his enslaved laborers were constantly sick or ran away in large numbers, but it is necessary to take Whiting's statements with a grain of salt. Perhaps his laborers were genuinely sick, perhaps they were feigning illness to protest impressment, or perhaps Whiting was exaggerating labor shortages at Wilmington (as he often did) to bolster his demands for additional workers.

Since their department employed most of the impressed laborers, the officers in charge of Confederate engineering operations were regular participants in slave impressment. Lieutenant John B. Stanard directed construction of the Richmond fortifications, working in close and regular consultation with Major Walter H. Stevens, chief engineer for the Army of Northern Virginia. Captain Thomas M. Talcott oversaw fortification work in much of southwestern Virginia. Colonel William Lamb arrived in Wilmington in July 1862, serving there as General Whiting's top subordinate until the fall of Fort Fisher in January 1865. On the administrative level, Major Danville Leadbetter served as acting chief of the Engineer Bureau from August 1861 to November 1861, followed by Captain Alfred Landon Rives. Both were eventually replaced by Colonel Jeremy Francis Gilmer, who would serve as chief engineer for most of the war.

A North Carolina native, Gilmer graduated from West Point in 1839 and immediately became an officer in the Army's Engineer Corps, a highly prestigious appointment. He resigned from the U.S. Army in June 1861 before beginning service as General Albert Sidney Johnston's chief engineer. Wounded at Shiloh in April 1862, Gilmer reluctantly found himself consigned to desk duty in Richmond that summer—he would have preferred to serve as chief engineer to the Army of Northern Virginia. On General Lee's recommendation, Gilmer accepted a compromise in July: promoted to colonel, he would serve as chief of the Engineer Bureau, a position he retained throughout the war and that facilitated his promotion to brigadier general and then major general. Captain Rives remained in the Engineer Bureau as Gilmer's primary adjutant, and he routinely acted as bureau chief during Gilmer's frequent illnesses and regular visits to fortifications outside of Virginia. The two men seem to have sustained a cordial working relationship; Gilmer also communicated and worked quite effectively with other military officers, government officials, and the various Confederate secretaries of war.[14]

Two commanding generals at key points of fortification had an especially significant impact on Confederate slave impressment. General Magruder began impressing slaves to build defensive works in southeastern Virginia in the earliest months of the war. Flamboyant, dramatic, and fiercely independent, Magruder, a native of Virginia's Tidewater region, graduated from West Point in 1830 and served in the U.S. Army until Virginia's secession in April 1861. Shortly after offering his services to the Confederate government, he took command of several thousand men stationed along the narrow peninsula separating the York and James Rivers, where he constructed a line of defensive works just south of Williamsburg, opposite the Union army's Fort Monroe. Magruder operated independently of the Engineer Bureau, although he usually sought its permission and assistance when impressing laborers. While local planters eagerly filled his earliest requests for slave labor, he began having difficulty obtaining sufficient workers by the fall of 1861. Conflicts between Magruder, Secretary of War Judah P. Benjamin, and slaveholders in southeastern Virginia shaped much of the slave impressment legislation that emerged in 1862 and 1863.[15]

General Whiting took command of the Confederate fortifications in and around Wilmington in the fall of 1862, eventually turning Fort Fisher, at the mouth of the Cape Fear River, into the Confederacy's most impressive fortress. A native of Biloxi, Mississippi, and a top-achieving graduate of West Point, Whiting was thorough, meticulous, confident, and firmly committed to achieving his objectives—in many ways, the ideal engineer.[16] But he may have lacked the ability to see beyond his specific objectives to the broader demands the war placed on civilians. From the time of his appointment until January 1865, when Fort Fisher fell to the Union,

Whiting demanded a nearly constant supply of laborers in order to carry out his extensive plans for fortifying Wilmington and its valuable harbor. In so doing, he caused serious political difficulties for state and national officials.

Whiting's incessant requests for labor sorely tried the patience of James A. Seddon and other War Department officials. Six different men served as Confederate secretary of war during the brief period that the office existed, but Seddon served the longest and was most actively engaged in the development of slave impressment policies and practices. Born into several of Virginia's wealthiest families, Seddon inherited his father's estate at a young age and invested in Louisiana sugar plantations before studying law at the University of Virginia. His impressive speaking skills brought him prominence in state Democratic politics, and he was elected to the U.S. House of Representatives in 1844 on an expansionist platform. He served in Congress for eight years, an ardent supporter of slavery and states' rights. By the eve of the Civil War, Seddon had largely retired from public life, but he eagerly served on Virginia's secession convention and then accepted a provisional seat in the Confederate Congress. After a second attempt at retirement, Seddon became secretary of war in November 1862. His primary role in the process of slave impressment was negotiating between the governors who controlled access to each state's workforce and the Confederate officers who demanded laborers.[17]

Virginia and North Carolina each had two different wartime governors, but three of these four men were strong supporters of slave impressment at both the state and national levels. John Letcher, a lifelong Democrat, had served in the U.S. House of Representatives for nearly a decade before taking office as Virginia's governor in January 1860. The son of a non-slaveholding carpenter from Rockbridge County, Letcher had established himself as a lawyer and newspaper editor before entering electoral politics and consistently defended the rights of Virginia's slaveholders against any encroachments by the federal government during his nine-year congressional career. Yet he expected Virginians to comply with all Confederate requisitions for slave labor.[18] His successor, William "Extra Billy" Smith, took office in January 1864 with a wealth of political experience, a passable military reputation, and significant popular support to his credit. He served in the U.S. Congress in the early 1840s and late 1850s, with intermediary stints in the California and Virginia state legislatures, and remains one of a very short list of Virginia governors elected to more than one term (1846–49 and 1864–65). Like Letcher, Smith proved an ardent supporter of slave impressment.[19]

North Carolinian Henry T. Clark rose to the office of governor quite unexpectedly, upon the illness and death of his predecessor John Willis Ellis in July 1861. While he had served ably as Speaker of the North Carolina Senate, there is no indication that Clark sought or welcomed the state's chief executive position, especially in the chaotic months immediately following North Carolina's secession. Clark took advantage of the U.S. arsenal at Fayetteville to provision militias and volunteer soldiers, and he encouraged all North Carolinians to unite for local defense, but he was reluctant to issue requisitions for slave labor and informed his constituents that they were not obligated to comply with impressment orders issued by Confederate military personnel.[20] Clark's successor, Zebulon Baird Vance, was elected in the summer of 1862 and quickly acted in favor of slave impressment. Like his Virginia colleague Smith, Vance's service in the Confederate army made him more supportive of policies that would expand the resources available for military use. Vance and Smith also enjoyed populist reputations that led many of their constituents to treat them as channels of protest against requisitions for slave labor, and so enforcing state and national slave impressment policies would occupy a great deal of their time and energies.[21]

Impressment, of course, was not the only means by which slaves rendered involuntary service to the Confederacy. Slavery was, as Vice President Alexander H. Stephens famously noted, the ideological "corner-stone" of the Confederate government.[22] Equally important, slave labor provided the physical cornerstone for the Confederate war effort. Private employers like the Tredegar Iron Works, railroad lines, salt mines, and iron forges, all of which sustained the Confederate war effort, hired increasing numbers of slave laborers as their white employees left for the army. Owners also leased their slaves to individual officers within the Confederate army or to larger departments like the Confederate Medical Department, which hired hundreds of slaves to work as nurses, cooks, and laundresses in army hospitals. Most slaves remained agricultural laborers, however, and their wartime production helped feed both civilians and soldiers, particularly after the Confederate Congress passed legislation impressing wheat, corn, and other foodstuffs. All of these slaves played a role in supporting the Confederacy. Slaves also filled a variety of noncombatant positions within the armies themselves, including those of teamsters, cooks, and musicians. By all accounts, the Confederate war effort would have failed long before April 1865 if these slave laborers had not freed white military-age men for service as soldiers.

The War Department's use of hired slave laborers extended one of the key developments in the Upper South's economy during the late antebellum era. Slave hiring was already an established facet of southern industry at the beginning of the war, and its prevalence helped smooth the transition to wartime production. In Virginia, for example, hundreds of male slaves were hired to or sold to iron manufacturers or railroad companies, and many of these slaves acquired skills they could use to protect themselves and their families from further sales. Using slaves as industrial workers, moreover, turned out to be just as profitable as using free laborers. Industrial work was only one potential application of slave hiring, however. Hired slaves most commonly worked as house servants or field hands. Some of the families who hired slaves did so to supplement their existing slave workforce, while others did so because they could not afford to purchase a slave outright.[23]

Slaves were almost always hired annually under the antebellum system, and both government and private hirers typically conformed to this pattern during the war. Owners and hirers negotiated the terms of a contract in late December or early January, and the slaves remained with their hirers from the beginning of the year until just before Christmas, when they returned home for the holidays. Some slaves would return to the same person who had hired them the previous year—this was particularly the case for slaves who had learned a trade or industrial job—while others faced the prospect of a new master every year. Moreover, the hiring trends of the 1850s accelerated dramatically after 1861. The war increased the importance of slaves with industrial skills in the Upper South's hiring market; the demand for hired field hands also increased as white men joined the Confederate army.[24] By 1863, impressment quotas began to disrupt standard hiring rituals. But the hiring practices of the antebellum period continued to shape military requisitions for labor because the Confederate attorneys general turned to state laws regulating slave hiring when seeking precedents for slave impressment.

Although the numerous enslaved men and women hired to the Confederate armies and War Department agencies by their owners provided vital labor to the Confederacy, they are generally absent from this study. Free blacks and Native Americans, two equally important pools of labor for the Confederacy, are largely silent here as well. While impressed free blacks, Native Americans, and slaves all performed similar duties, the vast difference in their legal and political status makes them incompatible subjects for study. Though neither citizens nor voters, free black and Native American men were legally persons, making their impressment more akin to conscription—or kidnapping. Slaves, however, were the property of full citizens and voters. Their status as chattel meant that slave impressment, from a legal standpoint, had more in common with the impressment of horses and mules than it did with the impressment of free blacks and Native Americans. At the same time, slaves' owners had a financial interest in protecting them, which prompted a concern that typically did not extend to free blacks and Native Americans. In many ways, it was therefore easier for government authorities to appropriate the labor of free non-white men than that of slaves. While the emotional and psychological experience of forced military labor differed greatly for free and enslaved men, their physical experiences often overlapped. Testimony from hired slaves and free blacks thus occasionally appears in order to provide a clearer view of impressed slaves' daily lives.

⁓ The *Richmond Whig*'s editor was perhaps correct to suggest that Confederate policies inadvertently devalued slavery over the course of the war. Slave labor on the Confederate fortifications served as the justification for the U.S. Confiscation Acts, which paved the way toward the Emancipation Proclamation and the Thirteenth Amendment. Rumored or impending impressment quotas may have encouraged slaves to escape their plantations and make the risky journey toward Union lines. But the vast majority of slaves in the Confederacy did not escape, and those who remained in servitude were forced to undertake a wide variety of labor designed to increase the chances of Confederate victory. Slave impressment, the most obvious example of that labor, brought tens of thousands of slaves into the direct service of the War Department and also illustrated both the vast expansion of the Confederate state and the high level of coordination between its various levels of governance. The centralization of slave impressment over the course of the war demonstrates the impressive growth and great effectiveness of the Confederate government as it struggled to achieve independence.

CHAPTER ONE

Hundreds Have Been Called

Slave Impressment at the Local and State Levels,
1861–1863

Throughout the summer and fall of 1861, Brigadier General John Bankhead Magruder called on the families of southeastern Virginia to send slave laborers to his defensive works along the James River. Jackson and Washington, two slaves from the Fleet family's plantation, traveled to Gloucester Point on orders from Magruder. The patriarch of the family, while complying with the requisition, wrote to his son Fred, a soldier at Gloucester Point, enjoining him to watch the slaves and "to try & get them off as soon as you can as we want to begin to seed wheat as early as possible in October."[1] Fleet was not the only Virginia slaveholder who hoped to limit the effectiveness of Magruder's impressments: slaveholders in Lancaster and Surry Counties openly resisted the requisition. Magruder complained that he could not properly fortify the Peninsula without slave laborers and threatened to send cavalry detachments to collect the slaves if necessary.[2]

The officers Magruder sent to impress laborers in King William County seem to have been more successful than those in Lancaster County. On September 17, 1861, Magruder ordered his subordinate Major H. B. Tomlin to begin collecting black men, both enslaved and free, from King William County; sensitive to at least one of the slaveholders' potential objections, Magruder mandated that while free blacks would work at Yorktown, the slaves would work at Gloucester Point, thus preventing any potentially harmful contact between the two groups of laborers. Ten days later,

Tomlin reported that most of the county's planters had sent the slaves requested, but the free black men were refusing to come. With some coercion, the free blacks of King William County arrived in Yorktown on October 8, prompting the dismissal of nearly fifty slaves who had been working there since late August.[3]

Confederate officers who attempted to impress slave labor during the first year of the war ran into numerous difficulties. Most had access to only a limited labor pool, sending their deputies into the counties immediately surrounding their headquarters but lacking the resources to work throughout the state. Overlapping requisitions from officers in contiguous areas confused planters and further limited each command's success. Procedures for compensating owners were cumbersome and inefficient. Slaveholders routinely complained that existing laws did not specifically authorize Confederate army officers to impress their slaves without permission from a corresponding state authority. Indeed, slaveholders generally sought to resist slave impressment by any means possible, and Confederate commanders found that some local and state officials were, at best, reluctant and unreliable allies. By the spring of 1862, it would become clear that the solution to all of these problems was legislative action on the part of state and national governments. Effective slave impressment would require centralized, rather than independent, action.

Military use of slave labor during the first nineteen months of the war revealed a series of questions and fissures that state legislatures would need to resolve if the Confederate army was ever going to meet its labor requirements. In addition to resolving any legal or constitutional objections to slave impressment, the legislation enacted by the Virginia General Assembly and the North Carolina state legislature attempted to centralize control over the slave labor force, create a consistent and efficient system for delivering laborers to the fortifications, and address slaveholders' concerns about the treatment of engineer laborers. Usually, in crafting these laws, legislators were responding to problems that arose in the earliest days of the war.

Virginia's General Assembly drafted a slave impressment law in the fall of 1862, an action prompted in large part by the Engineer Bureau's failed attempts to collect sufficient laborers on its own authority the preceding spring. A full year into the war, Virginia's slaves were already actively engaged in enforced labor for the Confederate armies as hospital nurses, commissary teamsters, and camp servants, while others worked for civilian-owned railroads and factories. In addition, of course, Virginia's farmers required slave labor if they were going to produce enough wheat and corn to feed the military and civilian populations of the state, especially after the April 1862 Conscription Act called large numbers of white men into military service. The extensive demands on slave labor in wartime Virginia certainly help explain why the Engineer Bureau turned to state government officials for help.[4]

As it crafted Virginia's slave impressment law, the General Assembly worked to grant the governor adequate authority to impress slaves for Confederate service while still protecting the property rights of slaveholders. Legislators also sought to create an efficient system of collecting and delivering slaves to Richmond that respected local authority. These priorities often operated in conflict with each other; in particular, county officials were quick to complain about each requisition. Yet county courts bore primary responsibility for enforcing slave impressment in Virginia, and Governor John Letcher's office eventually forced them to comply with his calls for 13,500 slave laborers from across the state between October 1862 and January 1863.

While fewer slaves were impressed under state authority in North Carolina, Governor Zebulon Baird Vance and the state legislature also needed to address statewide labor shortages prompted by frequent use of North Carolina slaves on Virginia fortifications. They did so by crafting legislation that gave the governor's office greater flexibility when issuing requisitions but put militia officers and the state's adjutant general in charge of enforcement. While compliance was far from perfect, especially in Virginia, implementing these two state impressment laws did afford Confederate authorities a larger and more reliable workforce during the second winter of the war than they had previously been able to muster.

◥ At the outset of the war, most observers would not have predicted the necessity of slave impressment quotas, as potential sources of labor seemed to abound. Military engineers expected Confederate soldiers to dig their own fortifications whenever possible but also assumed that the labor of hired slaves, free blacks, American Indians, and convicts would be sufficient supplements. In the initial flush of Confederate patriotism, some of the most prominent slaveholders in Virginia and North Carolina offered the services of their slaves to build defensive works. John Taylor of Culpeper County wrote to Virginia governor Letcher on April 22, 1861, offering 100 of his and his neighbors' slaves to labor "for the defence of the state."[5] Slaveholders from Hampton and Petersburg also voluntarily sent large numbers of laborers to Richmond in the first few weeks after the fall of Fort Sumter, while planters from New Hanover County in North

Carolina sent their slaves to build roads for military use in the vicinity of Wilmington.[6] It is unlikely that the slaves were as eager to go work for the Confederacy as their owners were to send them.

Free black men also played a prominent role in preparing defenses in both states, usually under compulsion from local authorities. Officials from Robeson County, North Carolina, sent free black men to work at Camp Wyatt, outside Wilmington.[7] In Virginia, prominent citizens from Northampton, Southampton, and Mecklenburg Counties brought hundreds of free African American laborers to Richmond in April and May 1861, while the leaders of cities like Lynchburg also offered the services of their free black populations.[8] Melvin Ely, in his study of free blacks in Prince Edward County, suggests that some may have even volunteered to perform labor for the Confederate army both "to avoid the suspicion of their white neighbors" and in the hope that volunteering—rather than waiting to be taken by force—might allow them to control the conditions of their service.[9]

State and Confederate officers in Virginia and North Carolina routinely appropriated the labor of Native American men, whom state laws classified as "free colored men." Members of the Pamunkey nation in southeastern Virginia complained when their friends and neighbors were put to work on the fortifications near Yorktown. Major Tomlin, the officer employing the men, insisted that the Pamunkeys had volunteered to help the Confederacy; he also suggested that the Native Americans in Virginia had intermarried so completely with the local African American population that it would be impossible to exempt them from labor requisitions aimed at free black men.[10] In southeastern North Carolina, Lumbee men from Robeson County were so frequently sent to work on the Wilmington fortifications that they mounted an armed resistance movement in December 1864.[11]

Black convicts from Richmond's penitentiaries formed another key component of the Confederacy's defensive labor force early in the war. Convict labor was probably the most useful option for engineer officers; once they obtained permission from state authorities, they could use convict laborers for long periods of time and without any interference from slaveholders. The convicts worked for several months on the entrenchments outside Richmond before traveling to Manassas in December 1861 to repair roads and bridges.[12] As Captain Alfred Landon Rives assured Governor Letcher, the Engineer Bureau was particularly careful to arrange guards and overseers for black convict laborers.[13]

Demand for manual labor quickly outstripped the supply available through convict labor, impressment of free blacks and Native Americans,

Figure 1.1. Slaves building fortifications, as depicted in Frank Leslie's Illustrated Newspaper, *January 31, 1863*

and voluntary labor provisions from Virginia's slaveholders, especially in areas that required extensive fortification. General Magruder, working to fortify Virginia's Peninsula in the summer of 1861, pioneered the practice of impressing slaves in his immediate vicinity, doing so as early as July and August.[14] In addition to the slaves and free blacks he impressed, Magruder appropriated the services of nearly 150 runaway slaves his forces captured in the vicinity of the Union army's Fort Monroe.[15] Early attempts at slave impressment drew on the antebellum practice of county and city labor levies, under which local governments called slaves into service to build or repair roads, bridges, and other public facilities. Magruder seems to have been the first Confederate official to impress Virginia slaves into service, however.

As a relatively autonomous commander, Magruder appears to have occasionally issued his requisitions without the authorization or even knowledge of the Confederate Engineer Bureau. In November 1861, Secretary of War Judah P. Benjamin denied Magruder's request for 500 additional laborers. Major Danville Leadbetter, as acting chief of the Engineer Bureau, informed Magruder that Secretary Benjamin did not anticipate a winter campaign along the Peninsula and felt that hiring or impressing a large force of laborers would both waste government funds and hinder agricultural operations in southeastern Virginia.[16] Denied the authority to hire or impress more slaves, Magruder impressed free blacks instead; he failed to inform the Engineer Bureau of this change, leading to competing labor requisitions in at least one county.[17] Recurring competition over labor resources would be one of the key motivations for implementing more organized statewide impressment quotas.

Magruder's February 1862 requisition for slave labor also overlapped with the Engineer Bureau's efforts. By that point, Magruder's former subordinate, Captain Rives, served as acting head of the Engineer Bureau; Rives had learned the importance of slave impressment from his time on Magruder's fortifications, and he would seek to use Virginia's slaves on fortifications throughout the state, not just on the Peninsula. Both officers encountered a planter population already heartily opposed to relinquishing its work force. Fred Fleet's father again faced the necessity of sending Jackson and Washington to work at Yorktown or Gloucester Point, confiding to his son, "I don't like their being as near to the Yankees."[18] From camp, William Aylett informed his wife that "Magruder is after the slaves of King William County again, to work on fortifications—and this time I believe it is proposed to take one half. I am not certain about *that*, however. Whatever may be the number required, get off with sending as few as possible."[19]

Magruder, realizing that he had placed a heavy burden on the slaveholders of southeastern Virginia, extended his reach into central Virginia and eastern North Carolina with mixed success. When Magruder requested one-quarter of the adult male slaves from each Halifax County plantation in February 1862, Catherine Edmondston readily complied, noting, "Prayerfully do I send them, hoping that their labour *there* may protect us *here*."[20] Yet Magruder found this requisition for slave labor was less successful than he had hoped, especially when a group of North Carolina planters hired a lawyer to protest the impressment with the War Department, which countermanded a portion of the order as having no basis in state law.[21] Based on General Magruder's experiences, legislative action had become necessary if work on the fortifications was to continue.

Further complicating matters, Magruder was not the only officer with designs on the slave labor force of northeastern North Carolina. In January 1862, Confederate engineers working to fortify Roanoke Island requested assistance from the state's interim governor, Henry Clark, to procure laborers.[22] Clark, however, acquiesced to the region's slaveholders, who had sent workers to Roanoke in the summer of 1861 and were reluctant to do so again. He agreed to impress free blacks, but only if the engineer in charge at Roanoke provided food and clothing.[23] Clark also authorized militia officers in Halifax County "to use as many negroes as may be necessary" to build obstructions on the Roanoke River.[24]

In addition to these calls for assistance, Governor Clark's office fielded requisitions from officials at Fayetteville and Wilmington. "In the event of Wilmington's falling into the hands of the enemy," Mayor Archibald McLean feared, Fayetteville would shortly be under attack. The town, situated along the Cape Fear River, was home to a large arsenal. To protect his town, Mayor McLean proposed that the state militia use trees to obstruct potential traffic on the river below Fayetteville. "As far as the labor necessary to do the work is concerned," he continued, "I have no doubt any amount of slave labour would be contributed from the Town & Counties, provided the work is enacted under proper & competent authority."[25] Unfortunately for McLean, Confederate officers at Wilmington also had their eyes on the slave labor force of southeastern North Carolina, and they did not hesitate to request help from Governor Clark. For his part, Clark adamantly refused to allow the state of North Carolina to bear the full burden of defending either place.[26]

Governor Clark relayed McLean's request to Secretary Benjamin in February 1862, arguing that river obstructions for Fayetteville, while easy enough for the militia to accomplish quickly, were more appropriately the responsibility of the Confederate government. After all, he wrote, "the destruction of that Arsenal would be a heavy blow and would give peculiar gratification in the Yankee's eyes, as the recapture of the Harper's Ferry Works." But Clark also pointed out that the best way to defend Fayetteville was to render Wilmington impregnable—a duty that, in his opinion, the Confederacy had neglected in favor of ports in other states. Two regiments and a light battery, he noted, "have been taken from the defence of Wilmington and set to Port Royal. They are not permitted to return, and no efforts are known to be made to supply their places; and there is the most painful anxiety for the safety of Wilmington and Fayetteville. If you have any disposable force, they could not be sent to any position where they are more needed or where they could render more valuable service."[27] Benjamin most likely did not have a "disposable force" in the spring of 1862, and equitable distribution of the Confederacy's finite resources in both soldiers and slave laborers would continue to plague the War Department, especially when governors called—loudly—for more manpower.

At least part of the problem facing Confederate officers as they struggled to obtain adequate labor forces was the great variety of engineer units in the field at any one time. At the outset of the war, each state had its own engineer department, although most of these were incorporated into the Confederate Engineer Bureau by the end of 1861. State authorities in Virginia, for example, transferred all engineering operations and officers to the Confederacy in November 1861. North Carolina state engineers retained control over most of the fortifications in their state until the fall of Roanoke Island on February 8, 1862, at which point the War Department took responsibility for the state's remaining defensive works. Even as it attempted to design a more centralized organization, however, the Engineer Bureau faced overlapping requests from both the engineer units attached to each field command and also the bureau's independent officers. These intersecting demands for laborers strained the ability of the department to keep track of all its resources and also made it much more difficult for masters to keep track of the slaves they sent to the fortifications. In addition, the procedures for lodging complaints and receiving payment mirrored the complicated structure of the Engineer Bureau and its attendant departments.[28]

The most pressing complaints of slaveholders often regarded payment for services their slaves had rendered. Indeed, slave owners had some cause for consternation at the very haphazard systems of payment that they encountered, although most of the problems that arose early in the war most likely resulted from inexperience and poor planning rather than malicious intent. For example, Confederate congressman (and former U.S. president) John Tyler suggested that slaveholders should get receipts indicating the value and service dates of impressed laborers.[29] By the next summer, impressment agents were carrying books of blank receipts to provide to slaveholders.[30]

Slaveholders who had sent laborers to Roanoke Island in North Carolina found obtaining payment equally perplexing. John B. Gilliam of Bertie County asked Governor Clark who would pay him for his slaves' work at Roanoke Island.[31] Clark told Gilliam to contact Confederate authorities, reflecting his understanding "that the Government and Officers who did the work, and employed the hands, would pay them or at least approve of their accounts for payments."[32] A few days later, Clark learned that Frank Vaughan, a commissary officer, would act as an agent for slaveholders and free black workers, collecting their pay from the Engineer Department and disbursing it when laborers left the fortifications.[33] It is not surprising that Gilliam found this plan for providing compensation difficult to navigate.

In Virginia, men whose slaves had served under the state Engineer Department had to travel to Richmond, send an acquaintance with a signed letter, or know when an impressment agent planned to be in their counties in order to collect wages due to them. When discrepancies arose, they had to navigate the process a second time.[34] As late as March 1862, some slaveholders still sought payment for work their slaves had performed the previous fall.[35] Some of these difficulties disappeared as the Confederate Engineer Bureau took over the impressment of slaves and payment of their owners in the spring and summer of 1862, but the myriad layers of the Confederate bureaucracy continued to perplex many slaveholders in both states. In addition, overlapping and local requisitions would continue even as the Engineer Bureau prepared to issue its first statewide slave impressment call in Virginia.

At the very end of March 1862, Captain Rives, acting chief of the Engineer Bureau, began contacting impressment agents throughout the state of Virginia, requesting that they collect slave laborers for service on the fortifications around Richmond. These agents were residents of the counties in which they worked but were employed and directed by the War Department. For months, they had been busy collecting horses, mules, and food supplies for the Confederate armies and so were already unwelcome visitors to most Virginia farms and plantations even before they began collecting slave laborers. The need for those laborers had become clear when Major General George B. McClellan began landing his army of well over 100,000 U.S. soldiers at Fort Monroe, approximately eighty miles southeast of Richmond, in the middle of March. McClellan clearly intended to move his army north toward the Confederate capital, so the Engineer Bureau scrambled to bring sufficient laborers to their defensive works.

For example, Rives instructed Christopher Gilmer, his agent in Charlottesville, to collect at least 100 slaves. He informed Gilmer and others that the bureau would employ most of the slave laborers "at Drury's Bluff, Chesterfield Co. about 8 miles below Richmond."[36] Acting with the authority of the War Department, Rives ordered Virginia's railroads as well as Confederate transportation officers to bring the slaves and their overseers to Richmond as quickly as possible.[37] While Rives expected all slave laborers to be in position by mid-May, some cities and counties failed to respond immediately, complicating Rives's efforts to provide laborers for all points of fortification. These communications in late March thus prompted the Engineer Bureau's first attempt at statewide impressment in Virginia, which took place in May 1862.

The Confederate capital was at a heightened state of alarm that month, as General McClellan's massive Army of the Potomac stood within a few miles of Richmond. Its advance had been delayed by General Magruder, whose famous antics at Yorktown made his force of 17,000 men seem much larger—although his less famous use of slave labor to build fortifications probably deserves more of the credit. But McClellan's glacial rate of advance was matched only by Confederate major general Joseph E. Johnston's penchant for retreating, and so the Union soldiers had arrived on the outskirts of Richmond in the middle of May. Every available black male laborer within the city was hastily thrown into the lines to dig trenches, joined in this work by disgruntled Confederate soldiers. Johnston was seriously wounded in the Battle of Seven Pines on May 31, 1862, and Major General Robert E. Lee took command of the Confederate Army of Northern Virginia the next day. While he began formulating a plan to push McClellan back down the peninsula, Lee also expected defensive construction to continue.

Defensive construction outside Richmond in May 1862 represented an example of redundant commands that was never resolved throughout the war. The work of the Engineer Bureau's chief of construction, Lieutenant John B. Stanard, overlapped with the work of Major Walter H. Stevens, chief engineer for the Army of Northern Virginia, whenever that army was in the vicinity of the Confederate capital. The Engineer Bureau thus had to divide impressed laborers between two distinct commands, and Stevens initially felt slighted. When Stevens complained, Rives responded, "I am expecting negroes every day but as yet have none to send you."[38] Unsatisfied with this response, Stevens appealed to General Lee, who immediately ordered Rives to assign Stevens an additional 300 laborers. Rives endeavored to refuse as respectfully as possible. "There are only about 100 negroes employed on the Richmond defences, completing works already commenced," he explained, and "Capt Clarke has a force of something over 100 negroes at Drewry's. These comprise all the available negro force employed on the fortifications. Quite a large number of negroes were called out a week since & are expected by every train. As soon as they arrive Major Stevens will be satisfied."[39]

This slave force did not arrive as expeditiously as Rives hoped. Governor Letcher allowed him to use black convict laborers on the fortifications until the impressed slaves could arrive in Richmond. In July, Rives assured Stevens that his laborers were on their way, noting, "Hundreds of hands have been called & will come in transportation being furnished by the Danville RR."[40] As late as September 1862, however, Nelson County impressment agent William Daniel Cabell was still working to fill the requisitions issued the previous May, so Stevens may have waited several months for the laborers he requested.⁴¹ The difficulty the Engineer Bureau and its impressment agents faced in filling these labor requisitions in the spring and summer of 1862 led directly into the Virginia state impressment legislation of October 1862. Those regulations would be designed not only to increase the potential pool of labor from which the Engineer Bureau could draw but also to show a clear chain of authority between engineer officers and national, state, and local elected officials. Finally, the regulations would need to find a way to cope with continuing—and indeed, mounting—slaveholder opposition to impressment.

Until the General Assembly crafted its first slave impressment law, though, Engineer Bureau efforts to impress slaves would remain piecemeal and would continue to be both supplemented by requisitions from individual commanders and roundly condemned by most slaveholders. For the Petersburg fortifications, for example, Major General D. H. Hill collected 1,000 North Carolina slaves in August 1862.⁴² While she had supported General Magruder's impressment call in February, Catherine Edmondston was far less inclined to comply with Hill's requisition, which she saw as "most rash, ill considered, and, as it is arranged, oppressive & unequal." Recommending that Hill use the slaves left behind by refugee James River planters, she argued that "to remove forty hands now from Father's and Mr E's crops is to destroy it."⁴³ Edmonston thus pointed to the most significant objection that slaveholders made when faced with impressment calls—removing slaves from the farms and placing them on fortifications endangered vital crops like wheat and corn. Without those food crops, neither Confederate armies nor civilians could hope to survive for very long. Yet Edmonston's father and husband sent their slaves as ordered.⁴⁴

John Pool, who lived east of Edmondston in Bertie County, raised a different fear. He worried that "if the Confederate authorities commence taking these exposed slaves, or any part of them, the enemy will then have a military excuse to take those that are left, and they will not be slow to do so."⁴⁵ Pool's concern was not unwarranted. The First Confiscation Act, passed by the U.S. Congress in August 1861, granted Union officers explicit permission to confiscate all Confederate property—including slaves—used in direct aid of the rebellion. By impressing slaves for military service, Pool feared, Confederate officials justified Union confiscation of slave property.

Another correspondent, militia officer David Clark, framed his objections to Hill's impressment call not in reference to protecting agriculture, forestalling runaways, or even preventing Union confiscation. Instead, he appealed to the governor's sense of state (and personal) pride. While he had complied with three labor requisitions from the governor's office, Clark objected to Hill's requisition not only because it bypassed state authority but also because it aimed to improve fortifications in Virginia, not North Carolina. He refused to send his slaves, declining "to give countenance to an order which will bring discredit on the State & which seems to imply that North Carolina is a conquered province or Territory—a footstool to be kicked by any one having a Confederate commission." Clark insisted that his objections reflected "state pride" rather than personal parsimony. To supply slaves under such conditions "would not be to the dignity of the State to me & might endanger the cause of the Confederacy. These filthy usurpations may be looked upon by some persons as of small moment, but it is always by insidious attacks that the liberties of a people are undermined."[46]

Governor Clark's response must have delighted this correspondent. The governor assured him that there was "no constitutional authority" for Hill's impressment call "and no statute either of the State or Confederate Government to authorize it, and consequently there is no penalty for a non compliance with it." Governor Clark suggested, however, that his constituents view General Hill's requisition as a plea for aid rather than a direct order; he further proposed that they interpret the imperious style of the requisition as "an assumed authority only justified by the emergency of the case," not as an insult to the state of North Carolina. He left it to the state's slaveholders "to decide for themselves how much aid they can contribute" to defensive projects in Virginia.[47]

Governor Clark further suggested that the Confederacy's military officers too often neglected the needs of the home front, a litany that his colleagues and successors would repeat regularly as requisitions for slaves mounted over the next three years. "After a community has freely sent forth all her citizens to the war," he proposed, "the slaves might reasonably be left to prepare a support for the soldiers on duty, and their families at home. This view of the subject seems never to enter into the consideration of our Generals," Clark concluded.[48]

On the subject of Confederate impressment of slaves or other forms of property, the governor adamantly proclaimed that such actions violated the state and Confederate constitutions. Clark's lack of support for slave impressment no doubt frustrated General Hill and other Confederate officers, but he was soon to relinquish responsibility for such questions: North Carolina's gubernatorial election loomed in the summer of 1862. Zebulon Baird Vance, colonel of the Twenty-Sixth North Carolina

Infantry Regiment and a former member of the Whig Party, entered the governor's office in September 1862 with an impressive electoral victory and a broad coalition of support to his credit.[49]

Vance immediately stated his intention to support the Confederate war effort more actively and more consistently than his predecessor. As governor of North Carolina, he announced, his first priority was "to beat back our invaders and establish the independence of this glorious Confederation of States," regardless of how many sacrifices that entailed on the part of his home state.[50] As a Whig, moreover, Vance was more inclined to support Confederate congressional policies that injected the national government into state and local economic affairs than Clark, his Democratic predecessor, had been. Thus, his election seemed to bode well for Confederate officials seeking North Carolina's help to procure enslaved laborers.

Indeed, Vance did nothing to stop them from taking slaves from North Carolina to fortifications in other states. North Carolina's largest and most prosperous slaveholding counties lay within easy reach of Confederate officers building fortifications outside Petersburg or on Virginia's Peninsula, much to the dismay of Brigadier General William H. C. Whiting, who took command of Wilmington's defenses in November 1862. With hundreds of North Carolina slaves working in Virginia, Whiting struggled to collect sufficient slave laborers for his own fortifications. The recent yellow fever epidemic had already substantially delayed these works before Whiting arrived, a difficult deficiency to correct.[51] Whiting's problems, including heavy planter resistance to slave impressment and overlapping requisitions, paralleled those encountered in Virginia a few months earlier. Meanwhile, Governor Vance's willingness to allow Virginia commanders to impress North Carolina slaves coupled with Governor Clark's previously stated aversion to slave impressment left Whiting without a clear understanding of the chain of authority in North Carolina and doubtful that he could depend on state officials for support. That skepticism did not prevent him from trying, however.

Throughout November and December, Whiting addressed numerous letters to a bevy of state and national officials, begging them to send soldiers and slaves to the Wilmington defenses. He even provoked reprimands from the secretary of war, who pointed out that the situation in Fredericksburg, just sixty miles north of the Confederate capital, where the Union Army of the Potomac stood poised to attack in early December, took clear precedence over Whiting's problems. General Whiting apologized but refused to back down, urging advance preparation so that the situation at Wilmington never became an emergency.[52] With Union forces in control of

New Bern, Beaufort, and Roanoke Island, Wilmington had become North Carolina's only viable port, and the rivers and inlets approaching the town served as a haven for blockade runners for much of the war. Yet they also provided multiple points of approach for the U.S. Navy, which meant that Whiting needed to build several forts at a time.[53] "After attack it will be too late to reinforce," he admonished Confederate officials.[54] In early January, Whiting sent Adjutant and Inspector General Samuel Cooper a full report of his activities at Wilmington, praising his officers and men for their hard work. He commended the navy and engineer officers responsible for constructing the fortifications but bemoaned their lack of laborers and resources. It would become a familiar refrain, one General Whiting repeated at least monthly in his correspondence with Richmond.[55]

Whiting did not confine his appeals to Richmond. Indeed, he was impressively ecumenical in his requests for assistance, favoring Governor Vance's office in particular—at least early in their relationship. Despite the lack of clear state laws permitting or prohibiting slave impressment, Confederate officials in general found that ignoring state authorities tended to alienate the men who had the greatest ability to provide potential assistance. After all, state and local officials knew far better than Confederate officers which slaveholders could best contribute labor to the Confederate fortifications. Thus, even when not faced with specific or determined opposition to slave impressment, national leaders quickly learned to respect governors' authority on the subject. In return, the governors of Virginia and North Carolina usually worked to fill each labor requisition.

The governors recognized that the state legislatures could be valuable allies in the process of slave impressment, and thus by the fall of 1862 both Vance and Letcher were urging lawmakers to craft clear guidelines and expectations. These laws would ideally address a number of crucial disputes that arose during early attempts by Magruder, Whiting, and the Engineer Bureau to commandeer slave labor for their fortifications. Many of these were proactive attempts to forestall planter resistance to impressment; some legislatures also considered punishments for noncompliance. In addition, many state lawmakers sought to place clear limits on the amount of time Confederate officials could hold slaves to service. Each governor also sought laws that would centralize the process of slave impressment at the state level, granting the state's leaders clear authority. Finally, rather than using impressment agents—employees of the national government—they sought to place the responsibility for collecting slaves in the hands of local governments.

All of the subsequent slave impressment laws no doubt fell short of what Governors Vance and Letcher envisioned in the fall of 1862. Yet they did represent a concerted attempt not only to address slaveholders' immediate qualms about impressment but also to establish a significant role for state and local authorities in a process ultimately designed to benefit the national army. Both of these were crucial: just as Confederate authorities could not possibly requisition slave labor without some cooperation from slaveholders, they knew that slave impressment would not succeed without the assistance of state and local officials as well. And because slaveholders resisted slave impressment wherever possible, it was the work of the governors, state militias, and county courts that ultimately gave Confederate officers access to slave labor.

The Virginia Senate first considered granting Governor Letcher the authority to impress slaves for work on the fortifications in August 1862 but did not immediately act on the proposed legislation. After periods of both debate and delay, the General Assembly passed its slave impressment law on October 3, 1862. This act "authorized and required" the governor of Virginia to call slaves for Confederate service when requested by President Davis. The legislation impressed slaves for a period of sixty days and stipulated that owners would receive payments of twenty dollars per month for each impressed slave. According to Virginia's impressment act, the total number of slaves impressed at any one time could exceed neither 10,000 across the state nor 25 percent of the number of male slaves between the ages of eighteen and fifty-five in each county.[56]

While state legislators in Virginia were among the first to address the subject of slave impressment, they were certainly not alone in this endeavor. Slave impressment was a hot legislative topic in the fall of 1862. Florida was actually the first state to enact a slave impressment law, although its law failed to specify either the length of impressment or the number of slaves eligible, and it appears that very few slaves were called into service under its provisions.[57] Alabama quickly followed Virginia's lead, enacting legislation in October 1862 that would allow the governor to impress not only slaves but also wagons, tools, and other property that those slaves would need to use while building fortifications. Alabama's legislature also appropriated $1 million to compensate slaveholders for slaves who died or escaped while working for the government.[58] Louisiana's impressment law, enacted in January 1863, stipulated that no more than half the adult male slaves in the state could be called into service at a time.[59] The Mississippi state legislature also enacted a slave impressment provision that month. Its law paid slaveholders thirty dollars—rather than

Virginia's twenty—for each slave and also granted planters who sent at least thirty slaves at a time the right to choose the overseer who would accompany those slaves to the fortifications.[60] South Carolina's legislature discussed slave impressment in the fall of 1862 but did not enact provisions regulating it until two years later.[61] Georgia enacted short-term impressment laws targeting specific needs, such as the fortification of Savannah, but did not provide for recurring quotas.[62] Tennessee, Arkansas, and Texas seem to have avoided the subject in their legislative deliberations.[63]

The Engineer Bureau used the success or failure of each statewide requisition in Virginia as a barometer for the progress of fortification work throughout the Confederacy. Examining the logistics of impressment in Virginia's first three impressment calls—a series of requisitions that sought to bring more than 13,000 slaves into short-term employment for the Engineer Bureau—helps translate the ongoing process of broad and unprecedented mobilization into a comprehensible microcosm. In particular, it demonstrates that while many slaveholders and local elected officials protested vigorously from the outset, at least as many complied quickly and with little fanfare. Moreover, the steps Governor Letcher and his aides took to force compliance on reluctant county courts set a pattern for strong support of slave impressment and similar policies at the state level.

The Engineer Bureau had already prepared impressment quotas for each county in anticipation of Virginia's October 1862 impressment law, and bureau chief Colonel Jeremy Francis Gilmer immediately sent his requisition for 4,500 slaves to Secretary of War George W. Randolph (see appendix, table 1.1).[64] As the law required, Randolph then transmitted the request to President Davis, who asked Governor Letcher to order the impressment. Letcher responded immediately, assuring Davis that his orders had conformed exactly to Gilmer's list of counties and instructed local officials to act immediately.[65]

Letcher made the first call for slaves under Virginia's impressment legislation within a week of the passage of the law, so it is impossible to gauge reaction to the law itself, separate from the first impressment call, among Virginia's slaveholders and newspaper editors. It is clear, however, that Letcher and his advisors anticipated little opposition to this impressment call, mistakenly believing that Virginia's slaveholders would respond quickly. In late October, Secretary of the Commonwealth George Munford assured Richmond mayor Joseph Mayo that the city's fortifications would soon have ample laborers, noting, "Four thousand five hundred negroes were ordered out, & are now being collected & will be furnished I doubt not promptly."⁶⁶ A clerk in Munford's office corresponded with county court officials to expedite responses to each quota. The Engineer Bureau also expected a quick response to the impressment call, directing Major Stevens and Lieutenant Stanard to prepare their officers to receive, manage, care for, and return the slaves even before Letcher had formally announced the requisition.⁶⁷

While Virginians' response to the October impressment call was perhaps not as smooth or efficient as Letcher and Gilmer would have liked, many counties furnished their quotas quickly and without significant complaint. The Louisa County Court began making arrangements to send its quota of slaves to Richmond as early as October 22, 1862, including assigning well-respected residents of the county to accompany the slaves as overseers. The clerk of the Cumberland County Court informed Letcher that the slaves from that county would arrive in Richmond by October 29. Impressed slaves from Campbell County boarded trains to Richmond on October 30. While the Campbell County slaves gathered at the Lynchburg train station, another group of slaves boarded a Richmond-bound train in Charlottesville. According to the *Richmond Daily Dispatch*, the number of slaves traveling to Richmond in late October caused great inconvenience to convalescent soldiers and other passengers by crowding the trains.⁶⁸

The slaves who boarded the train in Charlottesville in mid-October may have been from Nelson, Fluvanna, or Buckingham Counties, but they were clearly not from Albemarle County, which had not yet acted on the governor's requisition. Indeed, Albemarle County's response to the October call for slaves provides an impressive example of bureaucratic procrastination, as county officials sought to mediate between the local needs of their longtime constituents and the national needs of their new country. On November 6, county court officers appointed citizens from each district within the county to prepare a list of slaveholders and slaves in their district. These agents were to report back to the county court after one week. On November 13, the court determined that, due to imperfections in their census, they could not accurately apportion the county's impressment quota. They therefore adjourned and gave the agents another week to try again. When they met on November 20, the justices of the court decided that they should attempt to avoid the impressment call altogether, petitioning Governor Letcher for an exemption or postponement.⁶⁹

As a further stalling tactic, the Albemarle County Court drafted a letter to Governor Letcher in late November, arguing that between defects in its census of slaves as well as the approaching holidays and slave hiring season, it would be easier and more effective to wait until after January 1 to implement his requisition. In his four-page letter, presiding justice John J. Bowcock described the court's diligent efforts to obtain an accurate census of Albemarle County's slaves as well as its other work on behalf of the Confederacy. Not merely occupied with counting slaves, he noted, the county court had donated nearly $75,000 to the state to outfit new regiments.[70] Letcher, unimpressed with Bowcock's arguments or his attempts to take advantage of Albemarle County's relative size and wealth, ordered the county to send its slaves immediately, observing that "Albemarle is the only county that has not complied to some extent with the requisition."[71] On December 6—two months after receiving the governor's request—Albemarle County's officials finally crafted a list of slaveholders responsible for supplying the county's quota; the impressed slaves from Albemarle County made their way to Richmond in late December and early January.[72]

Albemarle County officials also sought to deflect blame for unmet quotas onto either the Confederate government or the slaves themselves. As an example, the court documented the difficulties Jason B. Douglass encountered when trying to send a slave to Richmond. Douglass took his slave to Charlottesville on December 12, 1862, but was ordered instead to report to Gordonsville a few days later because no transportation was available. He encountered a similar problem at Gordonsville on December 14 and so returned home. He finally delivered his slave Jerry to a sheriff's deputy at Gordonsville on January 1.[73] Other slaveholders claimed to have sent their slaves independently rather than wait for the sheriff; they argued that it was not their fault if the slaves never reached Richmond. No doubt the inability of some counties to meet their quotas promptly inspired renewed calls as well as the penalties imposed by the legislature for noncompliance with the governor's requisitions.

Engineer officers began preparing county quotas for the November 1862 impressment call even before they knew the full results of the October requisition. Gilmer and his subordinates needed to finish as much construction as possible before spring planting and spring campaigns commenced, which explains their eagerness to take advantage of the new impressment legislation. In the same letter he sent to Letcher describing each county's compliance with the October requisition, Stanard also presented the new set of quotas that was working its way through the War Department. The new list called for an additional 5,000 slaves (see appendix, table 1.2).[74] The counties included in the November requisition formed a broad ring around the Piedmont counties that had been targeted for the first quota.

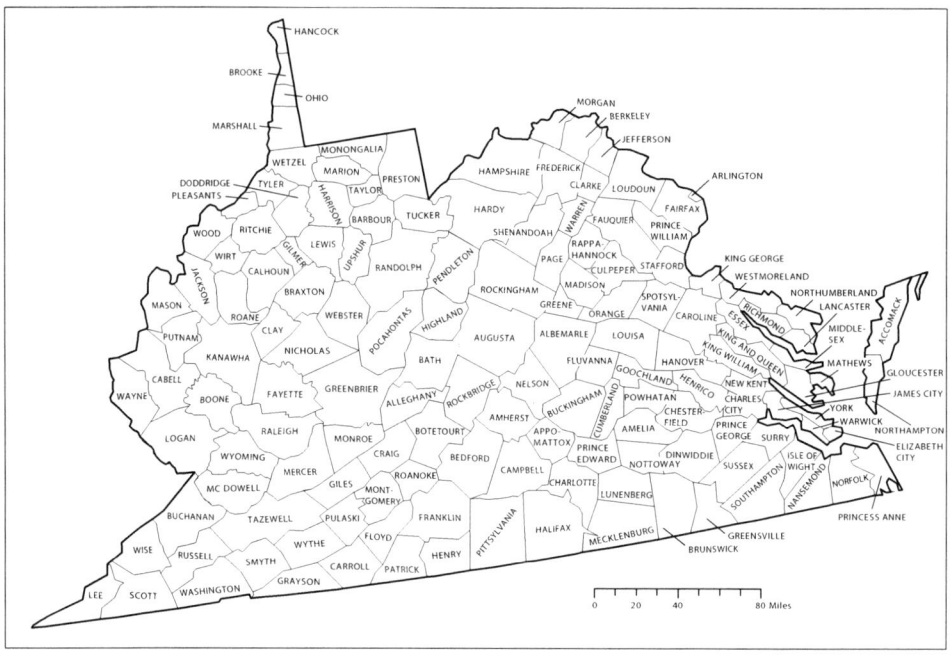

Map 2. Virginia counties, 1860

While the Nottoway, Pulaski, and Augusta County Courts responded to the November 1862 impressment call with relative swiftness, collecting their slaves within a month, most of the other counties moved more slowly, often communicating with Letcher to explain their delay.[75] The Hanover County Court protested that the sheriff and his deputies lived too far from the courthouse to communicate with the justices on a regular basis, especially in inclement weather. More plausibly, officials in Rockbridge County suggested that they could not meet immediately because both the sheriff and his deputy had traveled to Richmond to pay their county taxes. Officials from Culpeper County proposed that Letcher rescind their quota altogether because many of their male slaves had escaped to the Union army lines in northern Virginia.[76] Letcher's negative reply to all of these petitions was brief; he simply noted that he did not have the power to intervene.

Loss of slaves to Union army incursions was a particularly common complaint from the counties in the lower Shenandoah Valley, the Tidewater region, and the counties between Richmond and Washington, D.C. For example, slaveholders in King William County, less than twenty miles northeast of the Confederate capital, protested their quota of 100 slaves despite having been one of the most prosperous counties in Virginia before the war. According to the 1860 census, King William County's 5,525 slaves accounted for nearly 65 percent of the county's total population. Moreover, the county had held approximately 1,300 male slaves in the military age range.[77] Yet the King William County Court wrote to Governor Letcher in January 1863 to say that at least half of the county's able-bodied male slaves had escaped. In addition, slaveholders from King William had sent laborers to the Peninsula under several different requisitions from General Magruder in 1861. Under these circumstances, the county requested a reduction in its quota. Letcher agreed, forwarding the request to the Engineer Bureau.[78] A few days later, Captain Rives reduced King William's quota from 100 to 40.[79]

Rives and Gilmer regularly sought compromise measures, reasoning that it was better to receive some laborers, even if under restrictive terms, than none at all. As the spring of 1863 approached, they allowed some counties to meet their unfilled quotas by sending slaves to work on local railroads; others worked on the fortifications at Lynchburg or Saltville rather than travel all the way to Richmond. Sometimes these changes came at the request of Confederate officers rather than of the slaveholders, such as when Major General Samuel Jones asked to retain some impressed slaves from Pulaski and Montgomery Counties to work on local roads and fortifications, although the slaves' owners no doubt preferred these arrangements as well.[80] Compromise would be a recurring theme in Gilmer's efforts to obtain slave laborers for the Engineer Department.

As Virginia's counties once again petitioned and delayed their way out of sending their full impressment quotas in November 1862 (or at least doing so expeditiously), Gilmer and his subordinates began to prepare a third call on Virginia slaveholders. The January 1863 impressment call focused on counties not included in either the October or November requisitions, although some of these localities had contributed slave laborers to fortification projects before the state impressment legislation went into effect (see appendix, table 1.3). This requisition for approximately 4,000 slaves followed the same pattern as its predecessors, except that Gilmer this time communicated with newly appointed Secretary of War James A. Seddon; Seddon then passed Gilmer's letter to President Davis and Governor Letcher.[81]

Letcher's office noticed an immediate problem with the new impressment quotas: while Gilmer had listed some of Virginia's incorporated cities as individual localities, he had combined Henrico County and the City of Richmond on his list. Together, the 900 slaves Henrico County and Richmond were expected to send amounted to nearly one-fourth of the entire impressment call, so it was crucial that these localities respond promptly. But because the city and county had two distinct governing bodies, each needed a clear and independent quota. Noting a similar problem, Munford questioned whether Petersburg's quota was encompassed by Chesterfield or Dinwiddie County.[82] Captain Rives consulted census reports to make an equitable division, correcting the earlier requisition to require 550 slaves from Richmond and 350 from Henrico County. He also considered Petersburg's responsibility, noting, "The county of Chesterfield has been assessed independently of Petersburg; but then an equitable division of the Five Hundred and Fifty called for from the city of Petersburg and the county of Dinwiddie is necessary." According to Rives, Petersburg should send 230 slaves; Dinwiddie County, 320.[83]

Most of the slaves impressed in October and November 1862 had come from counties in the Piedmont or the Shenandoah Valley; the new impressment call in January turned to counties in the far southwestern portion of the state and to counties along the Chesapeake and Atlantic coasts. Most of the mountainous southwestern counties had slave populations accounting for no more than 20 percent of their overall population, and in many of the counties, this percentage was much lower. The coastal counties, while they generally had much larger slave populations than those in the mountains, had either contributed slaves to earlier fortification projects (such as Magruder's fortifications at Gloucester Point and Yorktown) or had seen many of their male slaves run away with each Union army incursion. Thus, resistance to this new call tended to be heavy and often continued well into the spring and summer of 1863. Two of the most common objections to slave impressment—that it would dramatically decrease the state's agricultural output and that it would encourage slaves to run away from already exposed areas—reached their peak of effectiveness during the summer and fall of 1863 in both Virginia and North Carolina.

North Carolina's slaveholders, like those in Virginia, contributed many slave laborers to the Confederate fortifications during the first two years of the war despite the absence of state laws regulating the practice of impressment. The most important fortifications in North Carolina were those surrounding the port city of Wilmington; North Carolina's slaves also built defensive works around railroad depots throughout the state. In addition, Confederate commanders in southeastern Virginia regularly crossed state borders to impress slaves from North Carolina's northeastern counties when the local labor supply had dwindled. Thus, slaveholders in North Carolina were already quite familiar with the process of slave impressment—and predisposed to object to it—even before the state legislature enacted its own laws in December 1862 and January 1863. Moreover, the law legislators eventually approved was much less dependent on local elected officials than Virginia's, granting more power to the governor and Confederate officers and almost none to county courts. The implementation of slave impressment in North Carolina would end up being far less predictable than the process in Virginia was, as well as more difficult to track. And while slaveholders in the state protested impressment just as vigorously as their neighbors did, they had almost no ability to resist a requisition.

By December 1862, the situation at Wilmington had reached a crisis point, and General Whiting feared the city would fall without a fresh infusion of laborers. Union forces had occupied New Bern, North Carolina, just ninety miles north of Wilmington; Union gunboats floated along the coast of South Carolina with relative ease. On November 26, Whiting wrote to former secretary of war Major General Gustavus Smith, describing the weakness of Wilmington's defenses; Smith shared these concerns with General Lee.[84] Lee recognized Wilmington's weakness but had no intention of sending his own soldiers to reinforce the city, as his army was fully engaged outside Fredericksburg, Virginia.[85]

The citizens of North Carolina, though fearing the outcome of a Union attack at Wilmington, expressed faith in Whiting. "We know that General Whiting is in command," the *Salisbury Carolina Watchman* intoned, "and that he will defend the place to the last, and we sincerely trust that the defence may be successful, that the enemy may be repulsed, and that our friends in Wilmington may be spared the scenes, trials and sufferings through which the citizens of Newbern passed."[86] North Carolina's newspapers may have been less favorably inclined toward Whiting if they had known that his preferred solution to defending the city was to impress more slaves to build fortifications, thus freeing his soldiers from that responsibility. Whiting, meanwhile, had little doubt that he was the man who could save Wilmington for the Confederacy.

Whiting's calls for increased slave impressment in early December 1862 coincided neatly with the peak of Vance's interest in the subject. During his first annual message to the North Carolina state legislature in November, Vance made a brief statement calling for a slave impressment law to cement the state's authority, ensuring that he, not General Whiting or the secretary of war, was in charge of slave impressment in North Carolina.[87] In response to the annual message, the *Salisbury Carolina Watchman* praised Vance's "deep and praiseworthy concern for the welfare of the

State"; William W. Holden, editor of the *North Carolina Standard*, opined that the governor's recommendations "should receive the cordial assent of the people's representatives."[88]

The state senate and House of Commons did, in fact, respond immediately to Vance's request for a slave impressment law. On November 20, House members introduced a bill authorizing the governor to impress slaves for defensive work. Two days later, the state senate referred a similar resolution to its committee on military affairs. Both houses debated slave impressment bills, with a series of potential amendments, in early December. On December 20, 1862, the North Carolina Senate approved its slave impressment bill and sent the law to the House of Commons. Rather than debate further amendments, the House immediately approved the Senate's version of the law.[89]

North Carolina's slave impressment law did not define new procedures for impressing and collecting slave laborers, but instead simply legalized the process already in place while attempting to give the state's leaders greater control. The law stipulated that the governor, upon request from Confederate officials, held the primary authority and responsibility to requisition slave labor for defensive work. In some areas, the governor's authority was absolute. For example, while slave impressment in Virginia, by law, could never exceed 20 percent of the adult male slaves, Governor Vance could, in theory, impress every enslaved man, woman, and child in the state of North Carolina. In other ways, however, the governor gained no measureable discretion over slave impressment. North Carolina's law failed to mandate that Confederate officials consult with Vance to ensure their requisitions did not overlap, and the law did not stipulate a maximum length of impressment. While Vance and the state legislature expected Confederate authorities to respect this new law and funnel all labor requisitions through the governor's office, nothing in the legislation actually required them to do so.[90]

While writing the impressment act, the state legislature did take a few steps to protect the power of North Carolina's local leaders and placate the state's slaveholders. First, legislators promised that owners would be compensated for any slaves who escaped or were captured or killed by Union forces. They also amended a section of the state's existing codes granting North Carolina's county courts, which met four times each year, fuller authority over local labor levies to repair and build roads. Finally, they ratified a series of resolutions allowing counties to send free blacks to the fortifications in place of slaves whenever they chose. This last provision was particularly important because it enabled many North Carolina counties to avoid sending slaves to work on the defenses in Wilmington and elsewhere.[91] In Virginia, by contrast, each requisition specified whether it targeted free or enslaved men, and local officials could not substitute one for the other.

Confederate officers in the eastern part of the state, eager to fortify the railroad lines connecting Wilmington to Petersburg, took immediate advantage of North Carolina's new impressment laws, calling for numerous slaves in December 1862 and January 1863. Whiting, with Vance's consent, ordered militia officers in Bladen, Robeson, Columbus, and Cumberland Counties to send him up to 200 slaves or free blacks from each county. Engineers at Goldsboro impressed slaves from Duplin, Lenoir, Greene, and Wilson Counties in December. In January, Vance ordered Warren County to send half its male slaves—1,200 men—to Weldon. He also issued an order for one-quarter of Halifax County's slaves, or 750 laborers. Franklin, Granville, and Wake Counties, rather than impressing slaves, sent most of their free black men to work at Kinston.[92]

As the spring of 1863 approached, Vance no doubt hoped impressment calls would diminish, leaving North Carolina's farmers a full slave labor force to accomplish their spring planting. Yet he received another urgent request from General Whiting at the beginning of March. Despite having impressed slave laborers at least twice since taking command of the Wilmington fortifications, Whiting felt he needed more men. In particular, he wrote Vance, "the negroes we now have ought to be discharged," but he could not send his current workers home without receiving assurances that he would have some way to replace them. "I am very loath to resort to *impressment* of the hands of the people immediately in this vicinity who have already done so much and made so many sacrifices to promote the defence," Whiting continued, "but unless I receive some assistance very speedily from elsewhere I shall be compelled to do it."[93]

Whiting issued the impressment call a few weeks later with support from Vance and at least one of Raleigh's newspapers. "We learn that a small number of slaves from each of the midland Counties have been called for and sent to Wilmington," Holden noted in the *North Carolina Standard*, "to work on the fortifications. This is a just and necessary measure." This "small number," nearly 800 laborers, amounted to 10 percent of the male slaves between the ages of eighteen and fifty-five in each county, compared to the 25 percent required from most Virginia counties during the same time period (see appendix, table 1.4). Adjutant General Daniel Fowle ordered state militia officers to collect the slaves, instructing them to arrest any slaveholder who resisted.[94]

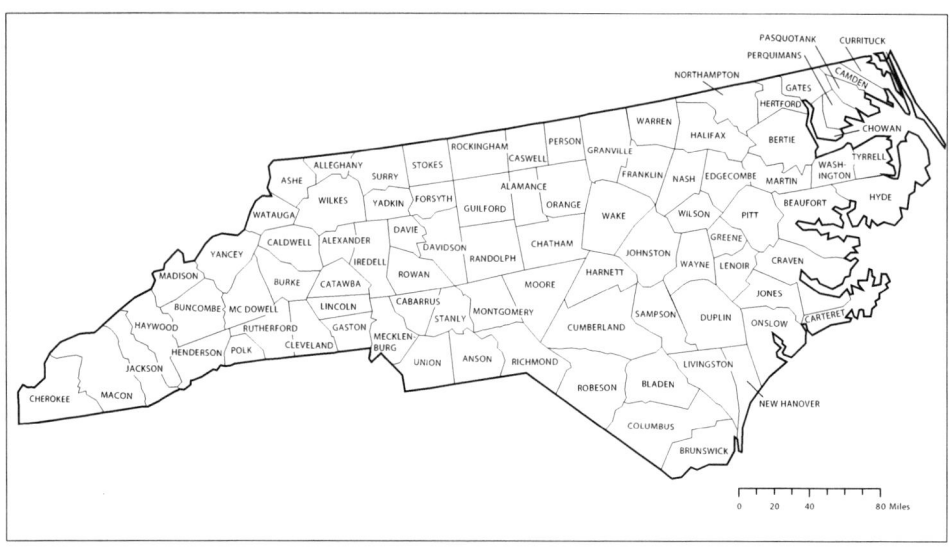

Map 3. North Carolina counties, 1860

According to the *Standard*, the March 1863 requisitions for slaves caused great dismay in the central portion of the state. Editor Holden was not particularly sympathetic to the slaveholders, noting, "The labor of these very slaves may save Wilmington—save the Railroad that runs by it—save Fayetteville from the gunboats of the enemy, and save Johnston, and Wake, and Cumberland from the presence of armies which would fall back to the interior if that Road should be lost." Thus, it was the duty of every North Carolina slaveholder, not merely those along the coast, to make sacrifices in order to defend the coastal fortifications. This article failed to take into account the numerous slaves and free blacks from the central portion of the state who had built fortifications in Weldon, Goldsboro, and Kinston just a few months prior to the new requisition.[95]

Holden did anticipate the key objection to this, and later, impressment calls in central North Carolina—that impressing slaves, especially in the spring and summer, would endanger the state's agriculture. Both Vance and his Virginia counterpart, Governor John Letcher, received regular complaints from farmers during the spring and summer of 1863 and proved more likely to rescind impressment calls to protect their states' farms than for any other reason. Protecting agriculture would also be the impetus for a number of amendments made to both states' slave impressment laws. As each state legislature contemplated those amendments, however, and as each governor sought to defend his state physically while maintaining agricultural output, they would face increasing interest in and control over slave impressment from the national government.

⁂ Localized, ad hoc requisitions gave way to state-directed impressment in the summer and fall of 1862 in part because the Confederacy's male labor pool was drying up. Once the April 1862 conscription law put most white men in uniform, the work of enslaved men became even more important, and planters were thus more likely to resist sending their slaves to build fortifications. Confederate officials no doubt hoped that state impressment laws could overcome this reluctance as well as many of the other difficulties they had encountered during the first eighteen months of the war: overlapping requisitions, murky authority, and noncompliance (and even outright obstruction) by local elected officials.

While the state laws enacted in October 1862 and December 1862 resolved some of the problems Confederate authorities and slaveholders encountered during the first year of the war, many difficulties still remained. Virginia and North Carolina eventually established the Confederacy's responsibility to pay slaveholders both a monthly wage for impressed slaves and full compensation for slaves who escaped, died, or were seriously injured on the fortifications, but doubtless many slaveholders failed to receive this compensation in a timely manner, if at all. Virginia's slave impressment statute gave specific authority and responsibilities to county courts and the governor far beyond the provisions of the North Carolina laws. This meant that Governor Letcher had considerably more power to oppose or restrict a requisition for slaves than did Governor Vance, although Letcher generally declined to take advantage of this authority. The laws put into place by the North Carolina state legislature and the Confederate Congress not only limited Vance's ability to oppose a requisition from General Whiting but also failed to require any clear line of communication between the two men—thus allowing Whiting to impress slaves without even informing Vance. Letcher, by contrast, received impressment quotas by county as well as regular updates on the Engineer Bureau's progress on collecting the slaves.

The difference between the two state laws would become clear in the spring of 1863, when Letcher successfully prohibited a requisition that he felt would endanger the state's agriculture. Vance was unable to prevent a similar call for slaves in North Carolina, prompting an outcry from his state's farmers. Diverging approaches to enforcement likely intensified their fervor. Denied the ability to exercise control over the local officials responsible for impressment, North Carolinians sent more individual letters to the secretary of war and to the governor's office than did their neighbors in Virginia. Virginia's slaveholders were more likely to allow their elected county court officers to communicate with state and national officials.

Slaveholders in both states protested impressment under the guise of state law as vehemently as they had protested ad hoc requisitions by Confederate officers. Their letters and petitions highlighted three major concerns: treatment of slaves on the fortifications, the possibility that impressment might encourage slaves to run away, and the damage that labor shortages might do to agricultural operations. In many cases, planters cloaked their resistance to early impressment quotas with benevolence, arguing that they did not want to send their slaves to the fortifications because they feared those slaves would be overworked, poorly fed, and exposed to bad weather and illness. Subsequent requisitions would become even more difficult to enforce when many of the nearly 18,000 slaves returning from the first round of calls in the two states confirmed at least some of these suspicions.

CHAPTER TWO

Throwing Up Breastworks

Slave Laborers under the Engineer Bureau

In 1937, speaking with Works Progress Administration interviewer Susie Byrd, Reverend Ishrael Massie recalled his experiences with Confederate slave impressment. A young teenager at the time of the Civil War, Massie once helped his master and the local impressment agent "catch men to carry to th' battlefield." When one slave attempted to run away rather than face service on the fortifications, Massie grabbed the man and tried to hold him. He recalled, "To weaken dis man down, one t'other men struck de bayonet in him. Dey missed his arm an' stuck mine right above de elbow." Eventually, the impressment agents pacified the slave and "put him to wuck on de breastworks." Massie received medical care for his arm and returned home.[1]

The enslaved man Massie fought was right to fear impressment and the weeks of difficult labor it entailed. Perhaps this man had already served a term with the Engineer Bureau and therefore had firsthand knowledge of work on the fortifications. Perhaps he had simply heard stories from slaves who had returned from earlier terms of impressment. This slave may have acted with the tacit approval of his master, a Mr. Young, because many slaveholders were also aware of the dangers slaves faced while on the fortifications. Neither Massie nor his interviewer had access to all of this information, but the anecdote suggests some key points in the story of slave impressment. Not surprisingly, impressed slaves faced long hours of extremely hard physical labor. In addition, the Confederate government routinely failed to provide adequate food, shelter, and medical care for impressed slaves. But most important, the widespread availability of information about these dangerous conditions made impressment both more necessary and more difficult throughout the course of the war and may have encouraged slaves to escape to Union lines rather than face a trip to the fortifications.

Slaveholders gleaned information about the living and working conditions of engineer laborers from a number of sources. Their first, and often most reliable, sources of information were the overseers who supervised both hired and impressed slaves. In particular, Virginia's planters trusted the slaveholding neighbors (often physicians or wounded Confederate soldiers) appointed as overseers in accordance with the state's impressment legislation. These overseers were in a position to provide slaveholders with detailed information about the daily routines, living conditions, shelter, and medical care afforded impressed slaves, especially after the slaves returned home. During each two-month term of impressment, overseers regularly sent letters to local newspapers with more general information about life on the fortifications; these letters most often contained appeals for additional food.

Newspaper editors also published reports about the Engineer Bureau's labor practices, often noting the most inflammatory or sensational stories in an attempt to indict the bureau for mistreating impressed slaves. One such story illustrated "the meagerness of the rations given [impressed slaves], by one of the negroes snatching a ration of meat from a comrade, and placing it with his own, swallowing both in one mouthful." Finally, slaveholders received reports from their own slaves as well as from the slaves of their neighbors as men returned from the fortifications. William T. Macklin told his representative that "reports from the sick servants returned to the [county] are that the sick in the hospital are very much neglected & almost starved." Governor Zebulon Baird Vance received a letter from a North Carolina slaveholder who complained that "the returned negroes say that my boy is without shoes or clothing and that he has been sick, and is very much swollen, still he is hard at work."[2]

These complaints—and dozens of letters just like them—reflected slaveholders' widespread assumptions that the Engineer Bureau either neglected or abused their slaves, and clearly owners hoped to capitalize on these perceived abuses to resist impressment calls. The governors uniformly rejected such appeals but also insisted that the Confederate government provide food, shelter, and medical care to all enslaved laborers. Most engineer officers recognized the importance of providing proper care to impressed slaves and frequently bemoaned their limited resources. Yet the charges of abuse and neglect, as well as the connections planters drew between labor requisitions and runaway slaves, remained remarkably consistent over time and space. While slaveholders' opposition failed to alter either state's commitment to slave impressment, they did force both the governors and Confederate authorities to keep slaveholders' rights as property holders quite high on their lists of priorities. Throughout the war, governors routinely pressured the national government to protect the interests of their slaveholding constituents by protecting their slaves' physical health; Confederate leaders responded by paying close attention to slaves' rations and medical care and eventually creating a claims board to help compensate owners for dead and escaped slaves. Thus, slaveholders' attempts to protect their property from abuse by the government prompted significant growth in the breadth and power of the Confederate bureaucracy. Tragically, that expanded bureaucracy still routinely failed to ensure the well-being of impressed slaves.

Former slaves who recalled working for the Confederate Engineer Department in Virginia and North Carolina spoke in very general terms about the work they performed. William I. Johnson, who had worked as a camp servant, stated that "sometimes, too, we were all put to digging trenches or throwing up breastworks." Robert Williams simply recalled, "I was pressed for service to make breast works over in Amherst." George Rogers remembered being sent from his master's regiment to Wilmington, where he worked on fortifications for more than three years. Cornelius Garner proudly insisted that slaves who helped build fortifications were "doin' soldier's wuk," but he provided no specific details of what that work entailed. Certainly, enslaved workers with the Engineer Department performed a wide variety of unskilled manual labor, but their primary responsibility was digging the long trenches that surrounded Richmond and other key Confederate towns.[3]

Confederate engineer officers, many of whom had received their training from the U.S. Military Academy at West Point, had very clear expectations for how the slaves would perform their work. Engineers on both sides of the conflict used Dennis Hart Mahan's *Treatise on Field Fortifications*, which suggested that excavation workers be organized into teams of three. While one laborer used a pick to loosen the soil, three to six feet deep at a time, two men would follow him with shovels, pitching the dirt twelve feet to either the side or the top of the ditch. Mahan avowed the importance of proper drainage for these ditches and also suggested that the

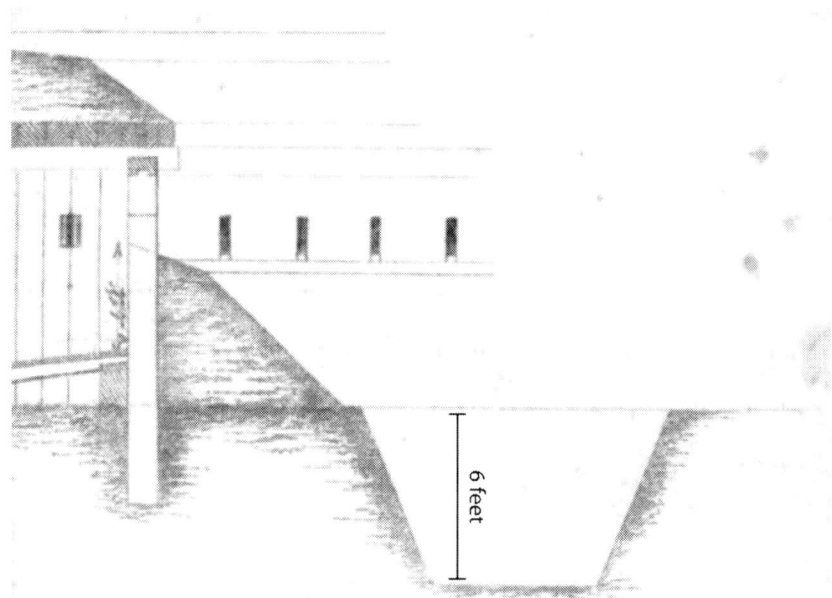

Figure 2.1. Layout of ditch from Mahan's Treatise on Field Fortification, *1846*

laborers could erect scaffolding if they needed to dig a particularly deep ditch. Finally, he enjoined, "From troops unaccustomed to the use of ditching tools, six cubic yards may be considered a fair day's work in ordinary soils."[4] Thus, an impressed slave working for the Engineer Department could expect to spend most of his time swinging heavy picks or shovels to move, in concert with two other men, roughly eight tons of dirt each day.[5]

Observing nearly 500 slave laborers near Gloucester Point, Fred Fleet described their work in a letter to his mother. First, the slaves felled all the trees in a fifteen-acre area. Then they began to dig deep ditches topped with embankments. Fleet reported that the embankment walls were at least two feet wide and two feet high. Once the walls were built, workers used large, heavy cylindrical implements to pack the dirt into place. From all indications, digging entrenchments was extremely difficult work, requiring long days in the field. Although the majority of impressed slaves normally labored as field hands and were therefore accustomed to long days of hard work, digging entrenchments probably required, if not greater effort, then at least more consistent and sustained effort than did most daily tasks on the farms of Virginia and North Carolina.[6]

Impressed slaves performed other tasks besides digging trenches. On occasion, the Engineer Bureau responded to requests from other Confederate departments and even civilian employers for additional

Figure 2.2. Slaves building fortifications, as depicted in the Illustrated London News, *April 18, 1863 (Courtesy of "The Civil War in America from the* Illustrated London News*": A Joint Project by Sandra J. Still, Emily E. Katt, Collection Management, and the Beck Center of Emory University)*

laborers. Impressed slaves loaded and unloaded supplies from trains and ships, hauled supplies from depots to camps, and helped construct pontoon bridges. Alfred Landon Rives, by this time lieutenant colonel and temporarily acting as head of the Engineer Bureau, sent a party of engineer troops and fifty slaves to the vicinity of Fredericksburg "to save the iron from the Warrenton R. R." in October 1863. The same month, an overseer from Rockbridge County told slaveholders from Lexington that their slaves were working in a stone quarry rather than building fortifications. While most of the slaves employed on the Weldon fortifications dug ditches and built embankments, others kept busy "cutting posts and holes for revetments and fraises, hewing timber for magazines and sills for platforms and carrying them from woods to works; [and] assisting carpenters in construction of magazines."[7]

The Engineer Bureau made consistent efforts to provide competent overseers for its enslaved labor force, thus calming slaveholders' fears about work conditions on the fortifications. The Virginia General Assembly, the North Carolina state legislature, and the Confederate Congress all continued this policy throughout the war. Rives mandated that overseers and armed guards accompany any movement of slaves from one location to another. For example, when detailing laborers from the fortifications around Richmond to Oakwood Cemetery, he instructed a subordinate to "send at once to Battery No. 17 on the Petersburg turnpike & have 100 hands & overseers brought over at once. They should report immediately on arrival at the office of the Provost Marshal who will send a guard with them."[8]

Early in the war, because the slaveholders were unable to choose or communicate with the overseers, most owners still did not trust the Engineer Bureau's management. Tales of the neglect and outright abuse of engineer laborers abounded. Sam, a slave belonging to Benjamin Hunter, was killed by a train when an unsupervised group of slaves attempted to cross the railroad tracks. The *Richmond Examiner* cataloged a series of abuses, including an instance "where a free negro on the fortifications had his back actually cut into a mangle of bleeding flesh, the driver having given him, as we were told by a policeman, *five hundred and sixty-one* lashes with the whip, until the poor victim sank exhausted under his fiendish rage." Benjamin E. Pope claimed that after his slave Tom fell sick at the Yorktown fortifications, "a Mr. James Bray who was a superintendent of the hands generally, went to the Shanty where this man 'Tom' was, when the Weather was very Cold, with a heavy sleet on the Ground, ordered him out, made him strip, lie down on the ground and whipped him, then made him go out to work."[9]

Eventually, Rives made provisions for each county to send community members to the fortifications as overseers, suggesting that "it would be well to content the owners." The slaveholders of Chatham County, North Carolina, for example, agreed to send the sixty slaves called from their county in March 1863 only if they could also send "Dr. Byrnum, a native of this county and discharged soldier, a good physician and young man of character," as overseer. The citizens of Mecklenburg County, Virginia, complained that the engineer officers at Richmond rejected one of the two overseers they sent with their slaves in April 1864. In response, Lieutenant William Hauser noted that Mecklenburg's overseer had "been on the works before and proved himself perfectly useless." Hauser reassured the slaveholders of Mecklenburg County that he had not dismissed their overseer from "a desire to do injustice to the slave owners, nor to push their slaves." Slave owners expected overseers not only to supervise slaves during work and leisure hours but also to ensure that slaves had sufficient shelter, food, and medical care. Drawing on often-scarce Confederate resources, the Engineer Bureau was never able to provide such things to the satisfaction of the slaveholders of Virginia and North Carolina.[10]

The Confederacy's slave laborers, like its soldiers, usually slept in tents. Captain Rives regularly communicated with the Quartermaster's Department in order to ensure that tents were available to the slaves as soon as they arrived at their destination.[11] This was not always easy, especially for the slaves working along rivers and on smaller fortifications, who were often moved from one point to the next without much advance notice. Overseers reported numerous instances where the slaves did not have access to tents. Accounting for the illness of Benjamin Pope's slave Tom, overseer Charles Bryant complained, "I with all my hands was ordered to a Battery near 'Bethel' Church during a storm of snow and hail & sleet where they were kept two or three days without any kind of Shelter, having no Shanties or anything of the kind to Shelter under." Another overseer testified "that the weather was wet and cold while he was there, and that the quarters were very uncomfortable—some few of them had old tents—the balance fixed some shelters by putting some poles on forks and covering them with leaves and dirt."[12]

Even those slaves and overseers who obtained adequate shelter claimed that they often were unable to build fires. One noted that while the slaves from Pittsylvania County slept in a hospital basement in Richmond, they lacked sufficient firewood to dry their clothes after rainy workdays. An overseer from Powhatan County indicated that the slaves in his charge were usually forbidden to light fires because of their proximity to Union forces. Discounting such claims, an overseer from Rockbridge County assured slaveholders that "the force from each County, has its own encampment and cooks. They lodge in tents with a large fire-place in close proximity and fronting the door of the tent."[13]

In addition to providing tents for its laborers, the Engineer Bureau assured owners that their slaves would receive army rations during their terms of service. Slaves and overseers who found the standard army ration insufficient sent messages to their owners through the newspapers. The *Staunton Spectator* reported, "Let the owners of slaves know that they are all well, near Drewry's Bluff. In fine spirits and cheering for Jeff Davis and the Southern Confederacy. Their rations are short—new corn meal sifted and bacon. Owners should join and send enough for one ration a day to the respective overseers." The *Lexington Gazette* published similar appeals. One overseer noted, "The hands generally were cheerful, and doing good service, but, they would like to have *a little more fat bacon*. The ration is ½ lb. bacon and 1 lb. 2 oz. flour per day. Meal is occasionally given instead of flour. They told me that they would not 'mind the work, if they had a little more hog meat.'" Another suggested that "so far the bread stuff has held out in weight, but I would say to all, who can send some bacon and a little meal or flour, with any sort of convenience, that it would be better to do so." The *Lynchburg Virginian* recommended to local slaveholders that in addition to sending their slaves, "it would be well to give an outfit to each, of a bushel of meal and some bacon, to carry with them."[14]

Other overseers and slaveholders painted a more dire picture of the slaves' rations. An overseer from Appomattox County testified "that the hands under my care were fed part of the time with unwholsome foods, Meat literally rotten & I have no doubt that it contributed much to the sickness among them." The editor of the *Lexington Gazette*, responding to such reports, thundered, "It is really uncivilized and barbarous to take negroes to work and give them nothing to eat. We hope that the Government will pay nothing to the owners of the negroes for their services, and spend the sixteen dollars for bacon and corn meal, and cease to starve our negroes."[15]

Slaveholders and county officials who feared their slaves received inadequate rations typically voiced their concerns to state leaders rather than to the Confederate government or the press. One appealed to Governor John Letcher of Virginia, asking him to "enquire into the matter and have the C. S. Government to give our negro's at least enough to eat." Letcher and his successor, Governor William Smith, maintained a regular correspondence with the Engineer Bureau and the Confederate secretary of war on the subject of rations for impressed slaves. In North Carolina, Governor Vance received similar appeals. One slaveholder complained that his slaves were "worked beyond their powers of endurance kept on food wholey unfit for use & but little of that," while another suggested that "we had rather furnish them with provisions from home than have their health injured by starvation." Expressing his frustration with such complaints, Vance responded, "I have reason to know that the negroes at Wilmington are faring better than our soldiers in the field & excite more sympathy."[16]

Interestingly, officers of the Engineer Bureau tended to agree with the slaveholders rather than with Governor Vance, considering the standard army ration inadequate for the amount of work impressed slaves performed on a daily basis. Colonel Jeremy Gilmer, bureau chief, assured slaveholders that he provided the standard army ration to all workers. "Whatever deficiency exists, if any," he argued, "is due to the inadequacy of the Army ration, which is thus composed or equivalent to $1\frac{1}{3}$ lb of flour or $1\frac{1}{4}$ of meal and $\frac{1}{2}$ lb of salt meat or 1 lb of fresh." Gilmer, after consulting with engineer officers in the field, asked Secretary of War James A. Seddon "to authorize and direct the Commissary General to issue a ration and a half daily to the slaves employed on fortifications, who owing probably to their *constant labor require the extra amount of food* to keep them in health." Seddon agreed with Gilmer and authorized the generals commanding major fortifications to purchase extra cornmeal for the slave laborers.[17]

The desire to provide extra rations for impressed slaves brought the Engineer Bureau into direct conflict with the Confederate Commissary Department. In the summer and fall of 1863, with the full support of Secretary Seddon, Gilmer instructed engineer officers Colonel Walter H. Stevens and Captain Charles H. Dimmock to purchase additional bacon and cornmeal to feed the slaves. Yet the following March, when the Commissary Department complained that the engineer officers were interfering with commissary agents, Seddon retreated from his promise. While he agreed with engineer officers and slaveholders that the laborers needed more food, he could not increase their rations without increasing Confederate soldiers' as well, and he simply did not have the resources to do both. This debate continued well into the summer of 1864, as both impressed slaves and Confederate soldiers faced mounting shortages. Seddon needed to balance the requirements of all Confederate military operations and could not place the claims of impressed slave laborers above those of white Confederate soldiers without alienating large portions of the Confederate voting (and fighting) population.[18]

Echoing the sentiments of Governor Vance, Seddon frequently reminded Governors Letcher and Smith that he could not give impressed slaves more food than Confederate soldiers. Such an action would no doubt have led to an outcry from the soldiers and their families, particularly the nonslaveholding families. In addition, impressed slaves were confined to army rations only for a period of sixty days at a time and, according to their owners, received more plentiful food at home. Thus, it is likely that impressed slaves were better nourished than many Confederate soldiers, especially by the last year of the war. Yet engineer officers had good reasons for requesting extra rations for their laborers. As they noted, "The labor here is very severe & exhausting." A slave employed constantly at digging entrenchments doubtless expended more energy than the average soldier during a comparable sixty-day period, especially in the winter months. Moreover, impressed slaves had almost no free time and were more closely supervised than soldiers in camp, which meant that they had few opportunities to supplement their army rations through scavenging.[19]

Beyond the claims of simple humanity or their desire to treat impressed laborers well, Confederate officers at key fortifications argued that they

Figure 2.3. Chaffin's Bluff fortifications (Library of Congress)

could not possibly retain a sufficient labor force without providing more food than the standard army ration. Engineers at points as diverse as Wilmington and Danville argued that slaves would escape rather than endure taxing labor without sufficient food—and that "their owners, knowing that they have not a sufficiency of food, rather encourage them in deserting." Slaves who deserted the Confederate fortifications, returned home, and told their masters that they had not received enough food while working for the Confederacy were all but guaranteed a sympathetic ear. Unless Confederate authorities threatened substantial fines, few masters went to extraordinary lengths to return their slaves to the Engineer Bureau's possession. It was crucial for engineer officers to provide sufficient rations and shelter if they hoped to retain their slave labor forces.[20] But as food became increasingly scarce, especially in Virginia, engineer officers found it impossible to provision slaves to the satisfaction of their owners, which exacerbated the difficulties they faced in enforcing impressment quotas.

⁀ The debate over medical care for impressed and hired slaves often paralleled the debates over shelter and rations. Planters, politicians, and newspaper editors were eager to criticize the army for inadequate medical care, although very often the standard of care offered impressed slaves was on par with that afforded Confederate soldiers—and thus superior to what many slaves could expect on the plantations. Yet slaveholders regularly expressed their fears that service under the Engineer Bureau would damage the health of their slaves, who obviously represented an important economic investment. One Albemarle County slaveholder used humanitarian terms when writing to Attorney General Wade Keyes to secure the release of local slaves, who he feared would die of exposure in the cold mountains of northwestern Virginia.[21] Most of all, slaveholders worried that reports of illness further disposed slaves to escape to Union lines rather than face labor on the Confederate fortifications. Providing medical care to impressed slaves thus not only ensured the engineers a healthy workforce in the present but also helped them forestall slave and slaveholder resistance to future impressment calls.

The Engineer Bureau, though eager to keep slaves healthy, apparently had difficulty gaining access to the necessary medical personnel. Captain Rives instructed Captain Thomas Talcott that "when army surgeons cannot be obtained to attend the Engineer force, physicians should be employed at plantation rates." Thus, Talcott employed three civilian physicians— John R. Pender, James B. Southall, and W. D. Southall—to care for the slaves working on fortifications in southwestern Virginia. Pender agreed to work for Talcott only if authorized "to visit the laborers at *least* once a day whether any be sick or not."[22]

Rives sought the help of civilian physicians, but Medical Department officers also provided treatment to engineer laborers. In February and March 1863, Assistant Surgeon John M. Sawing attended to over 600 slaves employed on the fortifications outside Richmond, requesting several common medicines as well as candles, tea, whiskey, bandages, and blankets to use at his station on the Manchester line of fortifications outside Richmond. Acting Assistant Surgeon N. B. Tuten made a series of similar requests while he cared for approximately 200 slaves working at Drewry's Bluff. Confederate army regulations allowed one surgeon and one assistant surgeon for each regiment of infantry, so Sawing in particular was responsible for more men on the fortifications than he would have attended to if accompanying an infantry regiment (although impressed slaves rarely, if ever, suffered gunshot wounds). Moreover, medical officers treating impressed slaves faced constant criticism from the overseers appointed by each county, who reported any perceived or actual neglect of slave laborers to their owners. Indeed, overseers regularly contacted civilian physicians from their home counties, requesting that they visit sick slaves on the fortifications and implying (or stating outright) that Confederate medical officers had been negligent in their duties.[23]

While the Engineer Bureau operated a hospital in Richmond solely for the care of black military laborers and medical officers regularly visited the fortifications, slaveholders routinely reported that Confederate authorities provided little or no medical attention to impressed slaves. Slaveholder Pharoah Richardson of Smithfield wrote to Governor Vance that one of his slaves "sickened and died from exposure whilst working down there [at Wilmington], which makes the *second one*, which I have lost by sending them to work on the Fortifications." Vance also received a letter from N. P. Wilkins of Roxboro, stating that his neighbor's slave, after suffering an injury, was left alone in his tent without medical care or food for four days. Officers at Wilmington then sent the slave home, where he died.[24]

Overseers, slaveholders, and the physicians in their communities proposed a pattern of unsatisfactory medical treatment and sometimes shameful neglect of impressed slaves. Dr. James Lysle of Prince Edward County noted that Charles, a slave of James A. Watson, had returned from the fortifications with a fever and died a few days later. Daniel Coleman of Pittsylvania County argued that his slave Bob died from a lung disease he contracted "in consequence of exposure while in the employment of the Government," although Coleman neglected to describe what, if any, medical care Bob had received. Jeremiah Earley of Albemarle County, with greater specificity, complained that his slave Zack became sick "in consequence of exposure at work and the want of proper accommodation at night" but did not receive medical attention for an entire week.[25]

A healthy man in his early twenties, Zack had left Albemarle County on December 13, 1862, and arrived in Richmond the next day. He worked for two weeks under the charge of Richard Shepperd, an overseer from Albemarle County. On December 30, he "complained of having a cold and stayed in camp some three days," according to Shepperd. Zack did not see a doctor or nurse during the three days he remained in his tent. On January 2, 1863, he attempted to join the other Albemarle County slaves at work but returned to his tent after only a few hours. Shepperd suggested "that he had a violent attack of Pleurisy or Pnuemonia attending with great pain." While Shepperd spoke with a doctor about Zack's condition, the doctor did not actually examine the patient. For the next three days, Zack remained in his tent without a fire during the day, receiving little food and no medical care; he probably also infected the other men who slept in the tent at night. An officer from the Engineer Bureau finally sent Zack to the Engineer Hospital in Richmond on January 6. Doctors there reported that "he was brought here in a dying condition," and Zack died on January 8. Zack's owner, Jeremiah Earley, called on Albemarle County delegate H. B. Magruder to remind Confederate officials that "our first act of Assembly makes the Govt. liable in such cases, unless they prove proper care & attention."[26]

Two other examples illustrate that Zack was not the only slave who suffered from such neglect. Isaac, another slave from Albemarle County, "was taken with a bad cold & remained at the camp several days in a tent lying on pine brush and a blanket receiving little or no attention from any one." According to Isaac's overseer, "Thus exposed his bad cold soon turned to Pneumonia he was then sent to Richmond to the Engineer Hospital, where he lived some thirteen days suffering much from neglect & want of attention." Dr. Benjamin F. Terry of Prince Edward County provided corroborating testimony for the claim of W. C. W. Crawley. He stated that he examined a slave named George, who was working on the Drewry's Bluff fortifications despite suffering from "Typhoid Fever of a low grade with Diarhea & Pneumonia attendant." Terry did not indicate whether or not Confederate authorities provided any medical care in this case.[27]

Zack, Isaac, and George received some medical attention during their time working for the Engineer Department, yet all three died in Richmond. Apparently, Engineer officers also kept some slaves working at the fortifications until their terms of service expired despite illness and then sent those slaves home without much attention or concern. After hearing that he was ill, Lindsay's owner, Mr. Thurmond, began traveling to Richmond to retrieve the slave. Thurmond discovered, however, that Lindsay had already arrived in Lynchburg and was staying at the home of Winfree Bradley. Thurmond described Lindsay's condition as "the most pitiable object I ever saw, filthy & emaciated to the last degree." Although Lindsay "was so weak he could not talk above a whisper, and that with so much pain and difficulty," he was one of the few slaves who had the opportunity to describe his medical treatment. Lindsay managed to tell his owner "that he believed he was hauled to the Depot in a wagon, that he traveled in great pain and discomfort to the junction, where he was left over until the next train or perhaps longer, spending the time in an empty car without fire or food. That he arrived in Lynchburg in the night, and not having any place to go to, or any one to care for him." Henry Alexander and Daniel Booth, overseers from Campbell County, confirmed Lindsay's story. In all of these cases, it seems clear that the Confederate Engineer Department neglected to provide its laborers proper access to medical care.[28]

Laborers who returned home with contagious illnesses presented a particular problem for slaveholders. One reported that some slaves from Albemarle County brought "typhoid fever, which has spread through the family to a most fatal and alarming extent." North Carolina slaveholders frequently reported rumored outbreaks of yellow fever in and around Wilmington. Each time, Adjutant General Richard C. Gatlin assured all correspondents that "there is no yellow fever at Wilmington. It is important that the negroes should be sent at once."[29] Slave owners from Prince Edward, Buckingham, and Nottoway Counties all objected strenuously to sending their slaves to Richmond in the fall of 1862 because they heard rumors of a smallpox epidemic. Most feared that their slaves would be exposed to the disease and then return home to spread it throughout the county. Colonel Gilmer assured the slaveholders and Governor Letcher that the Engineer Bureau was taking every possible precaution to avoid such a disaster, noting in a letter to Letcher, "The impressed force at work on the neighboring defences has been singularly free from contagious diseases." The slaveholders of Nottoway County, however, still refused to comply with the requisition, sending their slaves only after Gilmer assured them he would use the laborers on the defenses around Petersburg rather than at Richmond.[30]

Some reports indicated that, while the engineer officers and overseers had done their best to provide medical care for impressed slaves, the Confederate Medical Department was guilty of negligent treatment. Captain John J. Clarke, an engineer, contracted the services of Dr. J. W. Bronaugh, a civilian physician, to attend to some of the slaves working along the James River in December 1862. One of these slaves, Jim, was suffering from smallpox. Rather than move him to the Smallpox Hospital in Richmond, medical officers left Jim in a cabin near the other laborers. According to Dr. Bronaugh, Jim slept on a "damp dirt floor" in a cold and poorly ventilated cabin and had an enslaved nurse "who after the first 4 or 5 days shamefully neglected him; because I suppose he was afraid of contracting the disease." Bronaugh expressed no surprise that Jim died of smallpox under these conditions. He also noted that "if any other Physician than myself, or white or black man besides this nurse, visited or saw him during his illness, I am not aware of it."[31]

Slaveholders, of course, had a vested financial interest in demonstrating neglect when they presented these cases to the Board of Slave Claims. The Confederate War Department, with the cooperation of the Engineer and Medical Departments, established the board in 1864 to hear and adjudicate claims for slaves who died while in Confederate service or as a result of diseases contracted while working for the government. In general, slaveholders needed some evidence that the Confederate government had neglected their slaves in order to have a viable claim. This evidence usually came in the form of testimony from overseers that no medical officer ever examined the slave in question.[32] Medical officers did not respond to every claim and often provided no record of proper medical care, but the Engineer Hospital in Richmond housed at least several dozen slave laborers at any given point during the war.

The Engineer Hospital opened in June 1862 and was well appointed, suggesting that Chief Engineer Gilmer and Secretary Seddon recognized the political and practical value of assuring a high standard of medical care for impressed slaves. Under the supervision of Richard S. Vest, a civilian physician from Richmond, the hospital occupied a three-story brick warehouse adjacent to the Engineer Bureau offices at Nineteenth and Cary Streets. Its basement contained a kitchen and storage areas, as well as occasionally housed slaves impressed to work on the city's fortifications. The pharmacy, office, and staff quarters were on the first floor; two wards on the second and third floor had a combined capacity of 120 patients. In addition to Vest, the hospital employed one steward, two white nurses, thirteen black nurses, and three cooks.[33] The ratio of employees to patients at the Engineer Hospital, for the most part, compared favorably to hospitals operated by the Medical Department for the care of Confederate soldiers.[34] Vest, however, reported directly to the Engineer Bureau rather than to the Medical Department, and engineer officers reviewed and approved his almost weekly requisitions of medicines and supplies, including whiskey, tea, blankets, and bedpans.[35]

Part of the difficulty in providing medical care for impressed slaves was that the Medical and Engineer Departments shared this responsibility. Medical officers in the field with impressed slaves seem to have reported to the engineers in charge of construction rather than to the Medical Department. Surgeons Robert K. Carter and Alexander R. Medway supervised short-lived "Negroe Hospitals" in Smithville and Wilmington, North Carolina, but reported to the inspector of hospitals in Richmond rather than to the medical director of hospitals in North Carolina.[36] These sets of irregularities probably facilitated attempts to share information between medical officers and the Engineer Bureau, but they also created a situation in which negligent or incompetent officers would have had very little oversight. The most prominent example of this was the Engineer Hospital in Richmond. While Dr. Vest sent weekly lists of sick and injured slaves to engineer officers in the field, he communicated only rarely with Chief Engineer Gilmer, never sending him a formal report. Neither Thomas Williams, medical director for the Army of Northern Virginia, nor Surgeon General Samuel Preston Moore received regular communications from Vest. While the Medical Department provided supplies to the Engineer Hospital, it had no direct role in its daily operations.

The Engineer Hospital was the subject of great scrutiny in December 1862 and January 1863, as thousands of slaves impressed in the previous October and November arrived in Richmond and began working. Many fell ill in December as a result of exposure to both the cold weather on the fortifications and the new diseases in their living quarters. Clearly, the hospital failed to meet the stringent standards of John M. Daniel, editor of the *Richmond Examiner*, who reported that "the poor Negroes are dying off like penned sheep, afflicted with the rot." Daniel encouraged his readers to come to Richmond themselves, visit their slaves, and ensure that they received medical attention.[37]

Engineer officers were outraged by Daniel's suggestion that they had failed to provide adequate medical care. Engineer Hospital steward Charles H. Ryland responded to the charges in a public letter to the paper, writing, "The Hospital is thoroughly cleansed with water and broom twice every day and oftener if required." Ryland further assured slaveholders that nurses and stewards bathed the patients regularly, but noted that the hospital did not have sufficient clothing or laundry facilities to change patients' garments each day. Asserting that "as to the mortality, we can compare figures with any other Hospital in the Confederacy," Ryland invited slaveholders to visit the Engineer Hospital to judge conditions there. In a letter accompanying Ryland's essay describing the hospital, Lieutenant Stanard of the Engineer Department chided the *Examiner* for printing material "calculated to do much serious harm and mischief abroad, by impressing the owners with the belief that their slaves are neglected, &c, when the contrary is the fact, and they receive the best medical attention and treatment." The controversy these editorials created forced Surgeon General Moore to intervene.[38]

Acting on the instructions of the surgeon general, the Medical Department conducted an investigation of the Engineer Hospital in January

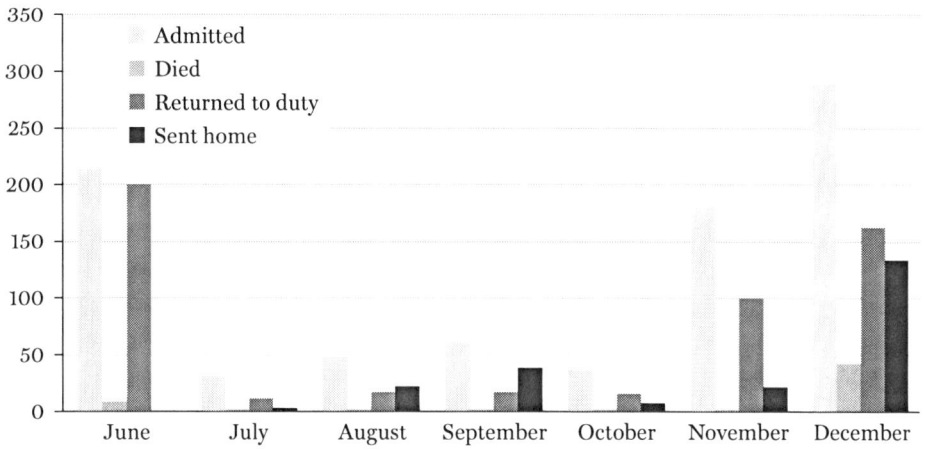

Figure 2.4. Slaves in Engineer Hospital, June–December 1862

1863. Surgeon William Carrington, inspector of hospitals in Richmond, was not impressed by Vest or by his hospital. Carrington noted that the slaves lacked hospital gowns and instead wore their work clothes, still dirty from the fortifications, and that many also lacked beds. Using Vest's weekly reports to Lieutenant Stanard of the Engineer Bureau, Carrington constructed a table of monthly admittances, discharges, and deaths, as well as those returned to duty. He also proposed a very preliminary mortality rate of .072, but he suggested this rate was not satisfactory as it failed to take into account those discharged men who died after returning to their homes. Carrington clarified the importance of the Engineer Hospital to the Confederate government: "57 negroes who died," he suggested, "are worth now at least $85,000, and dying in service, there is a question of whether their value could not be recovered from the Government." Moreover, curing the slaves quickly and returning them to the fortifications would prevent the Confederacy from having to maintain slaves it could not actually use. Finally, with the War Department struggling to find adequate labor, failing to provide swift and effective medical care to sick workers caused "inconvenience, delay, expense and miscarriage of Military operations." To ensure the best possible medical care for the engineer laborers at the least possible expense to the Confederate government, Carrington proposed the Medical Department take charge of the Engineer Hospital and replace Vest with a commissioned medical officer.[39]

Despite Carrington's suggestions, the surgeon general did not place control of the Engineer Hospital in the hands of the Medical Department, and Vest continued to run the hospital until the end of the war. Vest may have used Carrington's critiques to make changes and improvements to the hospital, and he must have retained the confidence of the Engineer Bureau, since they made no recorded efforts to replace him. Yet the Engineer Hospital remained subject to criticism by the owners of slaves who died while on the fortifications.

Vest responded to one such attack in December 1864. After explaining the circumstances under which William Macklin's slave Dudley had died, Vest took the opportunity to answer "the general charge of neglect at this hospital." He described his own daily visits to the patients before praising his subordinates, including a skilled pharmacist, a steward, and two ward masters. He noted that the two ward masters (both white men) and the nurses (primarily hired slaves) "remain constantly in the building day & night & give all necessary attention to the patients." Vest also defended himself against charges that the hospital starved its patients, claiming that "fresh beef & beef soup, chickens & chicken soup, eggs, milk, rice, stewed fruit, apples & peaches, potatoes, molasses Tea & sugar are furnished them in such quantities as the nature of the disease & the circumstance of the patient require." Finally, Vest repeated Ryland's earlier invitation, encouraging all interested slaveholders and government officials to visit the Engineer Hospital themselves and asserting that "the mortality of this Hospital will compare favorably with any in the Confederacy." Indeed, Carrington's estimated mortality rate of approximately 7 percent for the Engineer Hospital did compare favorably with the 11 percent mortality rate at Chimborazo Hospital in Richmond, although once again, doctors and nurses at the Engineer Hospital treated no gunshot wounds.[40]

Even under the best possible circumstances, the Engineer Hospital, like others, experienced chronic shortages of supplies and regular overcrowding, and Confederate medical officers and civilian physicians were unable to save every sick slave. Often, the only available history of a slave states merely that he was sent to a hospital for treatment and died while there. This is what happened to Elijah, the slave of James H. Evans; Jack, slave of Thomas A. Osborne; and countless other enslaved men from Virginia and North Carolina.[41]

Very few slaveholders from Virginia or North Carolina could follow their slaves to the fortifications and observe the medical care, rations, and shelter offered by the Engineer Bureau. Most had to rely on reports they received from newspapers, overseers, friends, and relatives near the fortifications, and sometimes from even the slaves themselves. Some went so far as to contact the Engineer Bureau, their governors, or other state or national authorities with inquiries about the well-being of their slaves. In general, slaveholders were not satisfied with the information they gained in this fashion. Most believed that the Engineer Bureau did not take proper care of its enslaved labor force, a perception that significantly hampered the bureau's attempts to field a sufficient workforce on a regular basis.

☞ The well-publicized hardships that impressed slaves faced, slaveholders repeatedly argued, encouraged them to escape. There certainly was some merit to this suggestion, and it is impossible to deny that slaves ran away at unprecedented rates during the war, especially in Virginia. The Caroline County Court, for example, reported in late December 1864 that they could not locate more than 225 male slaves between the ages of eighteen and fifty-five within their county.[42] Caroline County's slaveholders had reported owning a total of 1,889 adult men in the 1860 census. In Appomattox County, 470 adult male slaves remained, 55 percent of the 847 present in the county in 1860.[43] The Greene County Court claimed to have lost one-fourth of that county's slaves, while the Hanover County Court insisted it had lost more than half.[44] The increasingly vulnerable state of slavery even prompted Governor Smith to rescind his January 1864 impressment quotas for eleven counties in close proximity to the Union army, where the threat of mass escape was the greatest. And while the majority of slaves remained at home, slaveholders reported significant lapses in plantation discipline as well as mounting pressure to negotiate with slaves who now had more options for escape.[45] That process of negotiation included, on more than one occasion, pressuring the governors to protect slaves from being sent to the fortifications or at least to ensure better living and working conditions for those who were impressed.

Most historians now agree that emancipation was the most significant unintended consequence of the Civil War and that enslaved men and women helped make it part of the United States' war agenda.[46] Even as new studies emerge to shed greater light on the complicated priorities that slaves weighed and the often costly consequences they endured when they ran to Union lines, few doubt the importance of their unanticipated appearance in Union camps in the earliest days of the war.[47] Whether pushing emancipation to the fore or precipitating shifts in impressment quotas, then, runaway slaves shaped government policies in ways nobody expected when the war began.[48] The Virginia General Assembly, for example, issued a series of resolutions authorizing the governor to revoke slave impressment quotas for counties where more than a quarter of the slaves had run away, although Governors Letcher and Smith generally declined to exercise that authority as fully as they could have.

Work on Confederate fortifications provided some slaves with the opportunity to escape, while others viewed an impending requisition as the final element that tipped their mental balance toward running away. Still others used the threat of escape to pressure owners to resist impressment quotas. Slaves' actions also forced the governors of both Virginia and North Carolina to alter and occasionally rescind impressment quotas, as well as to quash rumors about new requisitions, rather than prompt a mass exodus of slaves in areas close to Union control.

A few slaves found their opportunities for permanent escape while in enforced service to the Confederate army. Ishrael Massie told WPA interviewers that his half-brother had run away to the Union army while impressed for Confederate service.[49] George Rogers of Wake County escaped from the fortifications at Wilmington near the end of the war and joined the Union army in Raleigh.[50] Lavinia Shepherd's slave Ben, put to work on the Richmond fortifications in February 1864, escaped the following month.[51] A slave belonging to William G. Wilkinson left his master's home but failed to report to the sheriff collecting slaves for impressment in August 1863, making his escape instead.[52] One of B. B. Walker's slaves ran away under similar circumstances in December 1864.[53] After the war, Warren White of Norfolk County told Southern Claims commissioners that he had been impressed to cut timber for Confederate forces in 1861 but eventually escaped to a Union hospital in Portsmouth, where he worked as a nurse for the rest of the war.[54]

William Benjamin Gould, a skilled and literate slave born in Wilmington in 1837, famously took advantage of the chaos caused by the city's yellow fever epidemic to escape to the Union navy via the Cape Fear River. On September 21, 1862, Gould and a party of seven other enslaved men boarded a small boat and rowed their way to freedom under cover of darkness. They were picked up by the USS *Cambridge* in sight of Fort Caswell, a Confederate fortification some thirty miles south of Wilmington. Gould then enlisted in the U.S. Navy, serving for just over three years. While the heavy Confederate presence at Wilmington usually limited slaves' chances for escape by surrounding them with armed white men, the disorder of the epidemic doubtless worked in Gould's favor.[55]

Slaveholders occasionally read about such runaways in the newspapers. A Prince George County slaveholder advertised for his slave Henry, who escaped from the fortifications outside Petersburg in September 1862.[56] More sensationally, the *Richmond Daily Dispatch* reprinted an article from the *New York Herald*, in which a U.S. Navy schooner near Fort Monroe "picked up a canoe containing six negroes in a bad condition. One of these being a very intelligent darkey, reports that the six of them having been impressed to dig entrenchments at Yorktown, planned their escape, which resulted as above stated by them, stealing a canoe and trusting to Providence for safety."[57]

Despite the presumably successful escapes of the slaves described above, there is little evidence that slaves were more likely to escape from Confederate fortifications than they were to run away from home. In fact, they may have been less likely to do so. Collin, a slave belonging to Thomas Bocock, Speaker of the Confederate House of Representatives, attempted to run away from the Richmond defenses in December 1864, but a group of soldiers detailed to guard impressed slaves caught him and put him back to work.[58] While impressment brought some slaves physically closer to the Union armies, it also brought them under far more stringent supervision than they experienced on most plantations. Surrounded by overseers, engineer officers, and Confederate soldiers with guns, most impressed slaves on the fortifications probably had few opportunities to escape. Tellingly, fewer than 10 percent of the cases adjudicated by the Board of Slave Claims involved runaways.

Many of the impressed slaves and free blacks who did escape Confederate service ran home rather than attempted to reach Union lines. For example, five slaves from Rockingham County who had gone to Wilmington in December 1863 escaped in late April 1864 and "returned to their owners in a bad condition."[59] Two slaves from Mecklenburg County and two from Randolph County escaped from the Raleigh fortifications together on September 19, 1864. Their owners sought payment for the slaves' service on the fortifications but not compensation for the slaves themselves, suggesting that the slaves returned home rather than ran away entirely.[60] When a number of slaves ran home from the fortifications at Weldon in November 1864, Adjutant General Gatlin wrote to militia officers to secure their immediate return.[61]

Slaves who returned home most likely did not act out of affection toward their owners, despite what many slaveholders would have liked to believe. Free black men like Robert Elliot of Norfolk County and Joseph Atkins of Henrico County escaped the fortifications to be closer to their wives and children, and no doubt many slaves went home for the same reason.[62] For those wishing to escape harsh working conditions, running home may have been far safer than attempting to run to Union lines, especially if they could enlist the help of a sympathetic master or one of his friends. Charles, a slave belonging to Andrew Grinnan, ran away from the government iron furnace his master had hired him to in July 1863; rather than going to the Yankees or his master, Charles went to Mr. Bryan, an acquaintance of his master, displaying "a deep cut on his knee" and requesting a break from his work. Bryan allowed Charles to stay with him for three weeks and recommended that Grinnan forgive the offense.[63] Charles thus manipulated Bryan's perception of himself as a benevolent slaveholder to earn a short vacation, a game many slaves played with proficiency borne of experience.

Finally, most slaves were practical enough to judge their surroundings and determine whether or not an escape seemed likely to succeed. Many slaves were impressed or hired to work in areas relatively far from any Union forces. Slaves and free blacks impressed in Cumberland County, North Carolina, for example, were regularly put to work in the Confederate arsenal at Fayetteville rather than sent to the fortifications at Wilmington.[64] James Dean, a slave in Bedford County, Virginia, was impressed and detailed as a blacksmith but never left the county. He later told a Southern Claims Commission interviewer, "I knew I was helping the rebels, when I was shoeing their horses, but I could not help it, they made me do it. I was about 200 miles from any Union forces and there was no possible chance for me to escape." Not only was he far from Union lines, but Dean, like most impressed slaves, was also carefully monitored by Confederate overseers and officers. The likelihood of a successful escape seemed slim.[65]

Still, impressment may have increased the likelihood that slaves would escape—from the plantations, not the entrenchments. With each new requisition, state and national leaders received new appeals from county officials who argued that their community's slaves would leave rather than serve additional terms on the fortifications. "Apart from every other consideration," the Madison County Court petitioned Governor Smith, "is it sound policy to enforce an order of this kind in the border counties when the negros have every facility for getting off to the yankees if they are disposed to go?"[66] The Henrico County Court objected to several impressment quotas on the same grounds. Yet in almost every instance, the governors deemed the threat of runaway slaves insufficient to revoke an impressment quota.

They acted quickly, however, to squelch inaccurate reports of impressment. In February 1865, for example, Catherine Edmondston complained that a militia captain had canvassed Halifax County, North Carolina, "calling on the planters to give a descriptive list of all their negroes between 18 & 50." The captain's presence, she noted, "has so excited & frightened the whole negro population that some of them went off without a moment's preparation, making a Hegira more sudden than that of the Israelites from Egypt."[67] Gatlin quickly instructed Colonel D. B. Bell of the North Carolina militia to stop counting the Halifax County slaves and assure local planters that the state had no current or pending plans to issue an impressment order.[68] Neither state could afford to lose slaves to the Union army under false rumors.

Slaveholders worked very hard to convince government officials that impressing slave labor for the fortifications exponentially increased the odds of a mass escape from their plantations. Correspondents in Virginia and North Carolina repeatedly justified their opposition to slave impressment by arguing that their slaves did not want to go work on the fortifications—while simultaneously, of course, asserting the overall loyalty and obedience of those same slaves. Typically, this justification appeared concurrently with other complaints, which suggests that slaveholders were more than happy to advocate on behalf of the slaves' preferences in this case because those preferences aligned with the slaveholders' desire to keep as many slaves as possible employed at home rather than working on the fortifications. And just as often, state and national leaders refused to rescind the requisition.

Like Andrew Grinnan's slave Charles, any enslaved men who asked their masters to protect them from impressment understood their circumstances. They sensed a common goal, as planters were no more eager to send slaves to the fortifications than slaves were to go, and they presented their masters with a convenient cover for resisting impressment. Slaveholders who objected to a requisition were being benevolent toward their slaves, not stingy toward their government.[69] In fact, asserting a connection between labor requisitions and mass escapes from the plantation allowed slaveholders who objected to impressment to present themselves as protectors of the Confederacy, for they could argue that their opposition prevented a wholesale loss of the agricultural workforce that fed Confederate armies.

Yet as slaveholders demonstrated each time they expressed surprise that one of their slaves would run away, they generally failed to understand their slaves' full motives for escape. Certainly, slaves had many reasons to object to impressment: grinding labor, difficult living conditions, short rations, distance from friends and family, and—especially for those going to Wilmington—uncertainty about when (or if) they might return home. For many, then, an impending requisition may well have tipped the scales in favor of running away. Among ex-slaves who spoke of wartime impressment, however, none mentioned it in conjunction with mass escapes, so perhaps slaveholders imagined or exaggerated the connection. Doing so both upheld the rapidly deteriorating fiction of slave contentment and provided useful fodder against new impressment quotas. Planters were no doubt disappointed to find that preventing one requisition was often not enough to prevent slaves from escaping.

Given that an impressment quota of some sort—national, statewide, or localized—was being announced, executed, or completed somewhere in Virginia or North Carolina almost every month during the last year and a half of the war, it was never difficult for a planter to find a requisition to blame if he awoke one morning to find that several dozen slaves had escaped. Temporal coincidence does not prove a causal relationship, however. And while most government officials believed that a causal relationship existed, they generally did not revoke quotas based solely on the possibility that impressment might prompt slaves to run away. Governor Smith's decision to exempt eleven counties from his January 1864 requisition on these grounds was the exception, not the rule.

"There is no doubt," Secretary of War James A. Seddon noted, "that the Call for slaves to work on the Fortifications from the Counties [near Union lines] tends to induce their running away to the Enemy. On the other hand, the less exposed counties have also been heavily drawn on for labor and cannot well have larger drafts, without seriously interfering with productive operations." Moreover, as Seddon frequently reminded slaveholders, from January 1863 on, the loss of Richmond and other major installations—the loss of the Confederacy—meant losing slavery entirely.[70] Under the circumstances, he was willing to risk some slaves for the defense of the entire nation.

Thousands of slaves seized upon the dislocations of war—including forced movements like impressment—to run away, thus pushing planters and political leaders to at least consider slaves' likely responses to Confederate policies designed to use slavery in support of the war effort. Yet planters shared slaves' preferences with government officials only when they coincided with their own, and the governors and secretary of war ignored both slaves' and planters' desires far more often than they acceded to them. The ongoing threat of runaway slaves was probably more useful for encouraging engineer officers to provide better living conditions for impressed slaves than for preventing impressment itself.

☞ Throughout the war, slaveholders from Virginia and North Carolina who objected to slave impressment frequently cited the conditions under which the slaves lived and worked as their primary concern. Like Jacob Bamhardt, who complained to Governor Vance that the slaves were treated "more like beasts of burden than like humans," slaveholders generally spoke in humanitarian terms, but it is clear that they also had a pecuniary interest in maintaining the health and morale of their slaves. The confluence of these two is most evident in the slaveholders' petitions to the Board of Slave Claims, in which they expressed paternal concern for the health of their slaves while requesting monetary compensation for slaves who died as a result of their work for the Engineer Bureau. Medical inspector William Carrington also exemplified this trend, bolstering his argument, by citing both the humanitarian and the financial benefits of such a change, that the Medical Department should take control of the Engineer Hospital. In a similar vein, the *Richmond Examiner* noted that "it is idle to attempt to get labour out of a half-fed negro, while the inhumanity of the evil complained of should insure its immediate correction."[71]

This convergence of humanitarian and practical reasons for providing food, shelter, and medical care to slaves in Confederate service mirrored antebellum and wartime arguments favoring the "ameliorative reform" of slavery. In particular, southern religious leaders who argued that the Confederacy would gain its independence only by eliminating slavery's "abuses" used practical rhetoric to achieve humanitarian ends, while slaveholders and engineer officers generally did the opposite, advocating careful treatment of slaves in order to achieve clear military goals. Moreover, while ameliorative reform movements generally concentrated on providing slaves with education, religious independence, and more stable families, those slaveholders who complained about the Engineer Bureau's treatment of its laborers were generally more concerned with the physical necessities of life. Attempts to improve conditions for engineer laborers were far more successful than most ameliorative reform efforts, suggesting that practical and material concerns took precedence over issues like slaves' family relations or religious proclivities. Yet while nobody explicitly proposed that failure to feed impressed slaves would bring Confederate losses due to divine retribution, the slaveholders who shared their complaints with local, state, and national officials uniformly strove to present themselves as benevolent masters. Their clear belief that this perception of benevolence mattered—that it was important for slavery to *seem* to provide its theoretical benefits—remained carefully balanced with slaveholders' financial interests in most of their letters regarding their slaves' well-being.[72]

Clearly, the Engineer Bureau did not provide food, shelter, supervision, or medical care on a high enough standard to please Virginia and North Carolina's slaveholders. Yet it would be unfair to accuse the bureau of malice, or even of incompetence, in all instances. Slave owners conveniently overestimated their own solicitude toward their slaves when condemning engineer officers for negligence. Moreover, some of the problems slave laborers encountered early in the war—especially the lack of proper tents and transportation to and from work sites—were less prevalent after the first year. The Confederacy's understandable lack of preparation accounted for many of the shortages in 1861, shortages that Confederate soldiers faced as well. By the same logic, as the Confederacy ran low on supplies, especially food, toward the end of the war, impressed slaves faced the same probability of starvation as Confederate soldiers. As Secretary Seddon and Governor Vance noted, it would have been difficult, at least from a political perspective, to justify treating impressed slaves better than Confederate soldiers.

As state legislators in Virginia and North Carolina drafted their slave impressment legislation in the summer and fall of 1862, slaveholders already possessed unfavorable opinions about the Engineer Bureau's treatment and care of slave laborers, and they soon became convinced that enforcing impressment quotas would lead to mass escapes from the plantations. This helps, in part, to explain the bureau's decision to adopt a more centralized impressment plan with the cooperation of state authorities, and then further intervention by the Confederate Congress, since slaveholders so vehemently resisted sending their slaves for engineer labor. Unfortunately, despite some improvements in health care and supervision standards as the bureau became more efficient, slave laborers at the fortifications continued to face difficult work and uncertain rations, shelter, and medical attention. Widespread knowledge of these conditions among both slaves and slaveholders would make Confederate slave impressment an arduous task throughout the war.

CHAPTER THREE

Provisions Are Needed Worse Than Fortifications

Slave Impressment and Confederate Agriculture

In December 1863, Francis McFarland faced a serious potential labor shortage. An elderly minister from Augusta County, Virginia, McFarland had depended on the labor of his sons and a hired slave to maintain his small farm before the war. By 1863, though, all three of McFarland's sons had joined the Army of Northern Virginia, forcing him to rely more heavily on the efforts of his hired slave, Moses. McFarland had hired Moses the previous December, paying $100 for the year, "with the reserve that if he goes to work for the Govt. a reduction must be made, or if he returns unfit for service." At the end of 1863, however, Moses's owner refused to hire him again on such easy terms.[1]

The slave impressment calls in late 1862 and throughout 1863 disrupted a profitable market for hired agricultural slaves in both Virginia and North Carolina. Farmers generally began negotiating in December to hire field hands for the next year, and the male laborers sought by the Engineer Bureau were also the most valuable in the hiring market. Some slaveholders caused further confusion by hiring slaves to meet their requisitions rather than sending their own workers. Jedediah Hotchkiss wrote to his wife, Sara, in January 1863 that he had been unable to hire a camp servant for the coming year because dozens of slaveholders in the Staunton, Virginia, area had hired male slaves to fill their impressment quotas.[2] Other slaveholders, like John Claiborne of Petersburg, simply hired their slaves directly to the Confederate government for a yearly wage. As Claiborne explained to his wife, "If I hire them to private individuals, the Government through its regular impressments will probably get some or all of them during the year—and work them I cannot tell where."[3] Hiring slaves to Confederate departments offered slaveholders some measure of control over their human property and often carried with it the promise that the owner would be shielded from future impressment quotas.[4] Between hiring and impressment, the *Richmond Examiner* noted, the Confederate army quickly became "the monopolist of the market for male negroes," limiting the number of male slaves left to do farmwork, especially in Virginia.[5]

In a testament to the centrality of this annual hiring ritual to the Upper South economy, newspaper editors frequently pondered the impact of slave impressment on the market for hired field hands. The editor of the *Republican Vindicator*, in Staunton, feared that the prices for agricultural produce would rise in the coming year due to the government's impressments of both food and slaves.[6] The editor of the *Lexington Gazette* concurred, noting, "Our impression is, that *men* will be more in demand than usual, because of the high price of the products of their labor." Furthermore, "the withdrawal of so much labor from the country by the army" had increased the importance of enslaved men in the local labor market. Slave impressment exacerbated labor shortages prompted by enlistment and conscription; it also exacerbated conflicts over who should contribute most heavily to the war effort.[7]

With each requisition, Confederate, state, and local officials sought to balance the country's need for food with its need for fortifications, and this balancing act was not always successful. The requisitions for over 13,000 male slaves between October 1862 and January 1863 obviously had an impact on agriculture in Virginia, even if each county failed to meet its full quota. While impressment quotas were initially much lower in North Carolina, the need to fortify Wilmington removed at least 2,000 slaves from the farms during the same four-month period. Tasks traditionally performed by male slaves during these months would have included slaughtering pigs, harvesting and threshing winter wheat, and then hauling that wheat to the mills; in March, male slaves would begin plowing land for corn and spring wheat. In the short term, then, slaveholders faced a labor shortage while they were preparing key food products. They also worried about the potential long-term implications of these slave impressments on the two states' agricultural economy. All of their concerns highlighted the necessity of slave labor for the growth and production of food in Virginia and North Carolina, suggesting that the states' governors might have to choose between fortifications and sustenance.

In their zeal to craft effective protests against slave impressment, some planters probably overestimated its real impact on agricultural productivity. Their letters frequently presented a fictitious world in which women did no farmwork, a rhetorical strategy designed to ensure male slaves' swift return from the fortifications. But if slave impressment alone did not irreparably damage agricultural work in the two states, it certainly was one aspect of a much more pervasive labor shortage that plagued Confederate farmers and often seemed the easiest problem to rectify. Farmers protested slave impressment in order to reinforce all the sacrifices they were making for the Confederate war effort.

The Richmond bread riot of April 1863, as well as similar protests in cities throughout the Confederacy, dramatically illustrated both the food shortages plaguing the country and the importance of a good harvest in the summer and fall of 1863. Thus, government officials had many reasons to take seriously farmers' suggestions that slave impressment, especially when enacted on top of conscription, the tax-in-kind, and the impressment of crops and livestock, crippled their farms' productivity, although those claims exaggerated labor shortages in most regions by erasing or minimizing the agricultural work that black and white women performed. In addition, a significant number of the communities that protested slave impressment did not, in the end, refuse to comply; in North Carolina, furthermore, numerous farmers pointed to agricultural necessity not to complain about the removal of their slaves but about the fact that General William H. C. Whiting failed to return them at the appointed time. State and Confederate officials collected the largest number of slaves with the smallest number of complaints when they demonstrated a clear respect for the value of agriculture to the success of the Confederate war effort.

While political, legal, and humanitarian arguments abounded when slaveholders protested slave impressment, their most frequent objections centered on the importance of slave labor to local agriculture. The agricultural objection, in addition to being the most common, was also the most effective. The governors of Virginia and North Carolina proved far more likely to interpose their power between the national government and the slaveholders of their states to protect agriculture than for any other reason. In the debate between the demand for fortifications and the demand for food, both sides seemed to agree that there simply was not enough slave labor to supply all of the Confederacy's needs.

The delicate dance of balancing agricultural and military labor needs generally worked well in Virginia. For example, while Governor John

Figure 3.1. Confederate fortifications at Drewry's Bluff, as depicted in Frank Leslie's Illustrated Newspaper, *December 13, 1862*

Letcher expected individual counties to fill their impressment quotas, he also took advantage of a joint resolution adopted by the Virginia General Assembly that authorized him to exempt from impressment any counties that had already lost enough runaway slaves to damage agricultural operations. The General Assembly adopted this resolution on January 27, 1863; Letcher immediately moved to exempt Sussex and Southampton Counties from slave impressment.[8] At the same time, Letcher encouraged the Engineer Bureau and Secretary of War James A. Seddon to schedule requisitions so that they interrupted agriculture as little as possible. In particular, both Letcher and Seddon agreed that all impressed slaves should return to their masters by the middle of April 1863 so that their absence would not prevent farmers from planting corn and wheat.[9]

Initially, the Engineer Bureau attempted a fourth impressment call in March 1863 but encountered strenuous objections from Virginia's farmers and their advocates in the state government. In preparing the March quotas, the Engineer Bureau revisited counties subject to impressment in October and November 1862; for many of those counties, the new impressment quotas included previous deficits (see appendix, table 3.1). Delegates from twenty-one of the twenty-nine counties encompassed in the requisition immediately petitioned the secretary of war to revoke the March impressment quotas, which they argued would cause irreparable delays to spring planting. For example, residents of Rockingham County noted that they had already lost many slaves to incursions by the Union armies in the area and that the Confederate draft's "drain upon the laboring population" had further diminished the number of fields in cultivation. Therefore, they needed the entire remaining slave population if they had any hope of planting a sufficient corn crop and suggested that the current impressment call "will further cripple and impair our ability to cultivate our lands, and to furnish aid to our Confederate Armies." While the citizens of Rockingham County acknowledged the importance of fortifying Richmond against further attacks, they called upon the General Assembly to place agricultural operations in a position of equal importance. Indeed, they argued, "we cannot believe that it is less important to prepare an ample supply of food for our armies, and we are painfully impressed with the apprehension that the greater danger lies on the side of a scarcity of provisions."[10]

Colonel Jeremy Francis Gilmer, head of the Engineer Bureau, denied these requests and insisted that the army could not finish its defensive preparations for the spring campaign season without receiving additional slave labor.[11] He assured Governor Letcher that the March impressment call was not only necessary for the Engineer Bureau to meet its obligations but also far less burdensome than Virginia's slaveholders represented. Gilmer worked with Col. S. Bassett French, an aide to Secretary of the Commonwealth George Munford, to prepare a comprehensive list of slaves impressed and received from each county prior to March 19, 1863 (see appendix, table 3.2). French calculated that only 16 percent of the slaves in the affected counties, about 30,000 men, were subject to impressment under the existing legislation. According to state law, only 20 percent of those 30,000, or about 6,000, could be impressed at any one time. The March requisition called for just under 3,000 slaves, or less than 1 percent of Virginia's slaves.[12] But French failed to note in his calculations that this 1 percent often represented the most productive portion of the enslaved agricultural workers, a loss that few counties could afford at a time when so many white men were in the Confederate army. According to one North Carolina slaveholder, one fifth "of the good hands is practically one half of the able bodied men upon most farms," suggesting that impressing 20 or 25 percent of the adult male slaves on each farm exponentially reduced agricultural productivity.[13] French also neglected to point out that while many of the counties targeted in the March call had failed to meet their quotas from October or November 1862, those quotas had been too high. Several counties had actually furnished more laborers than mandated under state law because the initial requisition exceeded 25 percent of their adult male slaves.

Letcher and Seddon displayed more willingness to revoke the March impressment call than they had on any previous occasion. Seddon, in particular, reiterated his commitment to Virginia's farmers that slave impressment would not interfere with spring planting. "I wanted the slaves dismissed by the 10th of April," he told Gilmer, asking, "Is it not too late to call for more now?"[14] In response, Gilmer acknowledged that any slaves he collected under the March quotas would be able to work for only a few days prior to April 10. He therefore revoked the request.[15] Fortification work would have to wait until the crops were in the ground, as ensuring a good harvest of wheat and corn was vital to the continued success of the Confederate armies.

Suspending the March 1863 impressment call did create a labor shortage for the Engineer Bureau and some Confederate field commanders. In June, when Major General D. H. Hill requested additional laborers for his defensive works near Petersburg, Gilmer refused to issue an impressment call for slaves because he assumed that Secretary Seddon would once again prioritize agriculture.[16] Eventually, Gilmer and Seddon decided to impress free blacks instead of slaves to meet the Confederacy's labor needs during the summer of 1863.[17]

While Seddon assisted Governor Letcher in working to return all Virginia slaves by mid-April and to prevent any calls that would fall over the summer months, Governor Zebulon Baird Vance of North Carolina was not so fortunate. Vance initially supported General Whiting's impressment call for the Wilmington defenses in March and April 1863, despite fears that this requisition would endanger agricultural operations in the state. He also encouraged Whiting to return the slaves to their farms as quickly as possible, and Whiting's repeated refusals to do so would endanger his hitherto cooperative relationship with Vance. Whiting indicated in late February that he would soon need more workers but was loath to call again on the counties closest to Wilmington. "Robeson & Cumberland have heretofore done well & supplied much free & slave labor," Whiting wrote. "They have certainly done their share. A vast deal of work is still required here & the labor of 400 to 500 negroes is essential to complete our works as rapidly as possible."[18]

Whiting therefore confined his impressment requests in the spring of 1863 to the counties in central North Carolina (see appendix, table 3.3).[19] The new call targeted both plantation belt counties, where slaves accounted for more than 50 percent of the population, and counties with notably smaller slave holdings. All of them were more significant producers of food crops than the southeastern region, which grew mostly cotton and tobacco. Vance did take one step designed primarily to protect the state's agriculture, authorizing militia officers to exempt farmers who held only one adult male slave from participating in any impressment quotas.[20] One farmer from Chatham County, objecting to a renewed impressment call, voiced his opinion that "we need something to eat worse than we do breast works and fortifications, if our negroes are taken from us, our corn cannot be tended, and our wheat, and oats will rot in the field, with the force left behind the grain cannot be saved."[21]

A number of newspaper editors in North Carolina and Virginia expressed their disgust with planters' objections to slave impressment, noting that nonslaveholding farmers and soldiers' wives had already sacrificed their agricultural productivity for the war effort. "With a knowledge of the fact that the institution of slavery was the chief impelling cause to a war which has devolved immense suffering and sacrifice upon thousands having no individual interest in such property," chastised the *Lynchburg Daily Virginian*, "we marvel that those who have a larger stake in it, can so far forget what they owe to the government that it [is] struggling to protect them in the enjoyment of their right of property."[22] The editorial further suggested that those of the planter class were making money from the war and therefore had a moral obligation to put their slaves to work building fortifications to protect the poor men serving in the Confederate army. Similar opinions came from both pro-Davis editors and those generally unlikely to support the administration.

Indeed, from its first appearance in state law, editors in both states heralded slave impressment as a measure that would help distribute the burdens of the war more equitably among the Confederate population. Nonslaveholding men were engaged in a war to preserve the institution of slavery, they argued, and putting their slaves to work building fortifications to protect those men seemed to be the least the members of the planter class could do. They failed to anticipate how even the short-term absence of those slaves from economic activities on the home front might affect nonslaveholding soldiers or their families. As the war extended and supplies dwindled, new petitioners began to suggest that slave impressment was placing an undue burden on the ability of communities to feed themselves and the Confederate armies, especially in areas where slaves also worked for a vast array of military employers and civilian contractors.

Officials of the Alleghany County Court, for example, told Governor Letcher that the county court was maintaining the indigent families of nearly 200 Confederate soldiers. "The support of these families requires every slave to be left," they argued, "as the slave owners alone have surplus provisions and upon them devolves the maintenance of our soldiers families. Take the slaves and you take their support." If Letcher did not revoke the impressment call, the soldiers' families might starve; then, the court feared, "we shall have what Alleghany would deplore—desertions from the Army."[23] Yet the failure to enforce slave impressment could be equally dangerous to the Confederate cause, as General Whiting told General Samuel Cooper. Whiting noted that the men in the heavy artillery force at Fort Fisher were not manning their guns because they were "compelled to labor constantly, owing to the backwardness of the people in furnishing negroes to work upon the fortifications."[24] The governors were more inclined to sympathize with slaveholders on this point, however, recognizing the importance of high agricultural yields to the continued viability of the Confederate armies.

Thus, while he was unable to prevent Whiting from impressing slaves in the spring of 1863, Vance repeatedly encouraged the general to return them by early June for the first harvest. In May 1863, Vance wrote to Whiting, "I promised the owners they should be returned in time to assist in planting the crops; they now ask them to be returned by harvest which begins on our southern borders by 1st June and will continue during the Month." The fortifications at Wilmington were important, Vance continued, but "I recognize no greater necessity to the common good, than the safety of the coming harvest: And must therefore insist on their being sent home next week."[25] Whiting finally conceded, "As you require the negroes, I will commence sending them back, though with extreme reluctance. I fully recognize the importance of the harvest." Vance therefore expected that impressed slaves would return to the North Carolina Piedmont by the middle of June.[26]

Yet while Whiting agreed to return the slaves to their homes in late May, many had not arrived by the second week of June, and Vance continued to receive letters from farmers anxious to complete their harvests. In mid-June, a Caswell County farmer begged, "You will please be so kind as to order my hands that has been working at the Fortifications about Wilmington and Fort Caswell &c home I am needing of them to save my crops of Grain and to make some Corn which I shall not be able to do without my hands."[27] At the same time, Vance received a letter from Stokes County bemoaning the waste of food that would result from the absence of slave labor in the county. "We have put in our crops on a larger scale than usual," one farmer wrote, "and our harvest is on us before we are ready. I shall have to turn the stock in some of my wheat for the want of force to cut it. The quality as well as the quantity is fine if it could be saved."[28] Throughout June and July, Vance continued to receive letters from farmers in central North Carolina, to whom he could only respond, "The negroes have been ordered home, and Gen Whiting informs me they are on the way."[29]

Secretary Seddon may have pressured General Whiting to keep his promises to Vance, as Seddon shared most farmers' interest in a good harvest. Whiting took every opportunity to protest this decision, reminding Seddon in late July that his work was behind schedule because he had returned 500 slaves to their owners for the harvest. "It is represented that there are upwards of 300,000 negroes in this State," he continued, "and yet I cannot procure without force 1000."[30] By late July, according to War Department clerk John B. Jones, Whiting was "squa[w]king loudly for the impressment of a thousand slaves, to complete his preparations for defense; and if he does not get them, he thinks the fall of Wilmington is a pretty sure thing." Jones noted repeated requests from Whiting over the next few months.[31]

Of course, North Carolinians may have found it easier to spare 1,000 adult male slaves for the fortifications at Wilmington if not for the fact that most adult white men were serving in the army. Whiting never acknowledged the enormous toll the war was taking on North Carolina's male workforce, or even the fact that he was not the only commander calling on the state's slaves to build fortifications. He expected to maintain a constant labor force, whatever the cost to agriculture.

While pinpointing that exact cost may not be possible, evaluating how slaveholders represented slave impressment's impact on agricultural productivity is a good starting point. In Virginia, while most farmers and planters were content to allow their elected county court officials to petition the governor on their behalf, they were also quick to act when they felt that local leaders had unfairly distributed impressment quotas. Slave impressment in North Carolina usually bypassed the county court structure, so petitioners went straight to the governor, but they were less likely to complain about initial impressment quotas than about the recurring difficulties they encountered getting their slaves back from Wilmington. All were eager to remind state and national leaders that food production played a role in military success and that food shortages could exacerbate mounting class tensions on the home front.

Letters from farmers bemoaning slave impressment's impact on agriculture suggest a number of important patterns that will help determine the validity of their claims. First of all, while they do constitute the single largest set of letters the three governors (Letcher, Smith, and Vance)

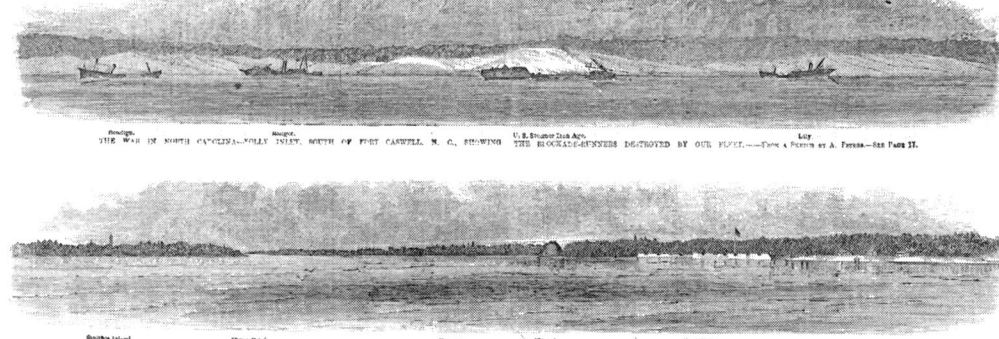

Figure 3.2. Wilmington coastline and Fort Fisher, as depicted in Frank Leslie's Illustrated Newspaper, April 2, 1864

received from individual constituents on the subject of slave impressment, their total number is still relatively small. Approximately 175 men and women in Virginia and North Carolina wrote letters to their governors protesting slave impressment solely or primarily because it would harm their agricultural work, a number that pales in comparison to the thousands of farmers and planters in those states who sent slaves to the fortifications over the course of the war. In Virginia, letters from individual farmers no doubt had less impact than the petitions originating in county courts, which became quite numerous in the last eighteen months of the war. Still, it appears that the vast majority of both states' slaveholders complied with slave impressment and kept their objections to themselves, perhaps indicating that most farmers could operate their farms while some of their male slaves occasionally worked on the fortifications.

Second, most of the men who wrote letters highlighting the danger slave impressment posed to agricultural production were older than fifty-five, thus exceeding the Confederate draft age, and so had valid reasons to be at home rather than in the army. Quite a few were in their seventies, lending credence to claims that they could not manage their farms without their male slaves. Moreover, in many cases their adult sons who had lived at home in 1860 served in the Confederate army for at least a portion of the war, further decreasing the agricultural capacity of their households. Many of the female petitioners were either widows whose adult sons had enlisted or wives of Confederate soldiers. Thus, the rhetorical flourishes from newspaper editors who lambasted these families for shirking their duties to the Confederacy were generally misplaced.

Another pattern reflects geographic location. In both states, the vast majority of letters on the subject of agriculture came from farmers in the Piedmont counties. The Piedmont region tended to have the largest slave holdings, calculated both in terms of total number of slaves and proportion of the population enslaved, so it is not surprising that those counties bore the brunt of most impressment quotas. In both Virginia and North Carolina, the eastern plantation belts were often exempt from state-directed impressment quotas due to their heavy participation in earlier ad hoc requisitions as well as to their vulnerability to Union army incursions (and therefore runaway slaves). The Piedmont was also the primary grain-producing region of each state, granting a special urgency to their letters deploring slave impressment's impact on agricultural work.

Finally, one interesting distinction between individual petitioners in the two states—a distinction that reveals much about how slave impressment operated—lies in the number of slaves they owned. Only one of the letter writers from Virginia owned the twenty slaves necessary to qualify for a draft exemption, and he chose to enlist in the Confederate army. In fact, most of the letters that Letcher and Smith received came from men who owned fewer than ten slaves, although Virginia county court officials, many of whom were among their community's wealthiest slaveholders, authored dozens of petitions over the course of the war. In North Carolina, where county courts played no consistent role in slave impressment, Governor Vance received letters from a much broader range of individual slaveholders, with a definite majority holding at least twenty slaves. (Many of these men, being above the maximum draft age, initially transferred their exemptions to adult sons.) Could this noticeable difference suggest class bias in the way Virginia's county courts enforced slave impressment?

Many petitioners certainly thought so, arguing that county court officers had shielded the Piedmont's planter class from full participation in slave impressment, placing a heavier burden on small-scale slaveholders—an argument that may have held true in some cases. Yet the planters of Virginia's Piedmont were just as likely to argue that they had contributed more than their fair share and to point to neighbors of similar class status who had sent fewer slaves. None of those letters, however, suggested that the absence of two or three male slaves would impede crop production on their farms. The impressment rolls that each Virginia county and city produced during the war, while often incomplete, indicate that most courts repeatedly targeted slaveholders with four or more men in the proper age range, turning to smaller slaveholders only when necessary. The burden of slave impressment seems to have fallen on the exact same range of slaveholders in Virginia as in North Carolina.

If class bias did affect the enforcement of Virginia's quotas, that bias may have originated in the state legislature rather than in the county court system. Legislators mandated that no more than one-quarter of a county's adult male slaves could be impressed at any one time, probably believing that this would limit slave impressment's impact on agricultural production. They seem to have assumed that most counties would be able to fill their quotas without turning to small-scale slaveholders—perhaps because many of their immediate acquaintances owned dozens of slaves. Yet few counties outside of the Piedmont and Tidewater regions had the kind of concentrated slave holdings that would have exempted men with only one or two male slaves. Even in the Piedmont, farmers with between ten and twenty slaves rarely held more than two or three adult men, likely a reflection of the Upper South's status as a slave-exporting region.[32] According to Samuel Saunders, very few of the farmers in his Piedmont Virginia community owned more than four male slaves. "If [you take] from the man who has only one hand (and as is the case sometimes the owner is in the army)," wrote seventy-three-year-old Saunders, "he can make no crop this year, and if from him who has four hands you take two you reduce his crop to one half and there will necessarily be suffering in consequence."[33] In North Carolina, however, where quotas rarely exceeded 10 percent of adult male slaves, the militia officers responsible for enforcing impressment could focus most of their attention on slaves belonging to the planter class.

Comparing the content of letters from North Carolina's small-scale slaveholders and larger slaveholders reveals an entirely different explanation for why Vance received so many complaints from men with dozens of slaves—many were protesting not the initial impressment of their slaves but the government's failure to return them, a problem that Virginia slaveholders rarely encountered. Men and women with fewer than ten slaves were most likely to appeal impressment quotas when first enforced, asking for an exemption or the immediate return of their laborers. The letters from the largest North Carolina slaveholders, in contrast, noted that they had complied with Governor Vance's request to send slaves in the weeks after spring planting under explicit promises from state militia officers that the slaves would return in two months, just in time for early harvest. Three, four, five, and in some cases six months later, General Whiting still held their slaves at Wilmington. These men objected not to the government's demand for slave labor but to the violation of an express compact between masters and the state. For many, their status as elite slaveholders had hitherto protected them from such treatment.

Class status reflected more than the number of slaves a man (or woman) owned; it also reflected occupation and lifestyle, and slave impressment exacerbated divisions between planters and those who employed slaves in manufacturing work or urban areas. Many farmers were frustrated by impressment quotas that, like conscription policies, routinely exempted industrialists from participation. "At a time when the question of bread & meat is so vital to the maintenance of our armies," it made little sense, officers of the Smyth County Court argued, "that the slaves of Farmers are required to work on the Fortifications while All slaves employed in Mining & manufacturing Iron, Lead, & Salt peter under Government contracts are exempted." Both impressment and conscription regulations, the court noted, had protected "consumers" of food while placing a heavy burden on its "producers."[34] "It certainly seems hard," a Raleigh resident complained to Governor Vance, "that a speculator or capitalist who has made $20,000 or $50,000 by the war should contribute nothing and a small farmer whose all may consist in a lot of negroes of 10 working hands, should leave his crop to suffer, and send his negro to work for the protection of the province."[35]

Rhetoric that compared consumers unfavorably with producers has figured prominently in discussions of class conflict in the Confederacy, yet the dichotomy it proposed was both artificial and subject to constant alteration. In a similar vein, the oft-reviled categories of consumer and speculator frequently, but not consistently, overlapped. Women engaged in bread riots, for example, were simultaneously producers (of food crops for subsistence and local sale or of manufactured goods for the military) and consumers (of cornmeal, flour, and textiles). Yet their scathing invective often targeted urban shopkeepers as consumers and speculators who produced nothing of value to the war effort while profiting from high prices on manufactured goods they sold to the civilian population. Most farmers depicted themselves as producers while castigating industrialists and urbanites as consumers.

In the case of slave impressment, the lines delineating producer and consumer were usually drawn between men with similar economic resources. The men on either side of this dividing line in Virginia and North Carolina typically owned or employed between ten and fifty slaves and forfeited an ever-increasing portion of their manufacturing or agricultural output to the Confederate government at prices far below market value. It would therefore be dangerous to treat Smyth County's proposed division between producers and consumers as unequivocal evidence of the destructive power of class conflict in the Confederacy, although it certainly points to a widespread perception that some people were failing to contribute their fair share.

Both planters and industrialists clearly produced goods of value to the war effort, yet slave impressment and conscription policies initially served to intensify distinctions between them. Manufacturers of iron, lead, and saltpeter were obviously less common than farmers, as were skilled workers like blacksmiths and tanners, and so while a comparable number of men from each group were probably granted exemptions and details under Confederate conscription laws, the percentage of farmers subject to the draft would have been much larger. A similar arithmetic could have been applied to impressment quotas for slaves employed in manufacturing versus agricultural operations, but instead, the Engineer Department chose to exempt industrial slaves almost entirely.[36]

Recognizing the vital importance of railroads, iron foundries, lumber mills, and other industrial operations—all of which required slave labor—to the Confederate war effort, Chief Engineer Gilmer usually responded favorably to requests from industrial employers that their slaves be exempted from impressment. A. I. Johnson's workers, though impressed by Halifax County officials, were detailed to his sawmill by Confederate authorities.[37] Appomattox County sheriff Wilson Hix reported that the county had filled its impressment quota with the exception of "two hired out on the Iron Mine Works, three to the [South] Side & five to the Va & Tenn R. Rds."; several others were in Lynchburg, "manufacturing flour for the government." Hix was unsure how to proceed in these cases, noting that "the companies refuse to give them up."[38] Charles Scott, owner of a large salt mine in southwestern Virginia, sought exemptions for the slaves he had hired from Roanoke County.[39] Joseph R. Anderson, proprietor of the Tredegar Iron Works in Richmond, petitioned Governor Letcher to release the workers from the M. S. Coal Mining Company, noting, *"we depend on [coal] for casting heavy cannon."*[40]

These requests for exemptions and details recurred with every impressment call, and those industrial proprietors lacking a powerful patron like Joseph Anderson often found themselves negotiating the combined state and national bureaucracies before they received a confirmed detail of their slave laborers. When L. B. Wetherall, whose shop produced harnesses and bridles for the Confederate cavalry, petitioned the Confederate War Department to gain exemptions for two workers, Secretary of War George Randolph replied that such requests were a matter for state authorities.[41]

Governor Letcher, however, usually responded to similar petitions with the succinct reply "no power" and forwarded the requests to the Engineer Bureau, as he did with letters from tanner F. M. Thacker and gun manufacturer Bilhartz, Hall, & Company.[42] These petitioners found a more sympathetic audience at the Engineer Bureau, where Gilmer reassured them that "we are very anxious to interfere in no way with the faithful and prompt execution of all [government] contracts."[43]

Gilmer provided exemptions and details to slaves working for Virginia's wide variety of industrial employers as well as for the Medical and Quartermaster's Departments of the Confederacy. In North Carolina, Governor Vance generally followed the Engineer Bureau's lead in exempting from impressment those slaves who performed industrial or skilled work necessary to either civilians or the Confederate war effort, including blacksmiths, shoemakers, and tanners. The adjutant general's office issued an exemption for the slaves that James Satterwhite employed "making waggons for the Confederate Government" as well as for slaves making flannel for the R. G. Wells Company.[44]

While Gilmer occasionally left exemptions to his engineers' discretion, Colonel Walter H. Stevens and Lieutenant John Stanard no doubt felt constrained by Gilmer's assertion that the Engineer Bureau should in no way interfere with either government contractors or the other Confederate departments. The rationale for exempting all industrial slaves was unclear, although a few likely possibilities exist. By virtue of their training and occupation, engineer officers were probably more aware of the labor demands of manufacturers than those of farmers, and they also made more regular use of products like iron and lead than did members of the population at large, so they may have simply been more sympathetic to the needs of industrial employers. In addition, mining and industry were less seasonal in their demands than was agriculture, and slaves with industrial skills and experience were far fewer in number than field hands, both of which suggest that industrial employers may have been less able to spare a few workers than farmers.

This policy no doubt delighted the slaveholders who had hired the men to these employers in the first place but greatly frustrated Colonel Stevens, who accused Virginia's county court officers of exploiting the exemptions to subvert the impressment process. Stevens had a point: as the number of petitions for exemption mounted, exemptions and details dramatically devoured the number of impressed slaves who actually worked for the Engineer Department. Moreover, county court officials' inability to fill their quotas with slaves who were not already working for the Confederacy began to look suspicious—perhaps they were deliberately choosing slaves hired to industrial employers in an attempt to keep as many slaves as possible from the fortifications. Industrial slaves who were impressed but then detailed to the factories and workshops of the county represented no net loss in the local labor force and allowed more agricultural slaves to remain in the fields harvesting wheat and corn.

Stevens also disagreed with the basic premise behind industrial exemptions. "I see no reason," he wrote to Chief Engineer Gilmer, "why a man contracting with a rail road should be favored any more than a farmer who wants to make corn or other crops."[45] As Stevens correctly articulated, both men employed slaves for the benefit of the Confederate armies—one to produce food and the other to transport men, rations, and war matériel. Policies that exempted one group of producers (industrial employers) from slave impressment increased the burden on other producers (farmers), thus aggravating resentments between the two pillars of the wartime economy, both of which needed to thrive if the Confederate military had any hope of success.

As the war progressed, the line between agricultural "producers" and industrial "consumers" became even more blurred, especially in Virginia, where a growing proportion of the male slave population moved from agricultural to manufacturing work. These slaves, owned by farmers but hired by industrialists, highlighted the permeability of the line between the two groups of employers and were also increasingly subject to impressment quotas as the process of collecting slave laborers became more centralized. Impressment policy continued to benefit those planters who could afford to hire their male laborers to War Department agencies, but by 1864 it was quite clear that wartime labor shortages affected farmers and manufacturers alike. At the same time, the long arms of the Confederate government reached into all of their business endeavors, requiring all slaveholders and employers, regardless of what they produced, to produce it almost exclusively for the benefit of the army.[46]

In addition to drawing arbitrary distinctions between two groups of producers, farmers routinely pointed to justified consumers—men and women deemed worthy of assistance—in order to bolster their arguments against slave impressment. Strictly speaking, for example, Confederate soldiers were consumers, but nobody doubted their right to demand sustenance, and farmers in Virginia and North Carolina routinely protested slave impressment by arguing that it would hinder their efforts to grow grain crops for the army. Asking Governor Letcher to exempt his slaves from impressment, a Louisa County farmer indicated that he had provided seventy-five barrels of flour to the army in the summer of 1863 and would be sending at least that much the next summer—as long as he did not lose control of his workforce.[47] Governor Vance heard a similar argument from a constituent who wrote, "Our soldiers are writing home now from many quarters, & are complaining of short rations, and it is bound to be worse another year," especially if Vance ordered slaves to the fortifications at Wilmington during planting or harvest season.[48]

Other farmers, especially those detailed to grow provisions rather than serve full-time in the Confederate armies, argued that they needed to maintain high agricultural production levels to serve an entirely different group of justified consumers—the white women, children, and elderly men left to fend for themselves in the absence of most able-bodied adult men. For example, detailed and exempt farmers from Chatham County pressured Vance to secure their slaves' return so they could "aid the soldiers wives in saving there grain," while those from Rockingham County claimed to need additional labor to help harvest crops planted by men who had since been conscripted into the army.[49] *North Carolina Standard* editor William W. Holden scoffed at this argument, proclaiming that the state's planter class had no intention of sharing their slave laborers with other farmers and that the slaves could therefore be put to better use digging fortifications outside Wilmington.[50]

Holden's skepticism was entirely reasonable. Antebellum patterns for hiring both agricultural and household workers, many of which persisted throughout the war, demonstrate that rather than serving the short-term needs of poor and middling members of a community, hiring contracts were written on an annual basis, generally to the financial benefit of those planters with sufficient labor to spare.[51] This does not preclude informal patterns of shared labor, however, especially between large-scale slaveholders and nonslaveholders with whom they shared kinship or other affective ties. Nelson County resident William Daniel Cabell, himself a small-scale slaveholder, routinely borrowed slaves from his father and other wealthy relatives; in turn, he lent a slave to a female neighbor when hers was impressed.[52] Francis McFarland's parishioners regularly sent slaves to perform a few hours' or even a few days' labor on his farm.[53] Exempted planters in Rowan County promised their slaves' labor to help female neighbors cut their wheat in the summer of 1863.[54] The desire to provide assistance may have been particularly strong among those men who received the twenty-slave draft exemption or were detailed as farmers, since they needed to constantly reaffirm their value on the home front or risk becoming targets of conscription.

Those same men frequently assisted women from their communities seeking exemptions from slave impressment. When the Augusta County Court ordered Margaret Ott to send her slave Alf to the fortifications, she asked her brother Enos and a neighbor named Mr. Black to help her request an exemption. When they failed, she asked another neighbor, Dr. McChesney, to hire a slave to replace Alf, but he was also unsuccessful.[55] W. Branch contacted Governor Letcher on behalf of Mrs. Thomas Omohundro, wife of a Confederate soldier, seeking an exemption for her slave Archer.[56] Judith Marr wrote her own letter to Governor Smith but sent it first to her representative in the General Assembly for his approval and assistance. Representative R. V. Barksdale endorsed Marr's letter and forwarded it to the governor's office.[57] Miss Powell's letter included references, urging Smith to "apply to Mr. Colin Bass former Representative of Roanoke Cty" to verify her need for assistance.[58] Edith Hobson sent her petition to John Goode, her representative in the Confederate Congress, and enclosed letters from a physician and a male neighbor as well as endorsements from Bedford County's two justices of the peace.[59] Taking a similar approach, Lucy Jeter wrote to state senator James F. Johnson to request the release of her slave Elim, "the only means of support in the world that I have for myself & four little children." Mrs. Jeter's soldier husband had been taken prisoner two months earlier.[60] Six men from Jeter's community signed her letter to demonstrate its veracity, and Senator Johnson forwarded it to War Bureau director Robert Garlick Hill Kean, noting, "I have no doubt the facts stated by her are true. The certifiers are men of high character."[61] The men who supported these petitions consistently represented female slaveholders as worthy of assistance—justified consumers—due to their moral purity and dependent status.

Underlying all the letters is an assumption that while women had typically owed nothing to the state—for, as women, their allegiances and civic responsibilities were covered by those of the men in their families—the state owed them a certain level of physical and economic security. As the war progressed, white women of all socioeconomic classes increasingly demanded that security. Most of the women protesting slave impressment were hardly poor, since, as slaveholders, their families fell within the top quartile of southern households, at least from an economic standpoint. Yet they typically owned too few slaves to truly be considered members of the planter class, and by 1864, many of those who lived in areas that underwent repeated contact with either side's armies probably hovered only slightly above bare subsistence. Keeping their slaves working at home would allow them to remain agricultural producers, even if only for their households, rather than become consumers in need of constant protection and assistance from their male neighbors. In addition, they consistently referred to themselves as soldiers' wives, suggesting at least a rhetorical unity with nonslaveholding women, who adopted that moniker in many of their protest activities.[62]

Most men who sought exemptions from slave impressment emphasized the vital contributions to the war effort and their neighbors that they (or their slaves) were already making at home. Soldiers' wives typically failed to make that argument when protesting slave impressment, in part because they did not have to. Their contribution was evident from their very status—and having sent their men (husbands, sons, or nephews) to serve in the army, they believed they had earned the right to be chary with their slaves. Men who remained at home, whether they qualified for the twenty-slave draft exemption or were detailed due to their vital importance to local economies, needed to reaffirm the services they (and their slaves) provided to the local community when seeking to avoid a requisition for slave labor.

In a few cases, these planters focused their collective energy on encouraging the governors to exempt the slaves of disabled men in their community, who also fit the definition of justified consumers. Joseph Davis, his neighbors in Franklin County wrote, "is a man of infirm health and utterly incapable of much bodily exertion and has twelve persons in his family consisting with one exception entirely of females and children. Mr. Davis has two sons in the army and has besides under his charge his widowed daughter and her orphan children his son in law having died in army."[63] Seventeen residents of Lunenburg County urged Governor Smith to exempt a slave belonging to a discharged soldier, "a man of infirm health, caused doubtless from service or exposure in the Army of the Confederate States, [who] has a wife and two Children, living on rented land for which he is to pay high rent. And his only dependence for a support is on the Negro man who has been drafted under the recent call for hands."[64]

These two protests on behalf of male slaveholders are a fascinating anomaly. In form, they bear great similarity to the petitions the governors and secretary of war frequently received asking that blacksmiths, millers, and other vital male laborers be granted exemptions from the Confederate draft. In content, they are more like men's letters asking political leaders to assist "helpless" widows or soldiers' wives. Interestingly, neither of the two male slaveholders described in these petitions sent a personal letter requesting relief from slave impressment, and it seems that both men were unaware of their neighbors' intercessions on their behalf. A task that prominent men seem to have routinely undertaken for women in their community—writing letters to government officials to request assistance—could be performed for another man only if done in secret. Openly describing a neighbor as "utterly incapable" of working his farm or wholly dependent on the support and labor of a black man was a violation of white manhood.

Healthy men, by contrast, typically wrote their own letters requesting exemptions and did so in ways that highlighted their work on behalf of Confederate military success.[65] As soldiers, as detailed farmers, as planters producing surplus grain for the army and civilian population, or as manufacturers, men served the interests of the state and often used their slaves to aid in that process. A few women also classified themselves as producers rather than consumers, writing letters to Smith that focused on their personal contributions to Confederate victory—typically, male family members and agricultural goods. Judith Marr protested, "I am a Widow and have two sons in the Army and the third made subject of an act of Congress taking all between 17 and 18 years of age I have made arrangements for a large crop and if my Negro is kept out untill the last of April I shall be compelled to abandon a portion of my crop."[66] Miss Powell requested an exemption because she had only two slaves (one male and one female) and was responsible for supporting two nephews, one fourteen years old and the other mentally disabled. Her two older nephews were both in the army. "I cannot hire for money," she continued, "and have let the county & government have all my surplus, which I have always done since the war commenced."[67] Edith Hobson's letters also emphasized her ability to serve her community (and the Confederacy as a whole) by producing a good crop.[68]

Hobson, Powell, and Marr took an unusual route, as most Virginia and North Carolina residents who wrote letters protesting slave impressment assumed—rather inexplicably—that women did not participate in agricultural work. This held true even in Marr's case, for while she described the large crop she (or more accurately, her slave) was busy sowing, Representative Barksdale, when forwarding Marr's letter to Governor Smith, focused on her status as a disabled and therefore "helpless" widow.[69] Maria Bagby, Nancy Webster, and Mrs. D. A. Puryear all argued that they would be unable to feed their children without the work of the male slaves on their farms.[70] None of these women took the time to consider how the wives of nonslaveholding soldiers managed to produce crops during the war, nor did they address the reality that helping maintain a farm was a common experience for even small-scale slaveholding women.

For example, Elizabeth Ellis Robeson was a slaveholding widow who lived in Bladen County, North Carolina. At the start of the war she owned nineteen slaves, three of whom were young men between the ages of fourteen and twenty. Her oldest living son, Raiford, worked as a physician in nearby Fayetteville, while her youngest son, Alexis, attended school, leaving the middle son, Evander, primarily responsible for running the farm. Yet even with at least seven slaves old enough to perform full-time agricultural work and an adult son living at home, sixty-three-year-old Robeson routinely helped maintain food crops, including collards and potatoes, for her household. Once all three sons enlisted in the Confederate army (taking slave John with them as a body servant), Robeson and her enslaved driver took over full-time management of the farm. Although most of her day-to-day tasks revolved around domestic textile production, she also kept track of her slaves' agricultural labor in her journal. When one of her male slaves was impressed in November 1862, work on the farm continued, despite the fact that his departure left her with only her driver and one other adult male slave. Obviously, women did agricultural work on this farm, which produced sugarcane, corn, and cotton for sale in addition to basic food crops and livestock for the household.[71]

Elizabeth Robeson's husband had died in 1845, so she was accustomed to running her family's farm by the time the Civil War began. For many women of the slaveholding class, while the war was their first opportunity to take such a sustained role in managing the plantation, it was certainly not their first experience as "deputy husband." Mary Bell wrote to her husband, Alfred, about the progress of their farm with a great deal of confidence and satisfaction in July 1864, suggesting that she enjoyed direct participation in agricultural work. Her letter implied that while her slaves seeded clover, peas, sugarcane, and potatoes and managed the horses, she had planted lettuce and onions herself, as well as cared for her cows. Bell predicted that her household would have "about as much to eat as most any person else" the next year.[72] Elizabeth Robeson's farm seemed similarly insulated from great scarcities prior to March 1865, when both armies marched through her community.[73]

Nonslaveholding women, for whom farmwork was nothing new at the start of the Civil War, did report more consistent scarcities beginning in early 1863, as well as difficulty finding and paying laborers to help them with tasks that required more than one adult to complete. One woman wrote to her soldier husband in October 1862 that she had not yet sowed her fall wheat crop because she had been unable to hire a man to help spread manure on the fields.[74] Another complained that due to the rapid depreciation of Confederate currency, she could not afford to buy dressed meat to supplement her children's diet of the corn and vegetables in her garden and that she was unable to butcher a hog without assistance.[75] So much of the work on their farms required two people that it is hard to imagine that these women did not perform at least some field labor before their husbands joined the Confederate army.

Despite the daily agricultural work that these farm wives, and hundreds of women like them, performed, opponents of slave impressment consistently depicted white women as incapable of operating their farms without the work of their (or their neighbors') male slaves. This reflects a broader regional as well as national reluctance to admit that married, native-born white women regularly did fieldwork with their husbands and families. While antebellum newspaper editors had increasingly praised the industrious farm wife—rather than the "ladylike" plantation mistress who avoided work—as the ideal white woman, they did so by emphasizing domestic textile production.[76] Wartime editors sang a similar tune, praising women's contributions to the war effort in nursing and textile production and enjoining them to spend more time in their kitchens and less time in their parlors.[77] But they all continued to uphold the fiction that farm wives spent no time performing agricultural work, in large part because to do so would have impugned the character and status of their husbands. In particular, small-scale slaveholders aspiring to the status of "planter" were expected to preserve their wives' distance from agricultural work.[78]

Many of the letters slaveholders wrote to protest impressment also seemed to suggest that enslaved women did little or no fieldwork, despite manifold evidence to the contrary. Sarah Cocke of Louisa County, for example, protested the impressment of "the only man I have to take care of my corn, feed my stock, and get wood for my family," despite the presence of several enslaved women and their children on her farm.[79] Petitioner after petitioner, even big planters, alluded to the damage that the loss of male slave laborers would do to the agricultural production of each community, in the process almost erasing slave women's farmwork from the historic record. Women's agricultural labors loomed large in ex-slave narratives, however, telling a very different story.

In fact, it appears that enslaved women did much of the routine agricultural labor on most large farms, in addition to being responsible for textile production during the evening hours, while men often had more varied work schedules.[80] Fannie Moore remembered that her mother tended crops in the field all day and then spent her nights spinning thread or piecing quilts.[81] Charity McAllister recalled splitting rails and digging ditches next to male slaves; Essex Henry reported that his mother spent the majority of her time planting and tending grain crops.[82] According to Henrietta McCullers, not only did the female slaves on her master's farm clear new ground, plow, plant, and harvest all the crops, but their mistress, Miss Betsy, worked in the fields along with them. Miss Betsy's husband, Henrietta reported, "was too puny to work."[83] So why did so many of the letters protesting slave impressment suggest that agricultural work would cease if male slaves were removed from the farms?

The explanation for this dissonance may lie in the fact that slaveholders consistently associated some specific types of farmwork almost exclusively with men. Men were far more likely to perform tasks that involved animals or heavy equipment, like plowing, and so it is not surprising that many slaveholders questioned who would operate their plows if the men were impressed.[84] (Many former slaves, however, reported that women frequently plowed fields, especially on smaller farms.)[85] In addition, ex-slave Chana Littlejohn recalled that women tended one set of fields while men worked another, so some slaveholders may have employed only men to grow specific crops.[86] Other farmers were slow to adapt; John Hughson complained that the enslaved women on his farm could not seed his crop, but it probably would have been more accurate for him to say that the women had not done so before and teaching them might be time-consuming.[87] For farmers seeking to increase production while coping with widespread labor shortages, experience mattered—the most effective slaves were the ones who needed little guidance in completing their agricultural tasks.

Most important, at key planting times and especially at harvest season, farmers expected that every able-bodied person, with only a few exceptions, would work in the fields. Planters calculated how much of each crop to sow based in part on the number of hands they expected to employ for the harvest, so their insistence that they could not spare male slaves during the harvest season reflects the fact that they could not realistically spare any slaves. Many of the letters, especially in North Carolina, protested not the removal of slaves but Confederate officials' failure to return those men in time for the harvest. Complaints from overwhelmed farmers, then, had far less to do with the gendered division of labor in agricultural slavery than with the larger problem of labor shortages across the Confederacy.

Interestingly, there is no evidence that state or national lawmakers ever considered impressing female slaves to build fortifications. Enslaved women were employed at various tasks for the Confederate armies, primarily as laundresses and cooks in hospitals, but never as engineer laborers. This may have reflected a widespread association of industrial slavery with men, as most antebellum industrial employers in the Upper South had hired few female slaves.[88] It may have also been a tacit acknowledgment that, in between planting and harvesting, enslaved women typically did most of the work involved in maintaining a crop. There were seasons of the year when planters could probably afford to send a few male slaves to the fortifications, but there was no time when they could keep their farms going without their female field hands.

If most farmers in the Upper South could continue to operate their farms while one-quarter of the male slaves worked on the fortifications for a few months, why the repeated outcry at impressment? What accounts for the consistent belief that slave impressment crippled wartime agriculture in both Virginia and North Carolina? Slave impressment was only one of myriad Confederate military and economic policies that affected agricultural productivity, and it is probably impossible to isolate the impact of any one regulation. It is best, then, to consider them all in relation to each other, especially because many petitioners did.

Farmers from western counties of both states were the most likely to highlight the relationship between conscription and slave impressment when discussing the labor needs of each county. The Tazewell County Court requested an exemption from slave impressment in February 1863, noting, "Since the white working population has almost to a man joined the army there is not now a sufficiency of labor to produce bread."[89] The officers of Smyth County similarly proposed, "A withdrawal of fifty labouring slaves from the agriculture of the County, in addition to the excessive drain of its men & provisions set forth, will but aggravate the danger not only of a deficiency of provision, but of famine."[90] Residents of counties with relatively few slaves generally proposed that they could afford to lose either the free farmers or the enslaved laborers to the war effort, but not both. Because the western counties had few farmers who qualified for the twenty-slave draft exemption, their effective enlistment rates tended to be quite high, leaving the burden of agricultural production on men over the age of fifty-five, women, and a fairly small slave population, so their argument does have merit.

From early 1864 to the end of the war, a growing proportion of the letter writers in Virginia and North Carolina lived in the tobacco-growing counties along the border between the two states, which suggests that policies designed to increase production of grain crops may have fallen particularly heavily on communities where decades of tobacco cultivation had rendered the soil unsuitable for wheat or corn.[91] Farmer R. A. Jenkins, for example, reported that enrolling officers were taking slaves first from men who grew tobacco. He objected to this because a portion of his land could not sustain grain crops, and so planting tobacco on that ground did not in any way reduce the amount of food he could produce.[92]

Finally, numerous farmers explained that their slaves' absence had left them behind schedule in harvesting their crops, which prevented them from meeting their obligations under the tax-in-kind. Enacted in April 1863, the tax-in-kind required farmers to forfeit 10 percent of their crops and livestock to government agents at various points in the year. This tax fell on top of any impressments of food or supplies that farmers endured from military officials, who paid for those supplies at below-market rates in rapidly depreciating Confederate currency.[93] "The 10th taken from what I shall have will leave me deficient in corn & meat," wrote a Rowan County farmer seeking his slave's return. Small-scale slaveholders, especially those who had not produced significant surpluses before the war, could not afford to hand over 10 percent of their crops while also losing between 10 and 25 percent of their agricultural workforces.[94]

So while slave impressment may not have destroyed the agricultural capacity of the two states' Piedmont regions, when combined with high rates of industrial and government hiring, conscription, the tax-in-kind, and military impressment of food and draft animals, slave impressment did amount to a significant drain on both the quantity of food each community could produce and the quantity left at home for civilians to consume. Not all communities had the same experience, of course. Proximity to the battlefield mattered. Counties and towns subject to frequent incursions by both armies lost more of their agricultural produce to impressment agents. Proximity to Union armies also increased the likelihood that slaves would escape from their farms and plantations, and so Virginia communities were more likely to argue that they would not be able to continue farm operations in the face of both impressment quotas and significant numbers of runaway slaves.[95] In this context, while slave impressment was only one of many limitations that Virginia and North Carolina farmers faced in their attempt to grow enough food to feed the military and civilian populations, it may have been the easiest to pinpoint as a cause of distress.

☞ Each time they issued a requisition for slave labor, most Confederate officials acknowledged the importance of the slaves' normal agricultural pursuits to the success of the army. Chief Engineer Gilmer assured the secretary of war that he fully understood "the great importance of not interfering more than is absolutely necessary with farming operations, in view of the vital necessity of liberal commissary supplies."[96] The Engineer

Department even committed its own laborers to agricultural work in the summer of 1864, sending a force of free blacks working on fortifications near the Pamunkey River to harvest local farmers' wheat crops instead. This ironic turn of affairs underscores the value that the Engineer Bureau placed on farming operations in Virginia and North Carolina.[97]

The value of both food and fortifications to the Confederate war effort, and the vital role male slaves played in producing both, gave slaves clear bargaining tools as the war progressed. By threatening to run away to Union lines, thus encouraging their masters to intercede with government agents, some slaves may have escaped the harsh living and working conditions associated with work on the fortifications. Others may have obtained concessions from their employers. Francis McFarland, after prolonged negotiations in December 1863 and January 1864, arranged to hire a slave named Zeke for the coming year. Zeke, however, objected to the arrangement because McFarland's home was too far away from the farm where his wife had been hired. McFarland thus had to negotiate with Zeke as well as with his owner, and Zeke most likely used his power in Virginia's tight agricultural hiring market to obtain extra time to visit his family. Slaveholders similarly sought to use the demands of agriculture to assert their power within the state and national impressment processes.[98]

Slave impressment required cooperation between national, state, and local governments and the slaveholders themselves, who responded most favorably when government representatives treated owners as partners rather than as adversaries. Just as Francis McFarland made concessions to Zeke, Secretary Seddon and Colonel Gilmer allowed Virginia's farmers to keep their male slaves at home during the most pressing agricultural seasons. Their inability to concede the same privilege to many of North Carolina's farmers prompted significant and recurring protests and eventually created a serious power struggle between Governor Vance and General Whiting. Indeed, it seems that Whiting was the only high-ranking military or political official involved in the process of slave impressment who did not place a good harvest near the top of his list of national priorities.

By contrast, Seddon, Gilmer, Letcher, Vance, and Smith all took remarkable care to avoid harming agricultural production as they enforced each requisition for laborers. Their careful timing and the continuing presence of large numbers of enslaved women on many farms and plantations suggest that slave impressment alone did not irreparably damage wartime food production in Virginia and North Carolina. But while many of the farmers' protests cannot be taken literally, they did reflect a mounting sense of frustration that political leaders had to take seriously.

Frustration with a war that was longer and more difficult than anyone had predicted, the continued absence of husbands and sons, and a series of state and national policies that limited the quantity of food available on the home front—all of these factored into how each slaveholder responded to impressment.

It may have surprised those slaveholders to learn just how much time and energy state leaders expended debating the relative labor and supply needs of the home front and the armies. On any given day, approximately two-thirds of the outgoing correspondence from the governors' offices addressed issues like access to and distribution of salt, obtaining additional corn from states less exposed to both sides' armies, and the impressment of slaves, horses, and agricultural produce. Letcher, Vance, Smith, and Seddon all recognized that while the army could not function without food and labor, it also could not function if starvation on the home front led to mass desertion. They therefore struggled to balance the needs of the soldier and civilian populations in order to achieve the result both groups desired: a victorious war for Confederate independence.

But because most of this correspondence was internal—taking place among government officials at the national, state, and local levels—ordinary citizens had limited knowledge of the daily balancing act their governors undertook. All petitioners knew for certain was that nobody responded to their letters, or if someone did, the response was generally unfavorable. In particular, because Governors Vance, Letcher, and Smith declined to exempt or return individual slaves on the grounds of agricultural necessity, slaveholders remained largely unaware of their commitment to securing good harvests for the benefit of both soldiers and civilians, a commitment they demonstrated whenever possible by timing and organizing quotas to limit their impact on each community's agricultural work. Slaveholders' demands thus shaped government policy, but usually in a proactive, rather than reactive, manner, as the governors sought to reconcile national defensive requirements with the information they daily received from petitioners on the home front.

Most important, the majority of slaveholders did not actively obstruct slave impressment but instead responded with reluctant compliance. They probably did not like sending their slaves to work on the fortifications, but they did it anyway. Those who voiced protests did so in ways that sent a message: farmers demanded respect for the harvest season and for their role as food producers. Political and military leaders who failed to grant that respect would find enforcing impressment quotas increasingly difficult over the course of the war.

CHAPTER FOUR

To Equalize the Burden

Slave Impressment and the Expanding Confederate State, 1863–1864

An anonymous citizen of Mecklenburg County, Virginia, while protesting Governor William Smith's January 1864 requisition on behalf of his female neighbors, encouraged the governor to take a more active role in the enforcement and distribution of each quota. "The wholesale enrollment of all slaves from 18 to 55," the correspondent suggested, "will operate most injuriously to the interests of certain persons," including two local widows facing an impressment order from the county court. One of those widows had "a family of five children and those women (one almost helpless) making in all nine persons who are almost entirely dependent on the labor of one negro man for support." The second widow, an older woman, lived with her three daughters (all soldiers' wives or widows), fourteen grandchildren, and ten slaves, only one of whom was an adult man. "To take him away at this season of the year so important to the farming interest," the petitioner continued, "is equal to leaving these women and children, the wives and children of soldiers who are fighting our battles, to want and almost starvation."[1]

This "Friend of Justice" neatly demonstrated some of the most ironic developments in Confederate governance. In a republic founded to protect the institution of slavery, few contested the basic right of governments to impress those slaves for military labor, although plenty of people complained about the impact of impressment policy on their individual households and communities. This federal republic of supreme states became increasingly centralized over the course of the war, often exercising its growing power to increase slaveholders' responsibility for waging war, developments that were neither universally condemned nor universally celebrated. Indeed, by 1864 many Virginians and North Carolinians agreed with the sentiments expressed in this letter, and especially with its culminating plea for more centralized intervention: "This matter should not be left to the entire control of [local] magistrates some of whom are too sordid and selfish to act justly toward all."[2]

The Confederate Congress tackled the question of slave impressment as one portion of a general impressment bill under consideration in March 1863. Sections 9 and 10 of the bill affirmed that the Confederate government had the right to impress slaves but also stipulated that impressment should be as rare as possible and that military officials should never impress slaves without first attempting to hire the necessary laborers. The earliest state and national laws on slave impressment failed to mandate both mechanisms for enforcement and penalties for noncompliance, suggesting that lawmakers at all levels assumed both slaves and slaveholders would obey the summons without question. Yet questions arose almost immediately, prompting state and national legislatures to respond with new laws. The resolution of each inequity or inconsistency seemed only to create new possibilities for protest, however, and so the complaints and negotiations continued.[3]

Congress issued a new impressment law in February 1864, one that further centralized the process of commandeering slave labor for military purposes. Legislators also established a Board of Slave Claims in April 1864 to review slaveholders' requests for compensation in cases where their slaves had died or escaped while working on the fortifications. Yet the new regulations and the board continued to respect state laws and local authority on the subject of slave impressment, indicating that uniformity was a means to an end rather than a goal in itself. The point of impressment was to turn slaves into military laborers when necessary, while exploiting their labor on the home front at other times. While centralized impressment processes often accomplished that goal most efficiently, state and local governments continued to play a vital role in enforcing national legislation.

By the middle of 1864, much of the communication that the governors received—whether about slave impressment or other topics—focused on questions of equity. Civilians and soldiers alike expected the governors "to equalize the burden [of the war], as nearly as may be," across the entire population of each state.[4] As this applied to slave impressment, they expected a lot from their governors: not only to devise quotas that evenly distributed the impact of impressment across communities but also to maintain an equitable balance of slave labor between the home front and the front lines. For Governor Zebulon Baird Vance, Major General William H. C. Whiting's insatiable appetite for slave labor on the Wilmington fortifications became another potential stumbling block to his political career, making him eager to distance his office from impressment. For Smith, mounting complaints about how Virginia's county courts distributed and enforced their quotas left him amenable to any new plans that Congress and the secretary of war might propose. The letters and demands that Governors Vance and Smith received from their constituents in the spring and summer of 1864 shaped how they would respond to Congress's plans for slave impressment, predisposing them to accept (and even welcome) greater central government intervention into and control over the process. The governors therefore served as a pivot point between individual slaveholding households and the Confederate government in the negotiated centralization of slave impressment.

During the first two years of the war, the Confederate attorneys general wrestled with the legal and constitutional questions prompted by slave impressment. Lacking a supreme court or clear national regulations, they were forced to rely on a hodgepodge of state laws, state court rulings, and their own experience in the U.S. judicial system. In particular, they turned to state laws regulating slave hiring and public use of private property as their two primary sources of legal precedent.

In November 1861, Attorney General Thomas Bragg clarified the government's liability for slaves who had escaped from Confederate service, arguing that the Confederate government was not legally responsible for compensating the expenses slaveholders incurred to apprehend the fugitives. "As a matter of policy," however, Bragg suggested that the government pay to recapture any slaves who escaped while performing military labor, regardless of whether those slaves had been hired or impressed. In addition, he recommended that the War Department compensate owners for the value of escaped slaves they were unable to recover. Although state laws regulating slave hiring, a practice that had increased significantly in the 1850s, placed all liability on the slave's owner, Bragg still recommended that the Confederate government compensate slaveholders as the best way to maintain their loyalty.[5]

Attorney General Thomas Hill Watts applied eminent domain laws to wartime impressment of all private property, including slaves, in October

1862. While states retained the power to claim private property for public use, Watts argued, the Confederacy's power superseded that of the states in wartime because only the national government had the power to wage war. "By virtue of this exclusive right to make war and raise and support armies for the defence of the States and people, the Confederate Government has the right to seize *private property for the public use*," Watts concluded. Even without a statute clearly granting Confederate officials the right to impress slaves, their impressments retained the force of law. Watts, unlike Bragg, failed to make a distinction in this opinion between the government's legal responsibilities and a politically expedient course of action.[6]

Watts saved this distinction for an opinion he issued in March 1863, when he also considered the government's liability for impressed slaves who died or escaped. Although slave impressment technically trespassed on the slaveholder's property rights, Watts reasoned, once the owner agreed to receive compensation for impressed slaves he had entered into a hiring relationship with the Confederacy. As such, echoing Bragg, he suggested that the War Department was not liable for the value of slaves who escaped or died unless the employer—the Confederacy—failed to properly guard or care for those slaves. Thus, in theory at least, North Carolina's and Virginia's state provisions requiring the Confederacy to compensate owners for slaves lost or injured on the fortifications would go into effect only if the owner could prove negligence on the part of Confederate officers. Yet Watts was hesitant to apply this legal opinion to the actual practice of slave impressment, suggesting that "how far this Government would adopt these principles in dealing with its own Citizens . . . is, perhaps, more a question for the Legislature than the Executive Department of the Government."[7]

Congress agreed and was simultaneously debating a slave impressment law that would seek to impose uniform, nationwide standards on the process of slave impressment. The different approaches to slave impressment contained in Virginia's and North Carolina's laws point to one of the key arguments in favor of a national statute: consistency. Six Confederate states—Alabama, Florida, Louisiana, Mississippi, North Carolina, and Virginia—had enacted laws permitting and regulating slave impressment by March 1863. Georgia, though never permitting widespread impressment, did occasionally enact limited requisitions. Each of these laws mandated different procedures for communication between national and state authorities, different rates of pay, and different lengths for the term of impressment; the effectiveness of slave impressment under these laws also varied with each state. In Tennessee, Arkansas, and Texas, slave impressment no doubt occurred without any explicit legal sanction, thus leading to disputes between state and national governments and also between slaveholders and Confederate officials. South Carolina repeatedly rejected attempts to impress slaves within the state. The need for a uniform national statute became particularly clear when slaveholders began to sue the Confederate government for compensation when their slaves ran away or died while working on the fortifications, since not all state laws established clear liability in those cases.[8]

Because the first national slave impressment legislation respected these diverging approaches, it failed to create any true uniformity in the process of slave impressment. Instead, Congress required that any impressment calls made under its March 1863 law conform to existing local and state regulations, thus reserving some power to the state governments. In particular, the governors of Virginia retained the authority to reduce or revoke quotas for counties in close proximity to the Union armies, where the threat of runaway slaves was most severe, although they did not usually invoke that authority on a broad scale. Congress also enacted its policy without truly considering the efficacy of any of the states' existing impressment laws. Recognizing this discrepancy, Assistant Secretary of War (and former U.S. Supreme Court justice) John A. Campbell asked Colonel Jeremy Gilmer to craft guidelines regulating the timing of calls, size of quotas, and dispersal and treatment of laborers. While Campbell urged Gilmer to design a plan that could be applied consistently throughout the Confederacy, he conceded that the regulations could not overturn state impressment laws, whose variations undermined the goal of consistency. Gilmer passed the responsibility for negotiating this conundrum to the engineers most directly affected by Virginia's slave impressments, Colonel Walter H. Stevens and Lieutenant John B. Stanard.[9]

Stanard, as chief engineer on the Richmond fortifications, knew better than almost anyone else the importance of a clear system for impressing and collecting slave laborers. He also knew that impressment would happen successfully only with the support of the Confederacy's slaveholders. Although unable to obtain copies of the slave impressment laws recently enacted in Alabama, Florida, Louisiana, Mississippi, and North Carolina, Stanard did survey the state laws in effect at the opening of the war, observing that no antebellum statutes addressed the subject of slave impressment. Thus, the Confederate government was free to regulate slave impressment however it chose. Stanard recommended that Congress adopt Virginia's impressment plan, "which is so stringent upon the

Government, and jealous of the rights of its citizens," that residents of other states could not possibly disavow it.[10] Amendments to the Confederate law did adopt some of Virginia's provisions; chief among these was a provision granting owners financial compensation for slaves who ran away, died, or were injured while impressed by the government.[11]

Recognizing the potential for confusion that the overlapping state and national slave impressment laws created, the Virginia General Assembly specifically amended its impressment act to say that if state officials chose to issue a quota for slave laborers at any time after March 30, 1863, that quota would serve as the state's tacit acknowledgment and acceptance of all provisions of the national slave impressment act. At the same time, the army, by accepting those laborers, signaled its tacit assent to all provisions of the state's laws. The General Assembly wanted to ensure that the Confederate government would respect the stringent, specific plans it had created for slave impressment and, most important, the protections the Virginia law put into effect for the state's slaveholders. This would certainly not be the last time state and national legislators encountered conflicts over the exact terms of slave impressment, but by March 1863 the existence of clear statutes permitting each requisition at least silenced slaveholders' complaints that slave impressment had no legal standing.[12]

Uniformity did not come immediately, as the impressment calls issued between August 1863 and January 1864 demonstrated. Even with the national law in place, Confederate authorities relied on state and local leaders to implement slave impressment. The fact that they chose to do so despite the inconsistencies and inefficiencies inherent in local enforcement suggests that they derived significant benefits from relying on state authorities. In particular, demonstrating respect for state authorities may have improved compliance among slaveholders—or at least forestalled their harshest criticisms of national policy—because individual property owners exercised more control over governments at the local level. In addition, state and local leaders were better positioned to assess the precise labor needs of each community and arrange quotas accordingly. Finally, authorities at all levels, but particularly governors and state officials, recognized the impossibility of drawing clear lines between the needs of the state and the needs of the nation. Neither institution could wage war without the support of the other.

In August 1863, the Engineer Bureau prepared to issue a new, comprehensive impressment call, the first one to invoke Confederate slave impressment legislation passed the previous March. Although individual commanders like General Whiting had impressed slaves in the months

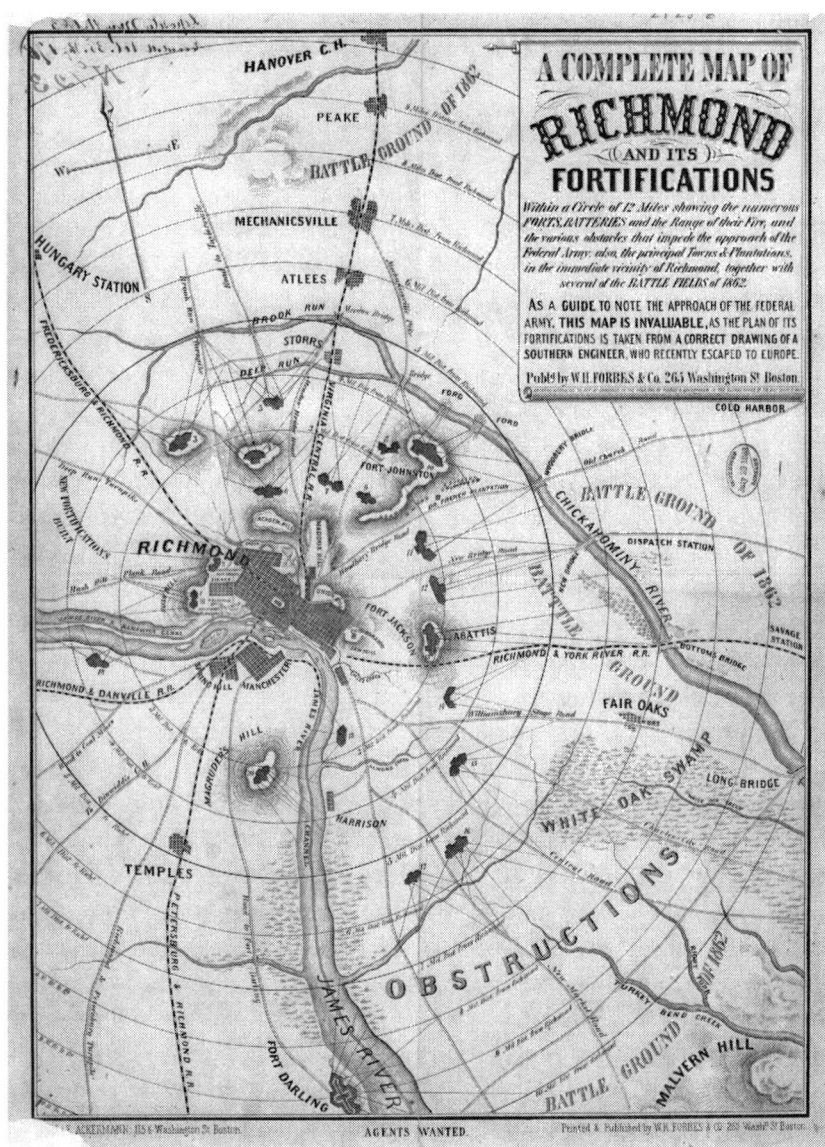

Figure 4.1. Map of Richmond fortifications, 1863 (Library of Congress)

between March and August, Secretary of War James A. Seddon had refused to authorize any statewide impressments that might interfere with the harvest season and further stipulated that any new call not require slaves to leave the farms prior to the middle of September, to cause as little disruption as possible to the Confederacy's food production. Food remained a priority, particularly in the aftermath of the bread riots that had swept the Confederacy the previous April, and local authorities had access to the information necessary to protect agriculture while meeting military labor needs. Thus, state officials played a key role in organizing and implementing the requisition. The new impressment quotas would call for the labor of 4,230 Virginia slaves for the fortifications in Richmond, Petersburg, Lynchburg, and Saltville, as well as 2,000 North Carolina slaves to work at Wilmington and Fayetteville (see appendix, tables 4.1 and 4.2).[13] Following the existing patterns for state-directed impressment still worked fairly well in these two states, underscoring the arguments against immediately imposing uniformity on slave impressment.

As always, Gilmer delegated most of the responsibility for preparing these impressment quotas to the commanders and engineers in charge of the fortifications. He instructed Colonel Stevens to consider each county's compliance with prior calls, as well as the likely number of slaves who had recently run away from each county, in order to craft equitable quotas. He also noted that Stevens should consider not only his own needs in Richmond and Petersburg but also any labor that might be needed on the Lynchburg fortifications as well as 300 slaves for the Saltville defenses. Gilmer further suggested that slaves, whenever possible, be put to work on the fortifications nearest their home counties.[14] After Stevens made his list of quotas, Lieutenant Colonel Alfred Landon Rives, acting as head of the Engineer Bureau, transmitted the list to the secretary of war, who then sent it to President Davis, who forwarded the requisition to Governor John Letcher.[15] Stevens also submitted a copy of the list directly to Letcher later that year, noting which counties had failed to meet their quotas.[16]

Interestingly, Rives not only continued using the chain of communication established under Virginia's state impressment legislation but also referred to the state law of October 1862—rather than the national law of March 1863—in his communications with Seddon. His decision to do so reflected both practical and ideological concerns. For one thing, the national law expected officials to respect existing state laws, and Virginia's laws mandated a clear and incontrovertible chain of authority on slave impressment. In addition, state and local officials had already collected the necessary information to start filling the requisition immediately;

replicating their efforts would waste both time and manpower. Finally, he probably expected that as much as Virginia's slaveholders resented slave impressment quotas delivered through state authorities, they would react even less favorably to those decreed from the national level. Respecting state authority thus helped improve compliance.

Governor Letcher published circulars listing the quota for each county and then distributed them to the county courts with a request that they comply immediately. Because all of the counties encompassed in the August 1863 requisition had supplied slave labor on previous occasions, the county courts already had lists of eligible slaveholders and could respond to the new requisition relatively quickly. The Albemarle County Court endeavored to draw on slaveholders who had not contributed their full quota of slaves the previous November, ordering its sheriff to collect the slaves in Charlottesville by September 21, when they would leave for Richmond.[17] Officers of the Nelson County Court met in a special session on September 10 to fulfill the impressment orders and in the regular session on September 28 compiled a list of slaveholders who had not complied with the requisition.[18] Halifax County Court officials began compiling their list in August, instructing the justices for each district to make any necessary adjustments to the existing census of male slaves in the county; they carried the impressment order into effect on September 29.[19] Augusta County made plans to collect its quota of eighty slaves in early October, and the *Staunton Spectator* urged the county court to act quickly, so that the slaves could return home before winter.[20] On the other hand, the slaveholders of Pittsylvania County appear to have ignored the new impressment order entirely, failing to send any slaves to meet their quota of 300.[21]

Pittsylvania County was not the only Virginia locality to shirk the August 1863 impressment call. Henrico County also failed to contribute any slaves toward its quota. In addition, while the Richmond City Council had eagerly forced free black men to work on the fortifications in July, they refused, one month later, to take any steps toward accomplishing slave impressment.[22] On September 15, the *Richmond Whig* addressed the city's new quota for slave labor, noting that the city council and hustings court had refused to implement the requisition due to insufficient information.[23] In a speech before the General Assembly, Letcher expressed his impatience and frustration with the tepid response of Richmond's leaders. "If nothing else will do," he threatened, "I will commence the impressment by taking the slaves of the members of the Court and its officers, by way of example." As late as December 1863, though, Richmond had still failed to meet its requisition. State-directed slave impressment worked—but imperfectly. Its imperfections, however, stemmed from different sources in each state, and in neither case did the governors seem to be at fault.[24]

Indeed, the governors of both Virginia and North Carolina repeatedly demonstrated their support for slave impressment, although the process of impressment continued to vary between the two states. Neither Letcher nor Vance revoked requisitions except under extraordinary circumstances, for example, and both clearly expected the slaveholders of each county to comply with the impressment quotas. Letcher regularly urged the county courts to act quickly. Vance delegated this responsibility to his new adjutant general, who admonished the militia officers of each county when they failed to meet their full requisitions. Adjutant General Richard C. Gatlin told several delinquent militia colonels to "impress the slaves required . . . *by force if necessary*."[25] This authorization to use force perhaps explains why North Carolina's slaveholders often objected to slave impressment to a greater extent than did those of Virginia. As elected officials, the justices of the county courts could not tell an intransigent slaveholder "that if they had orders to cut his throat, they would do so," as militia officers reportedly threatened a Henderson County slaveholder. Virginia's slaveholders also had a clearer channel of protest, since their first step was usually to approach county court officers, who could then write to Richmond on behalf of their constituents.[26]

Another significant difference between slave impressment procedures in Virginia and North Carolina was the level of cooperation between individual commanders, the War Department, and the governors' offices. Because General Whiting did not answer to the Engineer Bureau, he presumably took responsibility for preparing his own requisition quotas for the Wilmington fortifications, never formally submitting them to Vance, Gilmer, or even the secretary of war. Gilmer did, however, assist Whiting in communications with Governor Vance. Noting that "the works ought to be pressed forward without delay," Gilmer petitioned Vance "to call on the patriotic citizens in the neighboring counties, and elsewhere, to send a portion of their hands, say one-fifth of the negroes (male), to the city of Wilmington, to be employed under the command of General Whiting, on the fortifications." Whiting required a total of 1,000 laborers and would send his engineer officers into the counties to help local officials collect and chaperone the slaves on their way to Wilmington.[27]

The different approaches Secretary Seddon and Colonel Rives took to impressment in Virginia and North Carolina require some explanation. They chose to work closely with Governor Letcher of Virginia, seeking his explicit permission for all requisitions, while treating Governor Vance of

North Carolina as more of an advisor than a partner. Yet there is no evidence to suggest that Vance, in general, was less supportive of slave impressment than Letcher. Geographic distance may provide one explanation—Seddon, Rives, and Letcher all worked in the same city, which facilitated communication and interaction. More important, North Carolina's state law did not mandate that all requisitions come through the governor's office, so Seddon and Rives were simply obeying the laws of each state, as directed by the national legislature. But the decision to limit state officials' input in North Carolina may have led to higher levels of resistance, at least in proportion to the total number of slaves impressed in each state. It also routinely created confusion and inequity, as impressment calls from different areas overlapped with each other.

Following Whiting's call for 160 laborers from Cumberland County in August 1863, Adjutant General Gatlin issued statewide orders impressing 800 slaves in September 1863 and 1,040 more the next month, for a total of 2,000. Like Gilmer, Gatlin was concerned with equity. In particular, he encouraged each county's militia officers to focus their attention on slaveholders who had not previously sent laborers before asking anyone to fulfill a second requisition. Whiting received his thousand laborers at Wilmington, while the remainder went to work on fortifications outside Fayetteville, Kinston, and Weldon. Eager to avoid a repetition of events of the previous spring, when Vance and Whiting were unable to agree amicably upon a release date for the impressed slaves, Gatlin instructed the engineers at all points of fortification to send the slaves home after two months' service.[28]

On December 23, 1863, Gatlin issued Special Orders No. 115, calling on thirty-two counties to replace the 1,000 slaves he had sent to Wilmington in October. Twenty-two of these counties, mostly from the Piedmont area, had also sent slaves the previous fall. The ten new additions to Gatlin's list were all counties from the eastern portion of the state; their slaves would replace laborers drawn from the mountainous western counties in the requisitions of September and October.

Militia officers in North Carolina were typically able to collect slaves very efficiently, but Gatlin still received questions about how best to proceed with the impressment. The arrival of refugee slaveholders from eastern North Carolina posed a new problem for Piedmont militia officers, who pondered whether or not to include the refugeed slaves in their quotas. Gatlin instructed them to do so but to also assume that those slaveholders had complied with earlier impressment quotas in their home counties. They should not, therefore, be expected to bear a greater burden than the longtime residents of the county.[29]

Gatlin's assertion that the eastern counties of North Carolina had already furnished slaves underscores the extent to which Confederate commanders during the first two years of the war impressed slaves without the formal participation of state authorities. In fact, very few of the eastern counties furnished slaves under formal state requisitions in 1863, despite having significantly larger slave populations than the western counties. The northeastern counties, however, repeatedly sent slaves to the fortifications in southeastern Virginia, while General Whiting's requisitions for labor in 1862 had fallen heavily on the southeastern counties. Indeed, Whiting continued to make his own requisitions even after the state adjutant general's office took over this responsibility, which led to repeated disputes with Vance's office over the next two years. A slaveholder responding to the state's December 1863 call, for example, complained that Anson County had just sent 140 slaves to Wilmington in addition to its quota under the September call. North Carolina's militia officers thus had to navigate conflicting requisitions far more often than did county court officials in Virginia, where impressment calls were typically funneled through the Engineer Bureau. These conflicts proved exasperating to many slaveholders, and state officials no doubt shared their frustration.[30]

Gatlin and Vance also shared slaveholders' fear that additional requisitions would jeopardize the spring planting season. Anxious to protect the state's agriculture, Vance requested that Confederate officers in North Carolina release all impressed slaves by April 1, 1864. Indeed, in his correspondence with engineer officers regarding the December 1863 impressment, Gatlin consistently maintained that Governor Vance would not approve any new requisitions for slave labor after the start of the spring planting season. They should therefore make other arrangements to fulfill their labor needs.[31]

In Virginia, newly elected governor William "Extra Billy" Smith also sought to enact a requisition for slave labor before the spring 1864 campaign and planting seasons began. Though Smith was a Democrat and a strong supporter of states' rights during his years in the U.S. Congress, his experience as a brigadier general in the Army of Northern Virginia had rendered him more amenable to centralized governance in cases of great necessity. He supported slave impressment, as well as other forms of impressment, as absolutely necessary for the defense of both the Confederacy and his state. As biographer Alvin Fahrner notes, Smith supported slave impressment because "Confederate breastworks and fortifications were for all practical purposes also Virginia breastworks and fortifications."[32]

On January 22, only days after taking office, Smith issued a requisition for 5,070 slaves. This new call encompassed fifty-two counties as well as the cities of Petersburg and Richmond (see appendix, table 4.3). Secretary Seddon and Smith both extolled the value of strong fortifications, especially as the number of available soldiers began to dwindle.[33] Virginia's slaveholders were less enthusiastic. Because many of the slaves impressed in September 1863 had returned home only shortly before Christmas, Smith's first impressment call met with a great deal of resistance. Slaveholders protested not only the extremely short period of time between the two calls but also the fact that the new quotas did not exempt counties that had experienced sustained contact with Union armies. Again, it would fall to local and state leaders to determine the most effective way to meet the labor needs of both the front lines and the home front.

In issuing the quota, Smith took great pains to convince Virginia's county courts to comply quickly and without complaint. Smith encouraged court officers to act swiftly, forwarding the full text of the March 1863 state impressment law as a reminder that the courts were required to send slaves at the governor's request.[34] Secretary of the Commonwealth George Munford provided more explicit instructions and admonitions. In particular, he pointed out that sending the full quota of slaves immediately would increase the likelihood that Virginia's farmers would be able to retain their laborers during the spring planting seasons. He also suggested that both the governor's office and the Engineer Department anticipated needing no additional calls during the summer of 1864—as long as all counties complied with the current requisition. His deft combination of threat, incentive, and recognition for the county governments' other obligations was the work of a skillful and calculating politician.[35]

As the elaborate list that accompanied Smith's circular indicated, Munford and Colonel Stevens had considered both the total slave population of each county and that county's participation in prior impressments before determining the new quotas. Indeed, Stevens prepared the January 1864 quotas using Virginia's 1862 tax records rather than the 1860 U.S. Census returns, although he did not have a way of accounting for slaves who had run away since that tax assessment.[36] But this choice reiterates the best reason for vesting power in state and local governments: they usually had access to more accurate information about the slave population of each community. If they failed to act, however, local governments would now find themselves overruled, thanks to the growing power of the national state. In this circular, Munford explicitly reminded the county courts that if they failed to impress slaves, the Confederate government would assume that responsibility. "The cheerfulness with which the citizens of this State have generally heretofore furnished labor for the defences of the

Confederacy," he continued, "leads the Governor to hope that the officer of the confederate government may not find it necessary to apply any law but that enacted by the State Legislature." Munford clearly hoped that a mixture of optimistic entreaties and mild threats would produce the highest level of compliance with the new call.[37]

Stevens did not share Munford's optimism, and he immediately began to seek additional sources of labor for the Richmond fortifications. Smith's circular to the county courts included a letter from Stevens offering to hire 10,000 slaves for a period of twelve months at prices between $300 and $550 per year, depending on whether the slaves' owners or the Confederate government furnished rations.[38] Stevens also wrote to Munford in mid-March, seeking information about Virginia's laws regulating the impressment of free blacks, no doubt intending to issue a quota in the near future.[39] Stevens clearly anticipated that many of Virginia's counties would fail to meet their full quotas; he also recognized that he could count on the work of those impressed slaves only for a period of sixty days. Thus, prudence suggested he draw labor from as many sources as possible.

The slaves impressed in January 1864, whenever possible, remained on fortifications near their owners' home counties, thus employing strong traditions of local pride and "home defense" in the defense of the nation as a whole. For example, the Engineer Bureau again directed the slaves from southwestern Virginia to the fortifications at Saltville.[40] When the chief engineer at Saltville indicated that he did not need so many laborers, some were redirected to nearby Lynchburg. The Engineer Bureau also placed some of the slaves impressed from Augusta County under the control of the Quartermaster's Office in Staunton, where they hauled hay and other supplies for the cavalry and artillery.[41]

Rather than resist the January 1864 impressment call, some counties moved to meet their quotas as quickly as possible, thus ensuring that their slaves would return by the beginning of planting season in April. The Amherst County Court met in early February to issue its requisitions and sent Governor Smith a copy of its proceedings.[42] Cumberland and Pulaski Counties did the same, although both later requested an exemption from the impressment call.[43] More ambiguously, the citizens of Halifax County engaged in a little bureaucratic foot-dragging, claiming on February 8 that they had not received their instructions regarding the latest requisition. Instead of sending their slaves immediately, though, Halifax County's slaveholders withheld the laborers until forced to fill their quota in July.[44]

Finding their appeals to home-front labor demands less successful than in prior impressment calls, some of Virginia's slaveholders sought new grounds for protest. For example, the fact that several counties had failed to meet their August 1863 quotas provided ample fodder to those who claimed the new impressment call fell too harshly on their counties. The Botetourt County Court noted with particular displeasure that while the smaller counties had met their quotas, those with the largest slave populations were more likely to be delinquent.[45] To this new protest, Smith's aide S. Bassett French replied crisply, "It is not known to you as it is to this department that the inequality complained of is the rather apparent than real. The counties marked as having furnished 'none,' derelict as they have been, are now being summarily disposed of." In addition to expecting these counties and cities to fill their present quotas, French wrote, "stringent measures" had been applied to force all counties to meet delinquencies from previous requisitions.[46] Even when local authorities tried to avoid making sacrifices in support of national goals, state leaders worked to provide that support.

Court officials in Lunenburg County vehemently protested both the January 1864 impressment call and any attempt to make them fill prior requisitions. Conveniently ignoring its own delinquencies, the county court argued "that Lunenburg has already performed more than her quota of labour, having once voluntarily and three times under requisitions punctually responded to the calls made whilst other counties have refused & no steps have been taken to coerce."[47] In response, Smith noted that Lunenburg had not suffered as greatly as many other counties within the state. "Her fields have not been desolated, nor her houses burned, nor her negroes stock &c taken," Smith asserted. "Richmond is her protection. That lost she becomes a prey to the enemy, and with other counties similarly situated should raise no difficulty in those measures necessary really and in fact to her own defense." As Letcher had before him, Governor Smith refused to revoke any county's quota simply because it had contributed more slaves than its neighbors had. In addition, Smith reiterated that for Virginians in particular, national security was a local issue.[48]

Out of the fifty-two counties and two cities encompassed in the January 1864 requisition, twenty-three sent Smith petitions requesting exemption. Smith granted twelve full exemptions and reduced one quota; he rejected the remaining petitions. A small majority of counties sent their slaves without complaint. Even though most failed to meet their full quotas, this suggests that they recognized the importance of slave impressment, however unpleasant, to the continued defense of the Confederacy. Governor Smith typically denied requests from county courts that complained of unfair quotas, heavy local demands on labor by other Confederate departments,

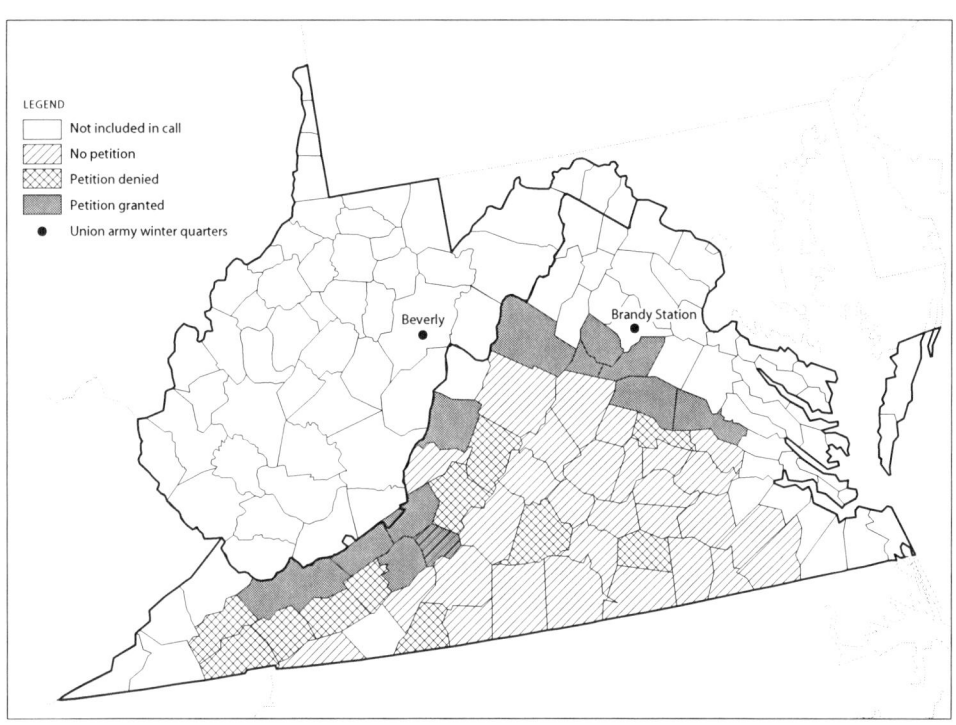

Map 4. Responses to January 1864 call in Virginia

and general concerns about agriculture, noting that no county could claim special hardships in these areas. His primary criterion for granting exemptions seems to have been a county's proximity to Union forces.[49]

Slaveholders in areas close to Union armies repeatedly worried that even a rumor of slave impressment would prompt an exodus of slaves from their counties. A Bertie County slaveholder suggested to Governor Vance, as early as September 1862, that an impressment order in his community would provide few laborers to the army, as it would prompt most of the slaves to escape.[50] Governor Letcher received similar reports in September and October 1863. The Rockingham County Court suggested that the proximity of the Union army in West Virginia—only a few hours' journey on foot—made slavery "a volunteer matter." Many slaves had already escaped, and others threatened to do so rather than go to the fortifications, so the court pleaded with Letcher to revoke his August 1863 impressment call.[51] Smith, Seddon, and President Davis all received letters making similar arguments on more than one occasion.[52] Fear that impressment would lead to mass departures from the plantations motivated Governor Smith to revoke some of his requisitions.

Smith extended exemptions primarily to counties in close and regular proximity to Union forces in western and northern Virginia. Many counties from these portions of the state demonstrated that the presence of Union forces had severely reduced their slave populations since the 1862 tax assessment. The Giles County Court described a raid that cost the county one-third of its adult male slaves in late 1862.[53] In a similar vein, citizens of Bath County claimed to have lost most of their slaves in a series of six raids in the previous year, while those of Craig County claimed to have "suffered severely by the Raid in December."[54] Meanwhile, Rockingham County sought an exemption under state law because more than one-fourth of its slave population had escaped in 1863.[55] The Tazewell County Court successfully resisted Smith's requisition by arguing that "Tazewell for some time has been & still is the border of the Confederate lines, all the Counties between her northern boundary & the Ohio & Kanawha rivers being held & occupied by Federal troops or Union men."[56] Slaveholders in Louisa, Madison, and Orange Counties, portions of which were behind Union lines by February 1864, also successfully resisted Smith's new call for slave labor. Smith agreed that these counties could not effectively collect slaves to meet his January 22 requisition and so revoked their quotas.[57]

This was the only time that Smith granted full exemptions to more than two or three counties involved in a single impressment call. More often, he followed Governor Letcher's precedent and reduced quotas rather than revoke them entirely. The Engineer Bureau had also learned to arrange its quotas more strategically, typically avoiding the counties closest to Union lines, although it would prove impossible to exclude from impressment any Virginia county with a noticeable number of runaways. Doing so would have exempted much of the state.

Governor Smith, though elected with widespread support, quickly found that debating and enforcing slave impressment absorbed a significant portion of his energy and popularity. As the war progressed and its burdens mounted, Smith received an increasing number of petitions from small-scale slaveholders (and their allies) accusing county court officials of shielding the wealthy and powerful members of their communities from full participation in slave impressment. The combined weight of these petitions would force Smith to contemplate intervention in early 1864 and then to support a more centralized approach to slave impressment that would bypass much of the county courts' authority.

Problems emerging with each requisition increased the appeal of a centralized approach. For example, Virginia's governors regularly found themselves mediating disputes between county governments and the mayors of incorporated towns when the Engineer Bureau's quotas failed to distinguish between the responsibilities of the towns and the counties that surrounded them. Mayor Thomas Atkinson of Danville, for example, protested the actions of the Pittsylvania County Court, which had drafted slaves whose owners lived within the town rather than in the county at large. The citizens of Danville eagerly supported the Confederacy, Mayor Atkinson assured Letcher, but they did not believe that the Pittsylvania County Court had any authority over them or their slaves.[58] In response, Secretary of the Commonwealth Munford referred Atkinson to Virginia's state impressment laws, which placed authority over labor requisitions in the hands of county courts in almost all cases. Since Danville fell within the boundaries of Pittsylvania County, town residents would have to obey the dictates of the county court.[59] Munford made similar pronouncements when disputes arose between Staunton and Augusta County and Charlottesville and Albemarle County. Although they echoed the rhetoric that pitted agricultural "producers" against urban and industrial "consumers," these disputes were primarily about political authority. Residents of small incorporated towns, many of whom were engaged in agricultural work, had their own elected leaders and did not want to answer to county officials whom they had played no role in choosing.

Disagreements between towns and counties occurred frequently because the Engineer Bureau did not have the time or information necessary to give every small municipality its own quota, but complaints that emerged within each county were even more common. Many petitioners suggested that the county courts granted special favors to some slaveholders but not to others. A resident of Prince Edward County, for example, wrote angrily, "I have four & only four between those ages & I have under the order of the court to send two of them. There are two of my neighbours that has five slaves each, of those ages, & they send one a piece."[60] A few days later, Letcher received a similar letter from a Pittsylvania County man who protested the impressment of his one male slave when several of his neighbors, though possessing twenty or more slaves, were excused from the requisition.[61] A similar supplicant from Albemarle County noted, "I am a poor man with only one negro man in the world, & he happening to be of right age is taken while my neighbors have more negroes than myself, but their ages not happening to be suitable, are all left."[62] The governor forwarded this letter to county court officials, who excused the man's slave from the impressment call.[63]

Some Virginians objected when county courts granted exemptions to individual slaveholders who had hired slaves to the Confederate government. Those who had the surplus laborers to do so, they argued, could better afford to send men to meet impressment quotas than could farmers with only one or two adult male slaves. One Lunenburg County resident protested, "I am willing to pay the last cent I have than the enemy should over run us, but Governor, the rich men are hireing their best hands out to the rail road, to keep from sending on the breast works."[64] Another reported that many of the "rich men" in question held seats on the county court and had thus found ways to avoid slave impressment themselves while enforcing it for their neighbors.[65] A Nelson County farmer complained that while his wealthy neighbors told the county court they had hired their slaves to Confederate authorities, they had not actually sent them.[66] Finally, one Campbell County slaveholder suggested that the local quartermaster, having hired dozens of slaves from county farmers, should have to send a portion of his workforce to the fortifications just like any other employer.[67]

On the other hand, numerous slaveholders who had hired slaves to government employers, often with the explicit promise of exemption from the next impressment quota, wrote to the governors in anger when their county courts failed to acknowledge that exemption. By 1864, government employers often struggled to hire sufficient slave labor, and one tactic they used to entice overburdened planters—Confederate paper money being of little use—was to promise that the planter could count slaves hired to the government toward any future impressment quotas.[68] The Engineer Department generally strove to honor these arrangements when made between slaveholders and other branches of the War Department but did not consider slaves hired out as camp servants sufficient qualification for the exemption. In addition, Colonel Stevens clarified that the slaveholder "is entitled to credit but *not the County*."[69] Hiring slaves to the Confederate government would not enable a county to evade filling its entire quota, but if a slaveholder had hired a slave to a legitimate military employer, like the Ordnance Bureau or Quartermaster Department, engineer officers could release that slaveholder's laborers from impressment. The practice of providing credits did mean that counties would have to rely more heavily on small-scale slaveholders (many of whom could not afford to hire out their workforces on an annual basis) to meet each requisition. Moreover, the heavy hiring demands that large military hospitals, mines, and factories placed on communities throughout the state meant that some counties really did struggle to find sufficient slaves to fill their quotas.

Like Virginia's governors, neither Colonel Stevens nor the Engineer Bureau overturned the actions of the county courts except in circumstances where the court had clearly ignored credits provided by a War Department employee. Stevens's reply to Dr. Crockett's request "to exempt his negro Chas" was more characteristic. If the county court was not willing to provide an exemption, Stevens wrote, neither was he.[70] To so blatantly undermine the authority of local elected officials would create chaos, thus complicating future requests for labor. Colonel Alfred Landon Rives, acting as head of the Engineer Bureau again in March 1864, agreed. Even when he believed a slaveholder should receive an exemption, Rives referred the case to the proper county court.[71] In upholding the actions of the various county courts in Virginia, both the governor's office and the Engineer Bureau demonstrated a proper level of respect for locally elected officials, respect that probably helped ensure them the continued cooperation of most county courts. But Virginians were losing confidence in the credibility and impartiality of their local elected leaders.

Complaints to Governor Smith often noted a slaveholder's previous sacrifices of his workforce, suggesting that some county courts relied heavily on a small cadre of wealthy planters while others spread impressments more evenly among small-scale slaveholders. Neither approach proved particularly effective at quashing protests. Slave impressment became the symbol of and the scapegoat for the vast array of sacrifices that Virginians were making on behalf of Confederate victory, and by early 1864 each person was convinced not only that his neighbors were contributing fewer slaves than they should have been but also that the county court was singling him out for unusually high quotas. Most of these deeply held convictions were erroneous, however. Isaac Carrington, for example, complained that of his twenty-eight male slaves in the proper age range, he had sent nine, thus exceeding the 25 percent demanded by state law. Carrington was (perhaps willfully) misinterpreting the law, however, which mandated that a slaveholder not send more than 25 percent of his eligible slaves *at once*. Since Carrington had never been required to send more than five at a time, his burden fell short of the maximum prescribed by law, demonstrating the extremely generous treatment he had received from Charlotte County officials.[72] Nathaniel Garland, an Albemarle County farmer who had sent a slave for both of Letcher's major calls, as well as having wagons, teams, and slaves impressed for short periods of time by the Confederate Quartermaster's Department, objected to the January 1864 requisition. Of the several local slaveholders who owned "as large a force of hands" as Garland, he wrote, none had been asked to send slaves more than twice, while he had just received a third impressment summons.[73] Indeed, petitions from Albemarle residents were frequent enough occurrences after every requisition to suggest that the Albemarle County Court's response to slave impressment merits close consideration.

Such consideration demonstrates that while some Albemarle County slaveholders did have cause to criticize the court's distribution of slave impressment quotas, Nathaniel Garland was not among them. In 1860, Garland owned seventy-three slaves, making him the seventh-largest slaveholder in Albemarle County.[74] He owned twelve adult male slaves and sent one under each impressment call in October 1862, August 1863, and January 1864, although under the letter of Virginia's impressment law the court could have required him to send three slaves to meet each quota. Of the nine slaveholders with approximately "as large a force of hands" as Garland, all but two had also sent at least one slave for each call, and all but one had sent more workers than Garland.[75]

On the whole, the Albemarle County Court was remarkably assiduous in its attempts to insulate the slaves of wealthy men like Garland from impressment. The wealthiest twenty-four slaveholders in the county, men (and two women) who owned fifty or more slaves in 1860, were never called upon to contribute disproportionately to the county's impressment quotas. Owning 12.25 percent of the adult male slaves in the county, they sent between 10.2 percent and 14.9 percent of the slaves included in each quota. Similarly, slaveholders with between fifteen and forty-nine slaves, who owned 37.5 percent of the adult male slaves in the county, usually sent about 40 percent of the slaves included in each impressment quota. By contrast, slaveholders with between one and fourteen slaves in 1860—too few to ever qualify for an exemption from the Confederate draft—sent between 26.5 percent and 35.6 percent of the slaves included in each draft, despite owning only 21.7 percent of the adult male slaves in Albemarle County in 1860. The Albemarle County Court thus shifted the overall burden of slave impressment slightly downward onto the slaveholders least able to bear it.[76]

Albemarle's process for distributing its quotas stood in marked contrast to that of nearby Bedford County. In October 1862, the Bedford County Court required wealthy slaveholders to send their full quota—one in every four adult male slaves—before turning to small-scale slaveholders. Then, the remaining slaves were chosen by a lottery system involving slaveholders with two or three adult men, as well as those with larger holdings not evenly divisible by four. (For example, a planter with eighteen male slaves in the proper age range would be required to send four, but then he also would be entered into the lottery at the same stage as a farmer with only two adult men.) The impartiality of this system led the editor of the

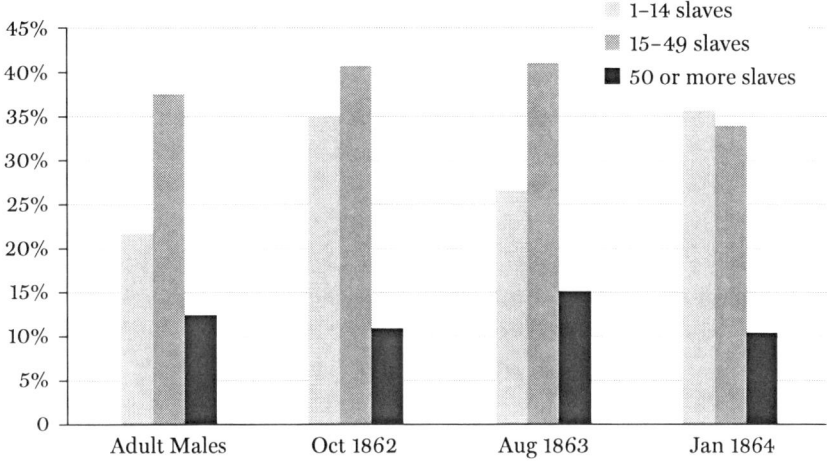
Figure 4.2. Albemarle County impressment quotas

Lynchburg Daily Virginian to pronounce it "the most satisfactory mode of allotment which could have been adopted."[77] Bedford County concentrated the bulk of its 1863 and 1864 impressment quotas on the wealthy slaveholders once again, forcing them to contribute one-quarter of their adult male slaves before asking small-scale slaveholders who had avoided impressment in the earlier lottery system to help meet the quota.[78] Albemarle County, by contrast, relied more heavily on a diverse group of smaller slaveholders to fill each quota. Bedford County's system seems to have forestalled slaveholders' criticisms of impressment more effectively, allowing the county to meet its obligations to the Confederate army with greater ease. Certainly, Virginia governors received far fewer letters of complaint from residents of Bedford County than from Albemarle.

Rather than drawing lots between slaveholders with only one adult male slave, the Albemarle County Court seems to have considered each person's ability to continue his or her work without that slave's assistance. Thus, they were less likely to take slaves from female slave owners (who were primarily widows) than from men, although this pattern is somewhat deceptive because many of the men listed as owners were probably serving in the Confederate army, leaving their wives to run their farms. Smaller slaveholders with wealthy relatives—members of the extended Cabell, Coles, Michie, Minor, and Randolph families, for example—were more likely to face impressment quotas than were their neighbors of similar rank, perhaps because the court assumed their extended families could provide assistance. This was the case for William Daniel Cabell of adjacent

Nelson County, whose father lent him a slave named John to meet his quota for the January 1864 requisition. Just like the governors, county courts recognized that deprivation on the home front could undermine civilian support for the war, so they strove to balance their constituents' needs for labor with their desire to support the Confederacy.[79]

Contradictions clearly abounded in the Albemarle County Court's approach to slave impressment, as they no doubt did for every county court. The court's decisions to rely heavily on some slaveholders while entirely exempting others suggest an attempt to meet the needs of its constituents, but the downward shift of each impressment quota indicates that the wealthiest constituents mattered more than others. Unlike the Nelson County Court, which aggressively prosecuted delinquent slaveholders to ensure full compliance with each requisition, the Albemarle County Court routinely exempted slaveholders it had placed on its impressment lists. Indeed, Albemarle County's original lists of impressed slaves fell short of its assigned quotas for the first three statewide calls even *before* such exemptions took place: the county court designated 533 slaves to meet its October 1862 quota of 540, 181 slaves toward its August 1863 quota of 200, and 177 slaves toward its January 1864 quota of 190.[80] This imperfect compliance, however, characterized most county courts' responses to slave impressment in Virginia. From the Engineer Bureau's perspective, it was better than no compliance at all.

Yet neither Smith nor the Engineer Bureau discounted the possibility that a different approach to slave impressment might have worked more effectively. Any plan that could reduce the competition among various War Department employers would probably create a more efficient distribution of labor resources. In addition, the growing volume of complaints about unfair treatment by the county courts certainly encouraged Smith to consider new options. Both issues made a plan hatched in September 1864 that would shift responsibility for enforcing slave impressment quotas to the Conscript Bureau especially attractive. If Virginia's slaveholders did not like the way county courts dealt with impressment, then Smith could resolve that problem—by removing those courts from the equation. The consequence of pushing the governor to intervene was that he would end up supporting plans for greater centralization, a step that was probably not what the voters had intended.

☙ The Confederacy's use of slave labor in the summer of 1864 typically conformed to preexisting patterns that placed a great emphasis on the role of local governments. While Congress strengthened the Confederate government's right to impress slaves with its act of February 17, 1864, events during the summer of 1864 illustrated the War Department's continued reliance on state and local governments to carry impressment into effect. In particular, as relations between Vance and Whiting deteriorated in the summer of 1864, the governor would relinquish most of his control over slave impressment in order to distance himself from voter discontent. Yet while voters and local elected officials were becoming more eager to avoid impressment, Vance continued to support the practice and even encouraged its further centralization.

The Congress that created the February 1864 slave impressment law differed quite dramatically from the one responsible for its March 1863 predecessor. In their 1863 congressional elections, Virginia voters had unseated a number of their representatives, replacing them with former Whigs who were more likely to support measures that strengthened the central government.[81] Voters in Georgia also ousted nine representatives, electing men who had campaigned for more active prosecution of the war on the part of the Confederate Congress.[82] On the other hand, the 1863 elections in North Carolina brought six additional peace advocates into the House of Representatives, men who would no doubt oppose more active measures on the part of the national government.[83] But the balance of the legislature seemed to be shifting toward nationalists, many of whom believed President Davis had mismanaged both the war and the economy. They would seek to construct a more centralized version of slave impressment that would also demonstrate greater respect for slaveholders' property rights—no simple task.[84]

The February 1864 law was designed to make the army's use of black laborers more efficient and effective. The Confederate Congress seemingly expected that a single, centralized authority would collect laborers both more efficiently and more equitably than decentralized county courts and militia officers would. Congress, no doubt reacting to concerns raised by military leaders, sanctioned the employment of black men in a widened range of noncombatant positions within the Confederate armies, thus freeing more white men for actual combat. This new law authorized the secretary of war to hire and then impress up to 20,000 slaves, but only after exhausting the supply of free black men through both hiring and impressment. The law also addressed some of the complaints Governors Letcher, Smith, and Vance had received from their constituents regarding the enforcement of requisitions at the local level, providing that owners with only one male slave between the ages of eighteen and fifty would be exempt from impressment. In addition, owners would receive credit against future impressment quotas for all slaves who died or escaped while working under earlier requisitions.[85]

The new law notwithstanding, Secretary Seddon continued to demonstrate respect for both local officials and the needs of the home front. He declined to exercise immediately the authority Congress had granted him with this new legislation, recognizing that Smith and Vance (and no doubt governors in other states as well) had made recent requisitions for slaves. Once those slaves returned to their homes in April, moreover, Seddon's general tendency to leave the slaves working in the fields during the summer prevented him from making an immediate call for slave labor on the fortifications. Indeed, in late April, Seddon directed the Engineer Bureau to return all impressed slaves "in view of the agricultural interests of the country" and then, in concert with the Conscript Bureau, to impress free blacks to fill their places.[86]

Despite the pressing importance of agricultural production, at least some slaves and free blacks continued to work on Confederate fortifications throughout the summer of 1864. A deserter from the Thirty-Fourth North Carolina regiment informed Union colonel George H. Sharpe in June 1864 that there were black men still at work on the fortifications in Fredericksburg and along the Chickahominy.[87] In August 1864, an escaped slave told Union officers that he had been working on the fortifications outside Petersburg with a gang of about 1,500 men.[88] Engineer officers on the fortifications outside Raleigh hired dozens of slaves and free blacks from North Carolina's Piedmont counties for several weeks at a time between June and August 1864.[89] This decentralized form of labor organization may have provided the flexibility needed to move slaves between fields and fortifications on short notice.

In addition to hiring slaves from their owners and hiring or impressing free blacks, Confederate officers found a more creative way to enhance their labor forces in 1864. Slaves who had run away to Union lines and were subsequently recaptured were regularly sent to work on fortifications, granting engineer officers a permanent workforce without alienating state or local governments. General P. G. T. Beauregard sent recaptured slaves from Plymouth to work on the Wilmington defenses in April 1864.[90] Engineer officers in Virginia used "negroes recaptured from enemy" alongside impressed slaves to repair railroad lines in the summer of 1864.[91] That July, Captain R. H. Fitzhugh received several dozen slaves recaptured from Union forces, whom he put to work building fortifications along the Staunton River. Colonel Gilmer informed him that while most of the slaves' owners lived behind Union lines and so were unlikely to seek their return, he should turn over any slaves to men who could provide proof of ownership.[92]

An urgent need for repairs to the Drewry's Bluff fortifications in October 1864 led the Engineer Bureau to take advantage of all available sources of labor. Gilmer and Stevens encouraged Governor Smith to issue a two-week requisition for both slaves and free black men from Goochland, Hanover, and Henrico Counties.[93] Apparently, they failed to complete the necessary repairs by the end of two weeks, and Stevens kept many of them for additional time. Stevens also gained laborers from the Medical Department, which ordered all slaves and free black men employed in Richmond's hospitals to work on the fortifications for the month of October.[94] Mindful of the Engineer Bureau's promises, however, Stevens returned the slaves by mid-November, although he may have kept the free blacks for a longer period of time. In all their efforts to gain a sufficient workforce during the summer of 1864, engineer officers in Virginia continued to cooperate with state and local governments despite the fact that the February 1864 law had granted Confederate officials greater authority over slave impressment.[95] This cooperation was less evident in North Carolina, however.

By April 1864, tensions between Governor Vance and General Whiting over the best distribution of North Carolina's resources in slave labor were threatening to boil over. Those tensions continued to mount throughout the summer, as Whiting held laborers well beyond agreed-upon release dates and slaveholders suggested that they would dash Vance's hope of reelection unless he convinced Whiting to return their workers. The constant wrangling interfered with Vance's ability to focus on other aspects of governance and took a toll on his popularity during his reelection campaign, but he found a sympathetic supporter in the secretary of war. All of these factors led him to welcome changes to the process of slave impressment that would relieve him of both the responsibilities and the political liabilities inherent in its enforcement.

The spring and summer of 1864 found Whiting as reluctant as ever to part with the workforce he received from North Carolina's slaveholders. The previous winter, Vance's office had quickly complied with Whiting's requests for laborers on the assumption that all impressed slaves from the state of North Carolina would be returned home by April 1, 1864, so that they could begin planting corn. While the Confederate officers using slave laborers to fortify key railroad depots elsewhere in North Carolina complied with this deadline, Whiting still retained many impressed slaves at Wilmington as late as April 28, refusing to return them without

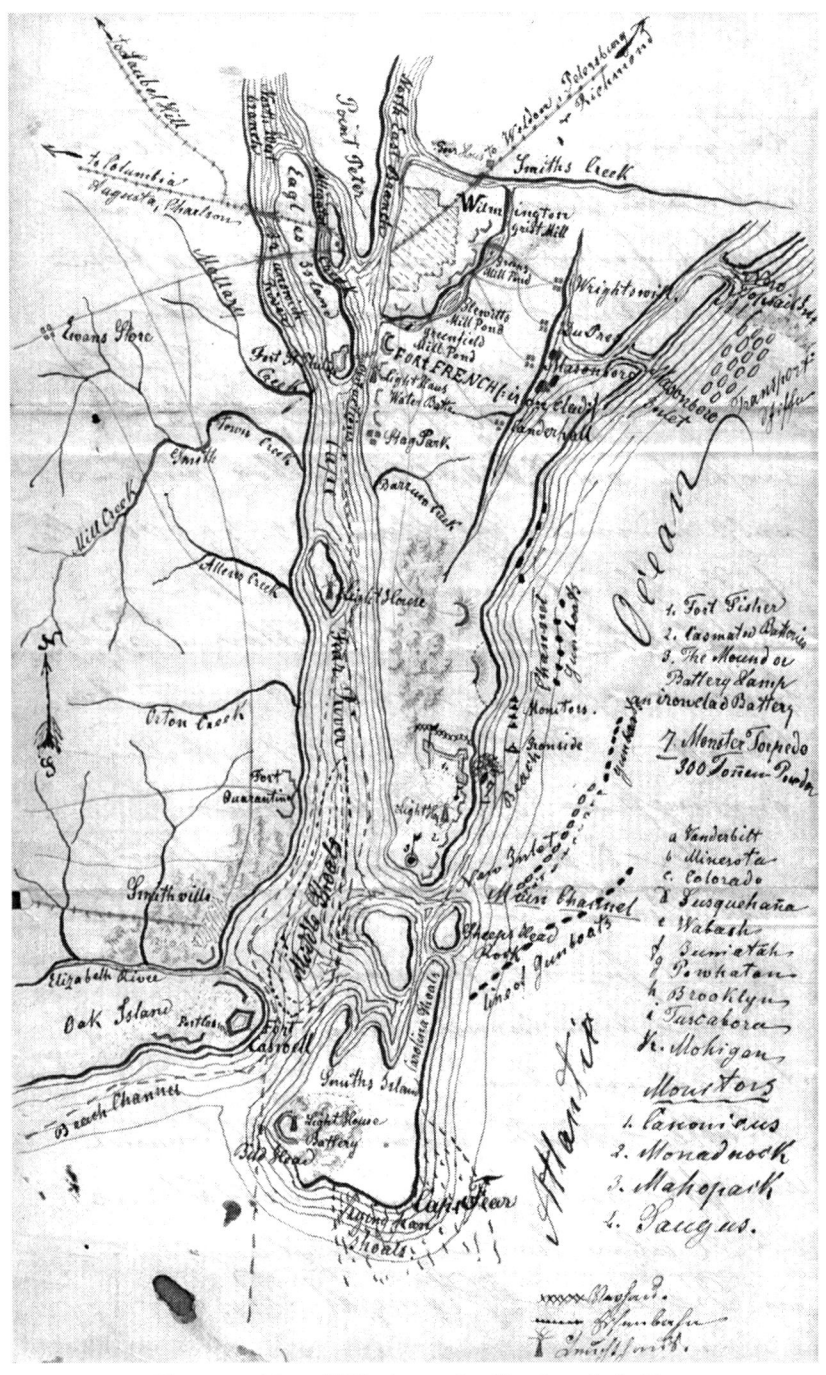

Figure 4.3. Map of Wilmington fortifications, including U.S. plan of attack, 1865 (Library of Congress)

replacements. Vance, meanwhile, received daily appeals from North Carolina's farmers to send their slaves home.

North Carolina's slaveholders were eager to tie Vance's job to his ability to prevent further slave impressment calls on the state, which gave them a great deal of power in the negotiations between local and national governments. In regard to impressed laborers from his neighborhood, one slaveholder wrote, "We can neither get them home or get a promise or satisfaction of any kind. Such treatment is well calculated to damage the patriotism of any people & distructive of all confidence in the authorities."[96] Another, after urging Vance to "take some steps" to ensure the slaves' prompt return from Wilmington, noted that "we should like to see your face up here—in a publick capacity—we will give you a harty welcome and do all in our power to promote your interests."[97] More explicitly, a farmer from Granville County wrote, "We through this section are great Vance men and intend to give you a unanimous vote, and hope you will do us the honor to send a dispatch sending [the slaves] home as it is the season to prepare to plant our crop."[98] These letters indicated that Whiting's failure to return the impressed slaves before planting season could imperil Vance's credibility as governor.

In the face of Whiting's refusal to return the impressed slaves, some of whom had been working at Wilmington for nearly six months by the end of April, Vance finally appealed to the secretary of war. On April 28, he wrote to Seddon, describing his efforts to collect slaves for General Whiting in December 1863, as well as his understanding that the slaves would be sent home after sixty days' labor. After detailing his unsuccessful attempts to secure the slaves' return, Vance asked Seddon to intervene. He further suggested that "if I cannot control [slave] impressments as contemplated by the [state] legislature, I of course want nothing to do with it."[99] At nearly the same time, Whiting wrote to Seddon requesting his help in ensuring a continued supply of slave labor for the fortifications at Wilmington, asking, "Can anything be done to insure a more rapid enrollment & delivery to me of negro labor? My work, at the very time most needed is almost stopped. I am unable to proceed with the very important outworks of Fort Fisher."[100] But Seddon granted Vance's request instead, forcing the general to return the slaves on the grounds that Confederate law required military officials to respect the authority and regulations of each state. In addition, Seddon did not instruct Vance to send any more slaves to Wilmington.[101]

Yet it would be hasty to describe this resolution of the dispute merely as the triumph of states' rights over the needs of the Confederacy. General

Whiting's frequent and overlapping requests may have convinced Seddon that Whiting had overstated his need for laborers. Indeed, some of Whiting's complaints were disingenuous, or at least hyperbolic: in January 1864, despite holding about 2,000 slave laborers from requisitions the previous autumn, Whiting assured General Samuel Cooper that "these last 5 months I have not been able to do any work at all for want of force, & this valuable time has been entirely lost."[102] From Seddon's perspective, Vance's consistent efforts to supply slave laborers to Wilmington and other Confederate installations inside and outside of North Carolina during the fall and winter of 1863–64 amply demonstrated his willingness to cooperate with Confederate authorities. Moreover, both Seddon and Vance had repeatedly acknowledged the importance of slave labor to agriculture within the state of North Carolina. If North Carolina's farmers could not grow corn and wheat, the Confederacy's soldiers would face even more severe food shortages in the coming year. Finally, Seddon recognized that Whiting's refusal to return the slaves could undermine Vance's popularity with North Carolina's voters.

Vance's opponent in the gubernatorial race, *North Carolina Standard* editor William W. Holden, promised to bring peace to North Carolina by negotiating with the United States, and some of his supporters called for the state to secede from the Confederacy, so Seddon could ill afford to jeopardize Vance's reelection.[103] (Interestingly, most of Holden's editorials on slave impressment had enjoined the state's planters to send their slaves quickly and without complaint for the benefit of the Confederate war effort, but those editorials had all preceded Holden's decision to run for governor.) Even General Whiting recognized, by June, that "the disgraceful state of politics in N. C." prevented him from issuing a labor requisition until after the election.[104] Indeed, Seddon probably agreed with Vance's assessment that his electoral victory in the summer of 1864 was "really a matter of congratulation to the whole country, as evincing the thorough loyalty of our tried & suffering people."[105] Denying Whiting's April 1864 request for additional laborers, and preventing any further slave impressments during the summer, was a price Seddon was willing to pay to maintain that loyalty.

Once Governor Vance secured his second term, though, his personal and professional disputes with General Whiting became even more acrimonious. In late September, Whiting petitioned Vance for more slaves, accusing the governor of conspiring to undermine his work at Wilmington by preventing him from maintaining a sufficient force of laborers the previous summer.[106] Meanwhile, in response to rumors that Whiting drank excessively, Vance asked General Robert E. Lee to assign General Beauregard to Whiting's command. Whiting furiously struck back, arguing that any failures of the Wilmington defenses were Vance's fault because he had not sent sufficient troops and laborers to the city.[107] While publicly denying Whiting's request for labor, Vance endeavored to repair the breach in a private letter. The rumors of Whiting's drunkenness had been largely disavowed, he reported, and he thus had perfect confidence in the general's abilities. Vance recounted more than one instance in which Whiting had violated state laws, prompting North Carolina's citizens to send dozens of angry letters to the governor's office. Yet, Vance wrote, "I believe you to be the man for the defense of Wilmington & have endeavored earnestly to get along harmoniously with that great end in view."[108] Soothing Whiting's ego thus became one more task Vance had to accomplish in support of the Confederate war effort.

It is not surprising, then, that Vance would eagerly relinquish control over slave impressment to the Conscript Bureau and other national authorities when the Confederate Congress enacted its new legislation in the fall of 1864. The transition indicated no change in his opinions on slave impressment, which he had always supported as necessary and beneficial to the defense of the Confederacy. But his well-documented frustration with the process of impressment—especially the extent to which it had failed to conform to his and the state legislature's expectations—made washing his hands of the endeavor seem like a very attractive option. In addition, he likely believed that the secretary of war, who had always demonstrated his appreciation for the economic contributions of the North Carolina home front, would have more success restraining General Whiting's demand for labor if the War Department directed every step of slave impressment.

This response from Vance was probably not what most North Carolina voters had in mind. Although they supported his reelection for a broad and complex array of reasons, at least one factor had to be their belief that he would continue to intercede for them against Whiting's tendency to indefinitely extend each labor requisition. Instead, he would choose to acquiesce to changes that completely removed the governor's office from the slave impressment loop, thus ensuring that, no matter what happened, at least the voters could not blame him. Yet Vance was hardly in a position to prevent all Confederate slave impressment, nor is there any reason to believe he would have wanted to do so. He responded to voters' concerns not by taking action to eliminate requisitions for slave labor in his state but by supporting a more centralized process that he believed would enhance the regularity and predictability of those requisitions. Vance's support for the highly centralized approach to slave impressment that would emerge in September and October 1864 was the unintended consequence of voters urging him to take action against Whiting during the reelection campaign.

Despite these heated exchanges between Vance and Whiting in the summer of 1864, communications between the state and national governments on the subject of slave impressment were generally harmonious. Governors Letcher, Smith, and Vance made consistent efforts to supply slave labor to the Confederate army, and in return, Secretary Seddon acceded to the governors' requests that slave impressment not interfere with agricultural production. Each time they enforced a new impressment quota, reduced an existing one, or contemplated a policy shift, the governors were forced to cope with mounting shortages, complaints, and uncertainties. Crafting proactive economic policies designed to promote equity and support the war effort was difficult, to say the least. In particular, the governors quickly discovered that their notions of what constituted an acceptable level of sacrifice on the part of civilians did not necessarily align with those of their constituents.

Whether they spoke of equality, equity, or fairness, by the summer of 1864 Virginia and North Carolina slaveholders presented a common message: filling another requisition for slave labor would be one sacrifice too many. Each petitioner, regardless of social status, wrote in full confidence that he or she had borne more than a fair share of the war's burdens and encouraged the governor to force others to make similar contributions. Some were probably right. North Carolinians who sent slaves to Wilmington for sixty days' labor were understandably outraged that General Whiting kept those slaves for an additional month or two—especially when neighbors' slaves who had gone to Weldon or Goldsboro returned on time. Virginians who watched more prosperous community members gain exemptions and credits for slaves hired to hospitals or railroads—and thereby keep four or five male slaves employed on their farms—had reason to feel injured when one of their two slaves went to the fortifications instead. While Governors Vance and Smith sympathized in all these cases and worked to correct overt injustices whenever possible, they did not have the resources to truly "equalize the burden" of the war. Furthermore, they had no intention of ending all labor requisitions within their states.

As the progress of slave impressment legislation and procedures between March 1863 and the summer of 1864 demonstrated, centralization in the Confederacy happened haltingly, with frequent compromises and renegotiations. Engineer officers worked with elected officials at all levels—national, state, and local—to cobble together the largest possible workforce. Slaveholders similarly relied on local, state, and national leaders to ensure that military demands did not completely overshadow the needs of the civilian economy and that they were fairly compensated when their slaves died as a result of impressment. In the end, a strong central government was not a goal but a tool that could be used or ignored, depending on the circumstances.

Secretary of War James A. Seddon probably best exemplified this compromise-based approach to national authority on the subject of slave impressment. Recognizing that Virginia's state and local leaders had developed a relatively effective—if imperfect—system for requisitioning labor, as well as good working relations with the Engineer Bureau, he only infrequently involved himself in the Commonwealth's process of slave impressment. In North Carolina, Seddon never found it necessary to enforce impressment quotas but did occasionally have to intervene to make sure Confederate officers (especially General Whiting) returned slaves to their owners according to schedule. Even as Congress granted a larger and larger role to national officials, Seddon chose to leave much of the responsibility for slave impressment in the hands of local leaders, imposing his authority only where he believed it would help impressment operate more effectively for both the army and the slaveholders.

Seddon, along with most engineer officers, chose to continue working through local and state leaders for a reason. They must have believed that the strengths local elected officials brought to the process of slave impressment—credibility, knowledge, and flexibility—outweighed any weaknesses of enforcement attendant in localized, rather than centralized, requisitions. Yet the fact that slave impressment worked reasonably well did not preclude the possibility that it could have worked even more effectively. Congress and other national leaders repeatedly centralized the steps of requisitioning labor in an attempt to perfect the process. At each stage, their goal seems to have been assembling the largest number of slave laborers for military purposes without jeopardizing either the economic activities of the home front or the legitimacy of slaveholders' authority over their laborers. Crafting a plan that met all these demands was a complicated task, one that required frequent revision and negotiation.

Viewed through the lens of slave impressment, the Confederate government was a highly activist state that combined unprecedented intrusions on its citizens' property rights with concerted efforts to respond to their demands for assistance. In a similar vein, the governors of North Carolina and Virginia expected their constituents to make sacrifices on behalf of the Confederacy but worked to mitigate the long-term effects of those sacrifices—in particular, to ensure that slave impressment did not lead to rampant starvation. Although neither state managed to achieve perfect compliance with the Confederate army's demands for slave labor, both provided thousands of workers to the war effort each year; both also found ways to channel slaveholders' complaints and acknowledge their rights as property holders.

Confederate officials in Virginia, on the whole, made more consistent efforts than those in North Carolina to ensure that slave impressment did not interfere significantly with slaveholders' ability to grow food crops. This reflected a closer sense of cooperation between state and national officials to regulate slave impressment in Virginia, perhaps borne of the two governments' proximity in Richmond. Another key difference between the two states' approach to slave impressment was the use of the militia in North Carolina. Impressment by militia operated more efficiently than impressment via the county courts in Virginia, but it was also more prone to abuses and thus to alienating the state's slaveholders. Virginia's county courts had the opportunity to provide their constituents with some safeguards against the indiscriminate impressment of their property and thus may have enacted slave impressment more effectively, if not more efficiently, in the long term. Like many aspects of the Confederate war effort, slave impressment in both Virginia and North Carolina worked only because it had the support of state and local governments.

While local support clearly waned long before the final year of the war, neither state's governor used this as an excuse to oppose slave impressment. Instead, Vance and Smith responded to the petitions and complaints they received in the summer of 1864 by supporting the more centralized plan for slave impressment emerging in response to recent congressional legislation. Rather than relying on state and local officials, this new plan would keep all responsibility for enforcing slave impressment quotas within the ranks of the War Department: engineers would submit labor requests to Secretary Seddon, and then the enrolling officers employed by the Conscript Bureau would collect the necessary free and enslaved black men. Governor Vance, still contemplating the implicit and explicit threats to his political career raised over the subject of slave impressment and having lost all patience for further interaction with General Whiting, was eager to relinquish his enforcement authority. For Governor Smith, the possibility that centralized enforcement could reduce competition for slave labor between various military employers and perhaps also limit the number of complaints he received from and about county courts made the War Department's new plan an attractive option. By petitioning the governors to intervene on their behalf in the process of slave impressment, slaveholders in Virginia and North Carolina had inadvertently encouraged Smith and Vance to take the opposite route and remove their offices from participation in favor of a more centralized approach.

CHAPTER FIVE

The President's Mishap

From Engineer Laborers to Potential Confederate Soldiers, 1864–1865

On November 7, 1864, Jefferson Davis delivered what would be his final annual message to the Confederate Congress. After discussing the efficacy of the February 1864 slave impressment act, Davis contemplated what he called "a radical modification in the theory of the law." Congress's actions to date had considered slaves only as private property, Davis explained, limiting their term of service to the Confederacy out of respect for their masters' property rights. He suggested that the country could no longer afford to place individual property rights above the needs of the state. Instead, Davis proposed that the Confederate government purchase approximately 40,000 slaves, who would be considered public property with the potential to become free persons, and put them to work for the Engineer Bureau and Medical Department. Slaves who served faithfully would receive their freedom after the eventual Confederate victory. At the same time, he cautioned, that "beyond this limit and these employments it does not seem to me desirable, under existing circumstances, to go."[1] The time was not yet right for the Confederacy to employ slaves as soldiers.

Yet even this modest proposal, which promised no immediate transformation of slavery, provoked a firestorm of controversy. Congressman John B. Baldwin of Virginia told one of his constituents that "the President's negro mishap has caused much feeling against him in quarters very near him." Not only were Davis's friends turning against him, Baldwin argued, but slaves were escaping in droves because they had no interest in becoming the property of the state.² In Raleigh, *North Carolina Standard* editor William Holden questioned, "How can Southern men and slaveholders, consistently with their oft-expressed opinions, regard manumission as a *reward*? We tell the world, what all experience justifies us in telling it, that the slave is far happier and better cared for, of better health and longer life, as a slave than as a freedman." Moreover, he doubted the constitutionality of the president's proposal.³ Finally, few observers drew a firm distinction between Davis's proposal to purchase slaves as military laborers and the idea of arming them as soldiers, and the president received letters indicating that some newspaper editors had interpreted his speech as a call for black Confederate soldiers.⁴ Despite Davis's assurances, white southerners feared the long-term implications of his suggestion that the central government pay less attention to their property rights as slaveholders.

While in theory all slave impressment legislation prior to November 1864 had held those property rights sacrosanct, in practice slave impressment clearly eroded the master's authority over his slaves, even those who were not subject to impressment. Congress created the Board of Slave Claims in April 1864 to protect slaveholders' economic investments in their slaves, and thus reinforce their mastery, but even this important step did not repair the damage. By forcing slaves to serve on Confederate fortifications regardless of their masters' objections, impressment shattered any illusion that the master held ultimate authority over his slaves.

Secretary of War James A. Seddon put the February 1864 impressment law into widespread use in September 1864, when he issued a requisition for 20,000 laborers. From this point on, slave impressment in most areas of the Confederacy occurred through the Conscript Bureau rather than through state governments, although the December 1864 and March 1865 calls in Virginia would prove notable exceptions to the pattern. The increasing centralization of slave impressment between February 1864 and March 1865 thus dramatically reduced the master's power over his human property because enrolling officers were less subject to political pressure from individual slaveholders than local elected officials had been. It also reduced—but did not eliminate—the governors' role in disseminating and enforcing slave impressment quotas. Another key trend in slave impressment during the last few months of the war was that the governors (especially Governor William Smith of Virginia) demonstrated far less sympathy toward their slaveholding constituents than they had in the past.

The final slave impressment calls in Virginia took place while Congress, meeting in secret sessions, debated the efficacy of enrolling slaves as soldiers as another means of averting a potentially disastrous defeat. Because Congress and many state legislatures had enacted specific provisions for collecting and organizing impressed laborers (as well as for compensating their owners), many of the practical mechanisms for using slaves as soldiers were in place well before 1865. Thus, from one perspective, the transition from using slaves as engineer laborers to arming them as Confederate soldiers did not seem to require a huge leap of imagination. On the other hand, southerners' longstanding ideological association of black men with manual labor—and nothing else—would prove difficult to overcome, especially when the laws of every state prohibited enslaved men from owning or using guns. Only the dire state of the Confederacy's military situation in February 1865, coupled with support from its most important general, would convince some white southerners that enlisting slaves in the army was an acceptable necessity.

Proponents of both slave impressment and slave enlistment would need to grapple with the rapidly dwindling pool of available enslaved men. Resisting slave impressment may not have served as the primary motivation for slaves to escape, but runaways certainly depleted the number available to perform Confederate military labor. Nationwide, some 500,000 enslaved men, women, and children—approximately 15 percent of the slaves held in the Confederacy in 1861—escaped from their masters over the course of the war.[5] In Virginia, especially in areas that experienced sustained contact with United States troops, most communities lost at least a quarter of their adult male slaves by 1864. There is little doubt that this deepening labor shortage shaped both white and black civilians' responses to new government policies that sought to harness slavery's power in the final push toward Confederate victory.

In most historical treatments of slave impressment, the Confederacy's white civilians stood monolithically opposed to the military and government officials who sought to use slave laborers to further the Confederate war effort, thus undermining the chance of victory.[6] Yet thousands of slaves from Virginia and North Carolina were put to work on the Confederate fortifications, most through a system of impressment that became more efficient and more centralized as the war progressed. Their work on those fortifications, coupled with slaves' industrial and agricultural labor, enabled the Confederacy to defend its major cities and maintain its armies in the field. Both the problems and the potential benefits of slave impressment became more pronounced during the last six months of the war, when many national and state leaders also began making serious plans for the enlistment of slaves as soldiers. The relationship between slave impressment and the long-term centralization of government power in the Confederacy also rose to the foreground in this period. Centralization was definitely an incomplete process, and Governors Smith and Zebulon Baird Vance continued to negotiate its terms. In very different ways, both demonstrated ongoing support for slave impressment and the stronger central government that enacted it.

Aside from the short-term impressments of slaves in limited areas in the summer and fall of 1864, by far the most important development during those months was the creation of the Confederate Board of Slave Claims. A perfect illustration of the growth of the Confederate government, the board met to adjudicate hundreds of claims between April 1864 and February 1865. Yet the board also demonstrated the steps a growing, centralizing Confederate government would take to accommodate voters and comply with state laws. By attempting to navigate between slaveholders' rights as property holders and the myriad ways that impressment restricted those rights, the Board of Slave Claims exemplified both the negotiated nature of Confederate centralization and the government's attempts to forestall the wartime deterioration of slavery.

The need for an adjudicating body had become increasingly evident after Governor Smith's January 1864 requisition, when the Lunenburg County Court expressed reluctance to send the county's slaves because the Confederate government had failed to compensate slaveholders for slaves who had died under previous requisitions. "The Virginia Bill of Rights declares that no man can be deprived of his property for public use without his own consent or that of his representatives, duly elected," the court proclaimed, and the Virginia General Assembly had acceded to slave impressment with the understanding that the Confederate government would be liable for all slaves who died or escaped while impressed. Since the Confederate Congress had neglected to appropriate funds to compensate slaveholders, the Lunenburg County Court proposed, unsuccessfully, that Smith suspend his call for slaves until Congress took steps to provide that compensation.[7] Lunenburg demanded that both state and national authorities work to protect slaveholders' rights and status as property owners. Governor Smith rejected Lunenburg County's reasoning, but the court's arguments had an impact on the General Assembly. In mid-February, the Virginia Senate instructed the state's congressional representatives to introduce a bill establishing the central government's liability for all slaves impressed to work on the fortifications.[8]

The Confederate Congress had already contemplated such a law in November 1863, seeking the opinion of Attorney General Wade Keyes, who argued that the government was liable for the value of "any slave impressed for temporary use." Keyes, however, urged Congress to consider each case individually, suggesting that "error lurks in generality."[9] Since Congress could not possibly listen to every claim while also conducting ordinary business, legislators established the Board of Slave Claims on April 1, 1864, appointing lawyer Colonel James D. Waddell, surgeon W. A. Spence, and Major J. B. Brockenbrough to serve on the original board. Richmond's newspapers noted the board's creation with a great deal of satisfaction.[10]

The board's authority extended to all impressed slaves, whether they served under state or national authority, who had escaped, died, or become incapacitated while working on the fortifications. The board could only recommend compensation, however; responsibility for repaying each claim remained in Congress's hands. President Davis encouraged Congress to appropriate the necessary funds even before the board began its sessions. He estimated that the board would need $708,000 to pay all Virginia's slaveholders who qualified for compensation, with an average value of $2,000 per slave.[11]

The creation of the Board of Slave Claims relieved state authorities and individual engineers from the responsibility of considering claims from slaveholders. Colonel Alfred Landon Rives instructed engineer officers at each point of fortification to send all claims to his office, and he would take responsibility for forwarding them to the board.[12] Noting the vast numbers of slaves who had worked on the Wilmington defenses, Rives asked the Conscript Bureau to detail a "perfectly reliable & intelligent man" specifically to assist in settling claims from Wilmington.[13] Any funds the Engineer Bureau received to settle claims were placed in the hands of engineer officers in charge of construction at various points of fortification—for example, Captain John B. Stanard in Richmond—who could then contact the slaves' former owners to arrange for payment.[14]

The Board of Slave Claims reviewed over 600 cases between April 1864 and February 1865, approving between 20 and 25 percent of the claims. To receive compensation, a slaveholder had to prove that negligence on the part of Engineer Bureau officers had resulted in a slave's death or severe injury. Most successful claims included testimony from an overseer affirming either that no Confederate surgeon had ever visited the slave in question or that such medical attention had occurred so long after a slave had been injured or developed symptoms of illness as to be ineffective.

Because the board returned all original paperwork and testimony to claimants and kept copies only of the successful claims, there is no way to evaluate its members' criteria for determining the justice of the claims they reviewed, but presumably the board dismissed many cases in which slaves unfortunately died despite receiving the rations, shelter, and medical care mandated by state and national laws. In such cases, the Confederate government rejected any liability for the slave's death.[15]

The three original board members—Waddell, Spence, and Brockenbrough—apparently found their responsibilities daunting enough to recruit several new members in the late summer and fall of 1864. One of them, Edgeworth Bird, feared that the salary attached to his appointment might not be sufficient for the support of his family but took the position because it seemed to offer a permanent refuge from active duty in the Confederate army. "Three millions of dollars have been appropriated for payment of these negro claims against the Government," Bird explained to his wife, "and they have not yet paid out fifty thousand. So it may exist a long time before the present sum is rid of—and as long as the war lasts new claims of a similar nature must continue to arise, and I suppose further sums be appropriated."[16]

The Slave Claims Board did indeed last almost as long as the war. Near the end of February 1865, board members requested a brief furlough from their duties and then suggested a change of venue. Board members would be able to feed themselves and their families more cheaply if they left Richmond; in addition, they also suggested that a new location might enable a different set of slaveholders to present their claims. Most of the claims they had received, noted board members, were from Virginia; slaveholders from other states might find it easier to communicate with the board if its members relocated to Colonel Waddell's home state of Georgia. It is unlikely the board ever resumed its duties after disbanding at the end of February.[17]

The Board of Slave Claims perfectly represents the growing strength of the Confederate government during the last year of the war. A highly specialized and organized bureaucratic committee, the board was empowered to pass judgment on the activities of local, state, and national government officials throughout the Confederacy. Moreover, Congress's appropriation of $3 million to compensate slaveholders for an unprecedented intrusion into their property rights demonstrated the willingness of the Confederate government to meet the needs of at least some of its citizens despite dwindling economic resources. Finally, it highlighted both the extent to which impressment undermined slaveholders' control over their property and the practical value of President Davis's plan to purchase 40,000 enslaved men. If the War Department owned outright all the slaves it needed for military labor, it would no longer need to waste time and manpower communicating with state authorities, collecting impressed slaves, compensating owners, and investigating liability for laborers' deaths. In addition to the labor force the government would gain, Davis's plan would put dozens of Confederate officers back into active field duty at a time when every man counted. A fully centralized approach to amassing military laborers — one that moved beyond impressment to outright ownership — could have been more efficient. By the end of 1864, it also seemed like the next logical move in the evolution of impressment policy.

The crucial steps in this transition from impressment to government ownership came in September 1864, when Secretary Seddon put into practice a new law authorizing the Bureau of Conscription, on orders from the War Department, to enroll slaves as military laborers. He did so with clear support from Governors Vance and Smith, who had both recently arrived at the conclusion that a centralized approach to slave impressment would probably yield the best results. Enrolling officers already in place in each county in the Confederacy would take responsibility for impressing slaves and transporting them to points of fortification. Those officers had already performed this task with free black laborers and slaves in some Virginia counties during the summer of 1864, but on September 22, Seddon issued a call for 20,000 slaves to serve for a period of thirty days on fortifications throughout the Confederacy. 5,000 of these slaves would come from Virginia; 2,000 from North Carolina. Seddon's disposition of these impressed laborers often reflected requests he had received throughout the summer.

For example, in July 1864, Major General William H. C. Whiting began submitting most of his requests for slave labor to national rather than to state authorities. In his letters to Seddon, Whiting suggested that North Carolina's authorities had lost all interest in supporting Confederate defenses, even in cases of dire emergency. Because he could not gain Governor Vance's cooperation in the summer of 1864, Whiting hoped for additional help from the secretary of war. Seddon, however, refused to issue any widespread slave impressment orders until the harvest season had ended, although he did encourage Whiting to impress a small force of free black men for the Wilmington fortifications.[18]

Whiting also sent General Robert E. Lee a detailed description of the fortifications at Wilmington, taking great pains to emphasize their incomplete state. He also assured Lee that any deficiencies in the works were not due to a lack of diligence on his part but rather to an ineffective supply of laborers. In particular, he noted that the governor had removed his entire labor force in the late spring of 1864, putting him four months behind schedule. (Once again, Whiting seemed completely unaware that fortification work in Virginia regularly halted or at least diminished during the summer months to enable the slaves to work in the fields.) Although Seddon had allowed him to impress free black men, Whiting continued, these impressments garnered him a workforce of fewer than 600 men, while he had "work for 2,000 and upward, and it is very pressing." Whiting concluded his letter by welcoming proposals from the Engineer Bureau to strengthen and extend the Wilmington fortifications but once again reminded General Lee that "the works about this city can only be taken in hand by a largely increased force of negroes."[19]

Whiting no doubt expected, as a result of this letter, that Lee and Seddon would designate a significant portion of the 20,000 slaves impressed by the Conscript Bureau in late September for work on the Wilmington defenses. Two weeks later, he encouraged the Engineer Bureau to order enrolling officers to impress slaves from outside the Wilmington area and bring them to the city. Unlike his engineer officers, Whiting argued, enrolling officers had experience gathering workers and conscripts and so were familiar with the population and labor demands of each district. Whiting also expressed reluctance to impress slaves from the counties immediately surrounding Wilmington, whose planters had already supplied most of his labor requisitions. Apologizing for his failure to complete the Wilmington fortifications, Whiting requested Chief Engineer Jeremy Francis Gilmer's indulgence and assistance. "You have no idea of the difficulty the delay & the obstacles," he complained. "Since the 16th when I wrote you so urgently I have not received 75 hands & that would not make up the deficiency incurred in the mean time by sickness & desertion." As a consequence of these appeals, all 2,000 slaves impressed in North Carolina in September and October went to the Wilmington defenses.[20] At least some of the slaves sent to Fort Fisher in the summer and fall of 1864 remained in Confederate service until the end of the war.[21]

Despite the importance of Weldon, Goldsboro, and Raleigh as railroad depots, Wilmington was the logical priority for Confederate authorities in North Carolina. By the fall of 1864, Wilmington's harbor was the only truly safe haven for the blockade-runners who supplied the Confederacy with meat, lead, saltpeter, boots, and coffee. In November alone, nineteen blockade-runners entered the harbor at Wilmington, all carrying essential goods.[22] Thus, as Union forces advanced on the city in January 1865,

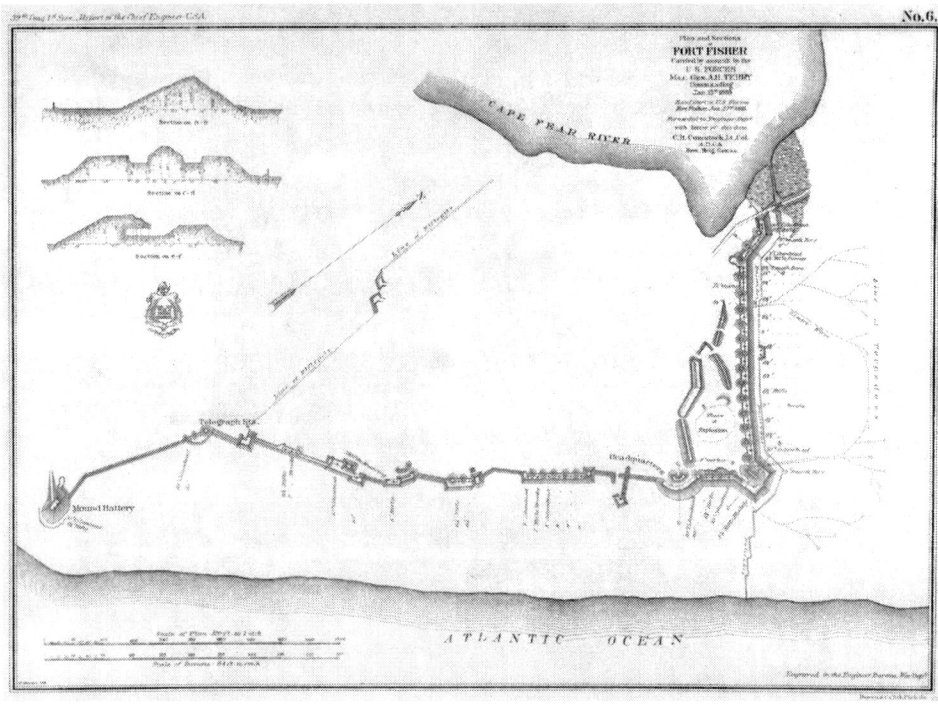

Figure 5.1. Plan and sections of Fort Fisher, 1865 (Library of Congress)

engineer Colonel William Lamb recalled, "General Lee sent me word that Fort Fisher must be held, or he could not subsist his army."[23] Though his repeated pleas for assistance may have annoyed state and national political leaders, General Whiting employed no hyperbole in his assessment of Wilmington's importance to the Confederacy. The 2,000 slave laborers he received in the fall of 1864 indicated a widespread consensus that Wilmington superseded all other Confederate installations in the state.

Impressment calls in Virginia, on the other hand, reflected a more diverse set of priorities. In early September, as the Army of Northern Virginia worked to strengthen and extend the Petersburg fortifications, General Lee urged Seddon to issue an impressment order for Virginia slaves. Unlike Whiting, Lee looked beyond his own labor needs to consider those of other commanders, suggesting that 5,000 workers be distributed among the fortifications outside Petersburg, Richmond, and Danville and along the James River and South Side Railroad. Lee enclosed a list, prepared by his chief engineer, Colonel Walter H. Stevens, designating impressment quotas and credits for each county, although Stevens's final list of quotas fell short of the desired 5,000 slaves by approximately 17 percent. While acknowledging that filling the new quotas would be a hardship for many Confederate citizens, Lee assured Seddon that it was "necessary for us to use our negroes in this war if we would maintain ourselves and prevent them from being employed against us."[24]

Seddon and General Samuel Cooper indeed lost no time in transmitting Lee's request to the Bureau of Conscription, which immediately instructed its enrolling officers to collect slaves based on Stevens's list (see appendix, table 5.1).[25] At the same time, Seddon went ahead with plans already under way to have the enrolling officers from nine central Virginia counties impress free blacks for railroad work between Richmond and Danville.[26] The swiftness of this nationwide call for 20,000 laborers took the Quartermaster's Department by surprise, as it was unprepared to provide clothing, blankets, and rations to so many slaves and free blacks on such short notice. If he had to choose, Quartermaster General A. R. Lawton asked Seddon, "shall soldiers in the field be supplied, or shall these indispensable articles go to the negroes? To meet the present demand for men in the field, blankets, shoes, and woolen goods have to be drawn in large quantities from abroad."[27] As the Confederacy's resources dwindled, the task of supplying both soldiers and laborers would continue to weigh on Seddon's mind. In particular, any impressment calls he issued in the fall and winter of 1864–65 would have to expire in time to return most laborers to the fields by the spring planting season.

In late October, finding that even a month-long extension of the September slave impressment would fail to meet all of the army's labor needs, Seddon ordered the Conscript Bureau to impress an additional 2,250 slaves from the state of Virginia. The newly impressed laborers would serve for a period of twelve months, predominantly under the Engineer Bureau, although Seddon could transfer them to another department to meet whatever needs arose. These slaves and free blacks would be organized into three Confederate Negro Labor Battalions under a plan Lee and Gilmer had devised. Each battalion included eight gangs of approximately 100 workers; free blacks and slaves would serve in separate gangs, and each gang had four white overseers. In addition to the overseers, a superintendent, surgeon, assistant purveyor, and clerk would be assigned to each battalion. Field grade officers would maintain muster rolls and service records for each worker and would conduct regular inspections. While the organization of gangs would reflect slaves' county of origin and the overseers may have been recommended by county authorities, this new plan effectively severed state and local control over impressed slaves—and by extension, their owners' control.[28]

Yet even this drastic step failed to end all state and local government involvement in slave impressment. Although the new approach was intended to replace all state-sponsored impressment procedures, state leaders were called on to supplement national requisitions on several occasions. For example, while General Whiting presumably received his 2,000 slave laborers at Wilmington, Confederate authorities initially slighted the engineer officers at Weldon, who instead turned to Governor Vance for assistance. Vance and Adjutant General R. C. Gatlin issued a requisition for 1,120 slaves on October 3, 1864, ordering militia officers to have the laborers in Weldon within a week (see appendix, table 5.2).[29] Gatlin chose the counties for this impressment call based on both their close proximity to Weldon and the fact that Vance had exempted them from many earlier calls in recognition of the slaves they had sent to General John Bankhead Magruder in the first year of the war.

Gatlin also expected the Confederate officers at Weldon to comply with standard slave hiring practices in North Carolina. On December 22, he asked the engineer in charge of the Weldon fortifications to send all slave laborers home for the Christmas holiday. They would return to Weldon on January 1, 1865, to finish their terms of impressment.[30] In addition, Gatlin issued a new impressment order, specifying that the new slaves would arrive at Weldon by January 10, at which time the first group would be sent home. This new order impressed 947 slaves from a different set of counties; their smaller quotas reflected smaller slave populations (see appendix, table 5.2). As always, Gatlin assured North Carolina's slaveholders that all impressed slaves would receive the rations and medical treatment prescribed by Confederate law and that the owners would be paid for both the slaves' time and the expense of transporting them to Weldon.[31]

Yet Gatlin and Vance quickly revoked their December 1864 order for slaves to work at Weldon when Confederate authorities issued a new impressment call on January 6, 1865. Since the enrolling officers would be collecting 2,500 slaves for work throughout the state, thus eliminating the need for supplementary efforts, Gatlin instructed his militia officers to cease their impressment activity. Gatlin also requested that engineer officers at Weldon send home all slaves impressed through the governor's office.[32] While these returns began in early January, as late as February 16 some slaves impressed under state authority remained on the fortifications at Weldon, and Gatlin ordered a militia officer from each county to visit Weldon and collect any slaves impressed under orders he had issued the previous fall.[33] "In future," Gatlin assured one correspondent, "the

Governor will not impress slaves to work on fortifications as the Confederate Govt is making impressments for that purpose."[34]

Political leaders in most other states seem to have taken Vance's approach, turning impressment over to the national government whenever possible. Alabama governor (and former Confederate attorney general) Thomas Hill Watts informed engineer officers at Mobile that he would not be sending them any additional slaves after Confederate authorities took charge of slave impressment in August 1864. Mixing state and national authority, he suggested, "would produce inextricable confusion." He further suggested that intransigence on the part of his constituents had left him eager to extricate himself from the slave impressment process, a sentiment that Vance clearly shared. Like Vance, meanwhile, he did nothing to prevent enrolling officers from collecting slave laborers within his state.[35] State authorities in Georgia had never been particularly involved in the impressment process, so the summer 1864 shift that put the Conscript Bureau in charge of gathering laborers portended little change from how impressment had operated the previous year under the March 1863 national law.[36] Several states, including Virginia and Georgia, enacted new laws prescribing harsh punishments for Confederate officials who attempted to impress slaves without proper authorization from the War Department but made no moves against impressment itself.[37] Only South Carolina seems to have undertaken significant resistance to impressment via the Conscript Bureau; the state legislature passed a resolution nullifying all slave impressment laws (state and national) in December 1864.[38]

Vance and Smith did not merely support the new requisitions under national authority; neither protested when the Engineer Bureau unilaterally extended thirty-day terms of service to sixty days. Perhaps the extension of thirty-day terms did not bother Smith because sixty days had typically been the term of impressment in Virginia. Perhaps Vance did not see extending slaves' term of service to two months as much of a problem in light of General Whiting's tendency to hold slaves at Wilmington for four or even six months. Or perhaps they simply assumed that protest would accomplish nothing and so saved their energies for other work. Slaveholding constituents in both states were no doubt frustrated by their governors' failure to admonish Confederate authorities for violating their initial promise, and many of their letters suggested that they viewed Governors Vance and Smith as coconspirators in an attempt to diminish slaveholders' authority over their human chattel. While Vance and Smith were hardly plotting the overthrow of slavery, neither gave any indication that they opposed the extended requisition or, more broadly, the increasing centralization of slave impressment. In fact, convinced by events in the summer of 1864 that a more centralized approach was necessary, both governors were eager to support that approach as it developed over the fall.

Even the highly centralized approach to slave impressment that emerged in September 1864 failed to completely overturn the importance of individual states as political and geographic entities. Each state received a quota based on the labor needs of fortification points within its borders; enrolling officers rarely took slaves across state lines, despite the fact that the Engineer Bureau's administrative districts generally combined two or three states. This approach intensified the burden of slave impressment on states like Virginia while limiting its significance in less exposed areas—a decision that reflected both military and political realities. Moving slaves hundreds of miles from a state that needed little fortification would have required resources the Confederacy needed to deploy elsewhere. Even more important, doing so would have damaged the credibility of both state and national leaders in the eyes of slaveholding voters. Thus, even the most centralized phase of Confederate slave impressment demonstrated the continuing salience of flexibility and negotiation.

The transition from state militia to Enrolling Office control over slave impressment probably changed little about the collection process in North Carolina, but Virginia's slaveholders no doubt noticed that enrolling officers—less subject to the demands of prominent local men—were more efficient at collecting impressed slaves than their county courts had been. Thus, it is surprising that Secretary Seddon and the Engineer Bureau turned to Governor Smith when they needed an additional force of laborers in December 1864 rather than relied on the Bureau of Conscription to again fill their requisition. They may have been responding to a proposed bill in the Confederate Senate that would have granted Governor Smith special authority to revoke any slave impressment order falling on a county that was located in close proximity to the Union army or had lost more than one-third of its adult male slave population.[39] By December 1864, this exemption would have applied to nearly every county in Virginia. While neither Seddon nor Gilmer made any reference to the proposed bill, they recognized that its passage would have given Governor Smith, a staunch proponent of state-directed slave impressment, grounds to override the Conscript Bureau.

While Smith's record of strong support for slave impressment certainly factored into the decision to place its operations back in his hands, this approach may have also served as a tacit recognition of the disproportionately heavy burden impressment quotas from the fall of 1864 had placed on Virginia's slaveholders. One-quarter of the 20,000 slaves impressed under national legislation in September came from Virginia; another 10 percent came from North Carolina. Requisitions for the remaining 13,000 slaves were thus divided among nine Confederate states. None contributed anywhere near as many as Virginia, and the state's voters were justifiably angry. The October 1864 request for an additional 2,250 Virginia slaves did not help matters. Even though Governor Smith never gave any indication that he would have wished to override nationally directed slave impressment, it is likely that his constituents, county officials, or state legislators would have pressed him to employ the new exemptions. Thus, it was most expedient for the War Department to solicit Smith's participation as an ally, rather than leave open the possibility that he would bend to popular disapproval of a new labor requisition.

On December 14, 1864, Gilmer asked the secretary of war to submit a sixty-day impressment request to Governor Smith.[40] Captain Stanard, chief engineer for the Richmond fortifications, sent Smith a list of quotas for each county (see appendix, table 5.3). Stanard also indicated that the Confederate government would pay sheriffs and their deputies a bonus of five dollars for each slave delivered to engineer authorities on time.[41] Perhaps the Engineer Bureau expected this bonus to encourage more active compliance on the part of county officials, but it is still not entirely clear why they chose to work through the county courts rather than through the enrolling officers at this point. County courts did lose some of their authority, however, as they no longer had the power to appoint overseers directly. Instead, Colonel George Munford would detail one reserved or injured soldier as overseer and supply manager for each group of thirty slaves. Munford also added that although the Engineer Bureau had promised to feed all impressed slaves, rations would probably be less plentiful than owners would like, so he encouraged owners to send food with their slaves, promising slaveholders additional monetary compensation in return.[42]

While some county courts immediately began to enact the new requisition, most looked for ways to avoid it. The Augusta County Court met and quickly assigned slaveholders to meet the requisition but seems to have made no effort to enforce these orders. In early January, the Nelson County Court assured Smith that they could not possibly meet their quota of 80 slaves because at least 150 slaves had already been hired to government employers.[43] The Charlotte County Court sent a delegation to

Richmond to protest the December requisition in person.[44] Smith could not have been surprised by any of the complaints he received from either county courts or individual slaveholders in the winter of 1864–65. All fell into familiar patterns, and all reflected protests Governor Vance was also receiving at roughly the same time. But at such a critical juncture, both governors maintained, national objectives took precedence over individual slave owners' labor requirements. Indeed, they repeatedly enjoined their constituents that consenting to slave impressment was a patriotic duty, one that could save the Confederacy from disaster. Slaveholders' objections to sending their slaves to the fortifications did not change, and county governments increasingly dragged their heels, but the governors' patience for those objections and delays clearly wore thin.

Smith did acknowledge some new grounds for protest in late 1864. Many counties argued that the Engineer Bureau's population estimates were completely inaccurate because they did not account for the numerous male slaves who had escaped to the Union armies during the previous summer. In order to achieve an accurate accounting of each county's slave population, Colonel Munford directed all county courts to send him their most recent estimates of the remaining slaves in the county. He also sought information on their compliance with past impressment quotas, noting significant discrepancies between each county's self-reported participation and the records of the Engineer Bureau. To correct those discrepancies, the governor's office asked each county court for a full tally of slaves submitted in response to each quota, as well as the current slave population of the county. At the same time, Munford insisted that this request did not exempt any county from sending slaves in response to the December 1864 requisition. While the information would help prevent future inequities in impressment quotas, the current situation was so dire that state and Confederate officials could not wait for a correct census. All counties needed to comply with their existing quotas.[45]

Most county courts responded eagerly to the request for information, hoping to prove that they had already fulfilled their responsibilities to the Confederacy and thus avoid future requisitions. The lists they sent to Munford and Smith certainly demonstrated the extent to which the war had affected each county's slave population, highlighting a wide variety of work on behalf of the Confederacy. Many of the counties' responses also demonstrated just how frequently slave impressment had occurred outside of the governor's official requisitions. Appomattox County, for example, sent 435 slaves under five calls from the governor, 65 under the auspices of the Bureau of Conscription, and 56 to meet various requisitions by the Quartermaster's Department, for a total of 556 slaves impressed throughout the war.[46] The Dinwiddie County Court reminded Smith that, in addition to his and Governor Letcher's requisitions, the county had sent slaves under "one or two calls made by Genl. Magruder and no evidence of the [number] sent can be found."[47]

Several counties challenged the Engineer Bureau's official lists of slaves furnished under each impressment call by arguing that other Confederate departments had kept the slaves away from the fortifications. Of the ninety-eight slaves Roanoke County impressed in November 1862, for example, the local quartermaster had detailed fourteen to work as teamsters, which meant that only eighty-four arrived in Richmond to work for the Engineer Bureau.[48] Officials from Appomattox County noted that engineer officers had released slaves working for the railroads and lumber yards from each impressment call.[49] Several of the slaves impressed from Dinwiddie County under each call were also detailed to work on local rail lines.[50] County officials insisted on receiving credit for slaves granted exemptions from impressment because they performed vital work for the Confederate war effort.

Finally, while some county courts reported past service, others protested the new impressment quotas by reminding the governor that large portions of their slave populations already worked either for the government or for private employers serving, almost exclusively, the needs of the Confederate army. The clerk of the Botetourt County Court reported that one-third of the county's 431 adult male slaves worked in the iron furnaces that supported Confederate manufacturing.[51] The Lynchburg hustings court informed Smith that the Quartermaster and Medical Departments had hired nearly 500 of the city's male slaves and that another 265 worked for the Virginia and Tennessee Railroad company. This left only 100 adult male slaves within the city not already working for the war effort in a direct capacity.[52]

Lynchburg's response, in particular, infuriated Governor Smith. "That there should not be more than one hundred and one slaves between the ages of 18 and 55 years in your large and crowded city is difficult to believe," he exploded. "At a time when the slave Institution itself is in peril, and our inability to hold Richmond would make our interest in slave property worthless," he continued, "a call made at the instance of Gen'l Lee to enable him to hold this city is too frequently responded to with such coldness and reluctance as to fill the hearts of those deeply anxious for our Liberty and Independence with anguish if not despondency."[53] Relaying a similar message to the Greene County Court, Munford wrote that the governor hoped "that when Gen'l Lee was calling repeatedly and earnestly for such aid, and the very salvation of the capital city of the State and the Confederacy might depend upon the promptness and completeness of this call for slave labor, all objections would be made to give way and the slaves be at once furnished."[54]

Despite his impatience with the county courts' objections, Smith agreed on January 14 to reduce his December 1864 requisitions. For most counties and cities, he reduced the quota to 10 percent of the slave population, rather than the 20 percent originally requested. Smith even granted four counties complete exemptions from the December call. Under the new quotas, the Engineer Bureau could expect to receive 2,315 slave laborers instead of 5,000.[55]

A few counties responded quickly, and happily, to their newly reduced quotas. The presiding justice of the Buckingham County Court appreciated that the reduced quota would allow him to exempt any residents who held fewer than three male slaves.[56] After determining that 551 adult male slaves remained within their county, officers of the Franklin County Court met in late January and selected 55 slaves for impressment out of the 131 "who have never been sent to the fortifications."[57] The Cumberland County Court also met during the last week of January, ordering the impressment of 105 slaves, who would arrive in Richmond on February 2.[58] On February 6, the Amherst County sheriff delivered his county's quota of 75 slaves to the Petersburg fortifications. As they often did, engineer officers detailed some of each county's impressed slaves to other departments, further shrinking the number who served on the fortifications.[59]

Despite a few favorable responses, most counties failed to meet even their reduced quotas, causing severe labor shortages on many Confederate fortifications. On February 9, General Lee informed Governor Smith that only 10 percent of the 5,000 requested slaves had actually arrived. "Unless I can get a strong force of laborers at once," Lee continued, "I see no prospect of having our extensive lines in the condition they should be. The troops are kept constantly employed in repairing the ravages of winter storms, &c., cutting wood, procuring supplies, and watching the operations of the enemy. They cannot be called off the lines of entrenchments to do the work for which I desired the negro force."[60] Captain Stanard confirmed Lee's fears one month later, when he noted the arrival of only 1,162 of the slaves impressed under Smith's orders (see appendix, table 5.3). "This number," Stanard insisted, "is entirely insufficient for the necessities of the service, as the need for labor on the fortifications and other works connected with the Public defences, is at the present moment great and urgent."[61]

Smith thus turned to the Virginia General Assembly, urging congressmen to draft new legislation that would grant him greater authority to enforce slave impressment quotas. The governor needed expanded powers of impressment to combat slaveholder resistance, he argued, as well as sufficient flexibility to cope with repeated enemy incursions and mounting demands for the state's industrial output. When the General Assembly failed to act quickly, Smith sent them an appeal for additional laborers from Lee's engineer Colonel Walter Stevens. "Without further legislation," Smith insisted, "it is impossible to comply with these requisitions. Surely some bill ought to be passed & that quickly."[62] The General Assembly responded on March 4 by passing a new law that would essentially override the national slave impressment legislation of the previous year, placing responsibility for enforcing requisitions in Virginia back in the hands of county and state officials rather than with the Conscript Bureau. The March 1865 state law provided slaveholders with increased incentives to send their slaves—compensation of sixty dollars per month per slave, rather than twenty—and reiterated that the Confederate government would provide rations and medical care to all impressed laborers.[63]

To this generous carrot, the General Assembly added several sizable sticks, prescribing harsh punishments for slaveholders or county officials who failed to comply with the governor's requisitions. Slaveholders who failed to deliver their slaves as ordered by the county court would face an extra impressment term of thirty days as well as a fine of three to ten dollars per day for each delinquent slave. Slaveholders would also have to pay the sheriff's wage of five dollars for each slave seized from recalcitrant owners. Delinquent sheriffs faced even more serious penalties, including fines between $500 and $2,000. Finally, any clerk, justice, sheriff, deputy, or sergeant who failed to comply with impressment quotas would be charged with "a misfeasance in office" and lose his position. Having lost their offices, most clerks, justices, and sheriffs would become eligible for the Confederate draft.[64]

Governor Smith responded quickly to this new law, issuing a requisition for 10 percent of the adult male slaves in forty-seven counties as well as in the cities of Lynchburg and Richmond on March 14, 1865 (see appendix, table 5.4). Anticipating the objections and complaints he would probably receive, Smith stated that he would not exempt any counties but would reduce quotas accordingly to those who could prove they had lost additional slaves since the last requisition. In addition, he mandated that in those counties that had lost at least two-thirds of their antebellum slave populations, only residents who retained at least three adult male slaves could be expected to comply. Smith's instructions emphasized the substantial fines that slaveholders and sheriffs could incur by failing to meet their quotas and also reminded county officials that he could remove them from office if they refused to cooperate with the requisition. "I regret to inform the counties that many of them wholly neglected to respond to the former requisition," Smith concluded, "and that the new act has been passed to prevent in future such delinquency."[65]

As if to illustrate Smith's point, engineer officers scrambled to lay claim to all available slave laborers. In the middle of March, Captain W. G. Bender of the Engineer Bureau petitioned Colonel Rives to send him ten additional workers to supplement the thirty-two he was using to repair the Staunton River bridge, which had been damaged in a midwinter flood.[66] When Rives asked the engineers at Petersburg to send ten slaves to Bender's command, Colonel Stevens responded that "our labor here is so *absolutely* necessary, that it is with great reluctance I can spare a single hand." Because most counties had failed to meet their December 1864 quotas, or even the reduced quotas of January 1865, every point of fortification in Virginia needed additional laborers.[67]

The harsh penalties connected with the March 14 requisition served their purpose. By the end of the month, the Conscript Bureau reported that 1,568 of the 1,843 impressed slaves had arrived in Richmond—a compliance rate of 85 percent.[68] Some counties did protest this quota, however. Campbell County officials wrote to Colonel Munford on March 23 that they not only were still in the process of filling the December 1864 requisition but also had received an ad hoc call from General Raleigh Colston to send slaves to Lynchburg. "We are thus, you see, between the devil and the deep sea," they protested, asking the governor to relieve them from filling at least one of the three requisitions they faced.[69] The Buckingham County Court also reported that Colston had impressed sixty slaves from that county to work at Lynchburg and thus requested an exemption from Smith's March call for slaves.[70] Justices from Powhatan County argued that since more than 10 percent of the county's adult male slaves already worked for the Confederate government, Powhatan should be exempt.[71] Smith refused every one of these requests, and all three counties forwarded slaves to Richmond.

What is immediately clear from both the General Assembly's March 4 law and Governor Smith's strict enforcement of the March 14 call for labor is that Virginia's state officials did not view these requisitions as a desperate eleventh-hour attempt to save a doomed Confederacy. The new impressment law, as Smith described it, was designed to prevent

Figure 5.2. Petersburg fortifications (Library of Congress)

delinquency in future requisitions for slave labor; he did not anticipate that March 1865 would be the last time he issued such a request. The Henrico County Court worked to fill its quota with equal confidence in the future of the Confederacy, meeting on March 29 to select an additional twenty-six slaves to send to the fortifications but postponing final decisions until April 1. County court minutes for that day contained only one incomplete sentence: "The Court having again met pursuant to their adjournment, to further consider the . . ."[72] Clearly, Henrico County never met its full requisition, as the Confederate, state, and local governments began evacuating Richmond on April 2. Unfortunately, no records indicate what happened to the slaves from throughout the state of Virginia who arrived in Richmond and Petersburg to work during the last few days before the fall of the capital.

Virginia's March 1865 slave impressment act was more detailed and far more punitive than similar laws in other states, or even the existing Confederate legislation. Governor Smith's active enforcement of the new law validated Seddon's decision to place the responsibility for slave impressment back into the hands of Virginia state officials in spite of many county courts' past intransigence. In North Carolina, granting the Bureau of Conscription more centralized authority for impressing laborers seemed to be more effective, even though, occasional rhetorical opposition aside, Governor Vance had never obstructed slave impressment. Although the trend toward centralization did not entirely hold true for both states, slaveholders in both Virginia and North Carolina saw their influence over the process of slave impressment—and thus their control over their slaves—decline during the last few months of the war. Finally, both state and national governments expected any changes they made to either the legal theory or the practice of slave impressment in early 1865 to have a long-term impact on the Confederacy's prospects for victory.

President Davis and Governor Smith likewise viewed the transformation of slaves into Confederate soldiers as a long-term plan for victory rather than the last gasp of a dying nation. In many ways, the practical steps they planned for enlisting slaves as Confederate soldiers were similar to those taken during slave impressment. In late March, Smith sent General Lee a list enumerating all black men, slave or free, within the state of Virginia (see appendix, table 5.5). This list relied on returns from both the county courts and the state tax assessors, and Smith assured Lee that the list was relatively accurate. He also reiterated his support of Lee's plans to expand the army's use of Virginia's slave population. Smith further suggested that instead of strangers, who would likely waste valuable time gathering redundant information, either local officials or the enrolling officers already present in each community should undertake the work involved in organizing the slaves.[73]

A few weeks earlier, in late February 1865, Governor Smith had urged the Virginia General Assembly to move beyond its recent legislation impressing slaves as laborers and authorize the enlistment of slaves as soldiers. In particular, Smith noted, General James Longstreet wished to place black Confederate soldiers into combat against black Union troops, believing the effect on both armies' morale would benefit the Confederacy. Unfortunately for Longstreet, even the Confederacy's expanded powers of slave impressment did not allow him to accept the services of black soldiers. State law prohibited arming black men.[74]

Once the slaves were enrolled, Smith predicted they could be arranged into either Negro Labor Battalions or fighting units; in fact, the two types of units could have been used interchangeably. By substituting company-grade officers for overseers, each gang of 100 slave laborers could begin to train as a company of Confederate soldiers. As Davis noted in his November 1864 message to Congress, impressed slaves had experience not only in performing manual labor but also in marching, setting up camp, and utilizing supply trains and thus had already completed much of the training necessary to fight as soldiers. Indeed, the black men who formed the "volunteer organizations" Smith described were probably drawn largely from the ranks of teamsters, nurses, and engineer laborers—men already performing compulsory labor for the Confederacy in some capacity.[75]

Still, most white southerners recognized a substantial ideological difference between employing slaves as military laborers and arming them as soldiers. The North Carolina legislature confirmed this assumption in February 1865, resolving that "the State of North-Carolina protests against the arming of slaves by the Confederate government, in any emergency that can possibly arise, but gives its consent to their being taken and used as laborers in the public service, upon just compensation being made."[76] North Carolina's legislature maintained this position until the end of the war, despite the fact that both the Virginia General Assembly and the Confederate Congress yielded to pressure from General Lee and approved bills allowing the enlistment of slaves as soldiers—though not their automatic emancipation.[77]

Lee's support for enlisting slaves as Confederate soldiers became public knowledge in February 1865 when a letter he wrote to Congressman Ethelbert Barksdale appeared in countless southern newspapers. Southerners could keep their slaves and allow General Grant to advance, Lee argued, or, "by timely action and judicious management, use them to arrest his progress."[78] Historian Robert Durden has suggested that while Lee's support of the measure convinced some southerners, especially the Virginia General Assembly, to enact plans for arming the slaves, "the South as a whole could not summon the intelligence, imagination, and moral courage to begin voluntarily to abandon the peculiar institution."[79] Yet the Virginia and North Carolina state legislatures' differing approach to arming slaves reflected their location as much as their ideas about race. White Virginians' proximity to the Union army made them more likely than their fellow citizens living in less exposed areas of the Confederacy to embrace the idea.[80]

While taking slaves from their owners to perform manual labor for the Confederate army may have violated many white southerners' theory of property rights, from an ideological perspective it was a fundamentally conservative policy. Though employing slaves in a wide variety of skilled occupations, white southerners mentally associated black men exclusively with unskilled manual labor, assuming that black men were somehow less than human and therefore incapable of performing acts requiring manly skill or courage. A fictional description of a slave's trip to the zoo that appeared in a North Carolina newspaper illustrated this belief. In the story, the slave encountered a baboon and was fascinated by the animal's ability to mimic human actions. Finally, because "the baboon seemed so intelligent and knowing, the negro addressed him some remarks, which the baboon only answered by a nod of the head. At length the negro was still more delighted and broke forth with the remark, 'You're right, don't open your mouth, kase if you spokes a word the white man'l have a shovel in your hand in less dan a minit."[81]

On a much more serious note, Confederate officers demonstrated their belief that black men should serve as laborers but not soldiers by placing black Union soldiers captured at Petersburg to work on southern fortifications. The commandants at both Libby Prison and Castle Thunder sent all black prisoners in their charge to work on the fortifications outside Richmond in October 1864. Secretary Seddon justified these orders by classifying the men as recaptured slaves rather than as Union soldiers, in spite of a report from Castle Thunder that eleven of the black Union prisoners sent to the fortifications were in fact free-born men.[82] Lee repeated Seddon's justifications in a letter to Lieutenant General Ulysses S. Grant, claiming (incorrectly) that the prisoners put to work on the fortifications were all runaway slaves, and that they were all employed in areas not regularly exposed to cannon fire.[83] Even so, it is not surprising that some Union officers were outraged by this treatment of the black prisoners, or that Major General Benjamin Butler actually responded in kind, forcing Confederate prisoners to fortify the Dutch Gap Canal.[84]

From the perspective of white southerners, the Confederate army's use of black Union prisoners—even those who enlisted as free men rather than as runaway slaves—to build fortifications was perfectly legitimate. Employing runaway slaves recaptured from Union lines had been a standard procedure for engineer officers since the first summer of the war, and this new approach struck most as a simple extension of that policy. Both were in keeping with their belief "that involuntary servitude is as indispensable to the moral and physical advancement, prosperity and happiness of the African race, as is liberty to the whites," as the Fifty-Sixth Virginia regiment wrote to the *Richmond Enquirer* in February 1865. While holding firm in this belief, however, the men of the regiment believed the time had come to arm any slaves willing to fight for the Confederate cause. Not only were they willing to overturn some of their racial ideologies to concede that black men might be capable of more than manual labor, but they also agreed that to secure the slaves' assistance, enslaved men who did fight for the cause of Confederate independence could earn their freedom once they had achieved victory.[85]

Richmond's newspapers presented the range of competing opinions in its editorials and readers' letters. Members of the Jordan Battery assured the *Examiner*, whose editor John M. Daniel was always critical of President Davis's policies, "that we view with the utmost abhorrence the idea of arriving at a settlement of our difficulties by sacrificing slavery or by yielding dishonourably in any way."[86] Other soldiers no doubt agreed with the editor of the similarly critical *Richmond Whig*, who in early January argued that arming slaves, especially with the promise of emancipation, meant "to abandon every object we had in view when we seceded from the government of the United States."[87] Only five weeks after publishing this statement, however, the *Whig*'s editor experienced an epiphany. "Must we be told that it is our duty to give every thing for independence—lands, houses, life itself—but not our slaves?" he asked. Losing the war also meant losing everything, he continued, and sacrificing slavery was surely preferable to being conquered.[88] Though earlier criticizing the pro-Davis *Enquirer* for arguing in favor of arming the slaves, he now agreed with editor Jennings Wise's suggestion that any sacrifice—even slavery—was preferable to "the unspeakable calamity of subjugation."[89]

In the end, many Confederate soldiers and civilians agreed that averting that calamity was a valid reason to relinquish a portion of their enslaved property, especially since black men had served so effectively as military laborers throughout the war. This shift in priorities was perhaps less momentous than it initially appears. In February 1861, delegations from the Lower South had endeavored to convince Virginians that subjugation under a Republican president meant the complete unraveling of the southern social order—not just emancipation but "black governors, black legislators, black juries, black everything," in the words of Georgia's Henry L. Benning.[90] By February 1865, President Davis had managed to convince Virginia's legislators that, rather than submitting to the Republicans' plan for emancipation, they should arm a portion of the state's slaves. An independent Confederacy could then severely conscribe the freedom they granted black men in exchange for their service. Confederate victory was not merely an ideological triumph but a means to an end and a practical way of preserving as much of the antebellum social order as possible.[91] By offering some slaves freedom in exchange for helping secure a Confederate victory, Virginians hoped to avoid the economic and social chaos of an emancipation plan directed by the "black Republicans" of the United States.

Like slave impressment, the national plan for enlisting black men required state support—but this time, the support was even harder to obtain. Only Virginia's state legislature enacted a law approving the policy; North Carolina was one of several states that issued clear statements opposing it. And so the only official attempts to enlist black men (all of them severely limited and largely unsuccessful) took place in and around Richmond. Davis likely recognized the futility of attempting to enlist black men in states where there was neither popular nor institutional support for the project. As with impressment, strong federal government action depended on supportive state leaders. Centralization was a negotiated and still incomplete process.

Some Virginians tendered their slaves to the government even before Congress passed the bill authorizing the army to enlist slaves as Confederate soldiers, echoing the enthusiastic slaveholders who sent their workers to the fortifications in the first flush of patriotic fervor in April 1861. Approving the idea of arming slaves, the *Lexington Gazette* assured its readers that "the planters, who have already evinced a patriotism above all suspicion of sordidness, and beyond all questions of property, will never HESITATE to yield up their negroes" for the good of the Confederate cause—despite the fact that many had hesitated to do so when asked to supply labor for the fortifications.[92] An Augusta County resident suggested one reason for the *Gazette*'s optimism in a letter to President Davis. "I feel satisfied," he wrote, that "unless the able bodied slaves are used by our Government they will be by the Enemy. I have already lost nearly half." This farmer's argument in favor of arming the slaves reiterated one many newspapers had used to promote slave impressment—it was better to lose some slaves to the Confederate army than to lose them all to the Union army.[93]

"Take all my negros that are able to fight, and I will go to work with the old men and women and children," a Nelson County farmer wrote to Thomas Bocock, Speaker of the Confederate House of Representatives, in February 1865.[94] Bocock, though an active participant in the legislative processes leading to both slave impressment and the enlistment of slaves as Confederate soldiers, could not quite match this level of devotion. Indeed, Speaker Bocock went to great lengths to avoid the penalties imposed by Virginia law when his slave Collin escaped from the Richmond fortifications.[95] Yet it cannot have escaped Bocock's notice that between impressment, hiring, and escape, many of his constituents lost all or nearly all of their effective slave laborers during the four-year Confederate war for independence.

The detailed estimate of Virginia's remaining slave population that Governor Smith submitted to General Lee in March 1865 amply illustrated these stunning losses (see appendix, table 5.5). Slave owners in the fifty-nine counties and three cities on Smith's list held no more than 26,196 male slaves between the ages of eighteen and forty-five, an estimate the governor himself admitted was probably too high.[96] According to the 1860 U.S. Census returns, those same fifty-nine counties and three cities had contained 65,720 male slaves in a comparable age range. Losing 60 percent of their most productive slaves to government hiring and Union army incursions had understandably prejudiced many Virginians against answering any further calls for assistance by the Confederate government.[97]

Losses in some areas even exceeded that 60 percent. Despite massive influxes of refugees from the countryside, the adult male slave population of Richmond and Henrico County in March 1865 reached only one-third of its prewar total; Rappahannock County, which spent much of the war behind Union lines, lost 72 percent of its slaves. A disabled ex-soldier from Louisa County, which matched the average loss of 60 percent, complained to President Davis that he could not hire a male slave to work on his farm because the army was employing all of them.[98] Even the tobacco-producing counties along the border with North Carolina, one of the more sheltered regions of Virginia, lost nearly half of their adult male slaves in the last two years of the war. There was more than a grain of truth to the county courts' assertions that they did not have enough slaves to fill all of their needs on the home front and to send laborers to the fortifications.

Without a detailed record similar to that produced by Virginia's auditor of public accounts, it is difficult to determine the extent of North Carolina's labor shortage. Since most areas of North Carolina faced little or no exposure to Union armies until the very last weeks of the war, most North Carolina slaveholders probably lost fewer runaway slaves. Still, slaves had composed only one portion of the antebellum workforces in both states. Of eligible white Virginia men, 89 percent served in the Confederate military, as did approximately 82 percent of the eligible white men in North Carolina.[99] As each white man left for the army, each slave's labor became more valuable. Meanwhile, as male slaves ran away, were impressed, or were hired to Confederate employers, the burden of maintaining the farms of Virginia and North Carolina shifted more and more to black and white women.

Thus, it is difficult to condemn as pure selfishness the efforts of slaveholders in Virginia and North Carolina to resist slave impressment and keep their remaining workers at home. Many of these slaveholders had been detailed as farmers and grew food crops almost exclusively, contributing to the Confederate war effort by feeding both soldiers and civilians. Others hired their slaves to railroads, iron forges, armories, hospitals, and salt mines. Despite mounting labor shortages, many continued to supply workers for each impressment call, whether under state or national authority. In the end, there simply were not enough workers to fill every open position.

While slave impressment clearly failed to meet all of the Engineer Bureau's labor needs, thousands of slaves from Virginia and North Carolina worked on Confederate fortifications over the course of the war. They built the walls that protected Richmond, Petersburg, Wilmington, and Saltville until the last few months of the war, often serving multiple terms despite harsh working conditions. The success of slave impressment, while incomplete, testifies to the high level of integration between local, state, and national governments during the Confederacy's four-year life span.

EPILOGUE

Black Confederates?

Slave Impression and Confederate Memory

Once the war ended, slave impressment became a subject of contested memories rather than intense and practical political debate. John Bellamy of Wilmington incorrectly remembered that his father and other prominent North Carolina slaveholders sent their slaves to build fortifications without hesitation, complaint, or any sort of coercion.[1] Numerous ex-slaves told WPA interviewers that their fathers or uncles had been taken to work on the fortifications; a few of the older men interviewed had been impressed themselves, although most provided little, if any, information about the experience. For a time, however, the wartime activities of slaves impressed to work for the Engineer Bureau largely disappeared from postwar memory, while Lost Cause ideology lauded the body servants of Confederate soldiers and the faithful mammies on the home front. This selective memory was deliberate, for impressment reminded white southerners that many slaves had to be forced to work for the Confederacy rather than voluntarily gave their support. Moreover, erasing the memory of the thousands of enslaved laborers who sustained the Confederate war effort also masked the essential dependency of white households on black labor, thus easing any potential threats to white supremacy.

But impressed slaves have returned to the forefront of Civil War memory as "evidence" to be wielded by those who insist that thousands of black men served as Confederate soldiers. Sadly, some of those who engage in this debate are no more concerned with the actual experiences of impressed slaves than were the government officials who directed requisitions or the slaveholders who opposed them. In February 2011, for example, the commissioners of Union County, North Carolina, considered a Sons of Confederate Veterans (SCV) proposal to etch the names of ten black men from the county (nine slaves and one free man) who had worked for the Confederate army onto the Confederate monument at the Old County Courthouse in Monroe. All ten men worked as camp servants, cooks, teamsters, or impressed engineer laborers and were awarded state pensions in the early twentieth century.[2] While rejecting the initial proposal, the county reached a compromise in August 2012, approving plans to place a new granite marker on the courthouse grounds. The language for the marker, dedicated on December 8, 2012, does not explicitly call the men Confederate soldiers but instead hews to a more accurate, if suggestive, rendering: "Confederate Pensioners of Color."[3]

The debate over this particular monument has created some surprising alliances, heroes, and villains. Sons of Confederate Veterans member Tony Way has joined forces with Greg Perry, great-great-grandson of one of the nine slaves listed on the monument, to promote the new marker. Perry even allowed the SCV to place a marker on his ancestor's grave with the completely erroneous claim that Aaron Perry, who was forced to dig trenches outside Wilmington under the control of the Engineer Bureau, served in the Thirty-Seventh North Carolina regiment.[4] Meanwhile, the county commissioners and historic preservation advocates who rejected the initial proposal did so out of an apparent distaste for affirmative action, suggesting that adding the names of black men to a Confederate monument that listed regiments but not individual white soldiers from the county would change the "race-neutral" character of the existing monument.[5] And thus when historians—well aware that a Confederate monument erected in the early twentieth century could never be characterized as neutral on the subject of race—attempt to dispute the accuracy of Way and Perry's claims, we are painted as opposing a laudable attempt to acknowledge the shared history of black and white southerners. For who could possibly object to a monument that honors "the courage and service by all African Americans during the War Between the States," as the text of Union County's new marker reads?[6]

The problem, of course, is that the courage and service of so many men is being misrepresented, often deliberately, and we should be wary of the purposes this particular set of misrepresentations will be used to serve. While the new monument does not actually call the ten men Confederate soldiers, people are certainly reading that construction into it.

One newspaper article describing the monument used the phrase "black Confederate Army veterans" in its headline, while local television news anchors who covered the ceremony unveiling the monument repeatedly called the men soldiers.[7] Online comments suggest a significant portion of *Charlotte Observer* readers believe that thousands of black men served as Confederate soldiers, the Confederate government and army had no interest in protecting the institution of slavery, and emancipation was just a convenient cover for a transparent power grab by the Yankee tyrant Abraham Lincoln.[8] Greg Perry, meanwhile, publicly describes his great-great-grandfather Aaron as having "fought for the Confederacy."[9] While I have no objection to honoring Aaron Perry or bringing his story to light, surely as historians it is our job to oppose such significant misinterpretations and to interrogate the motives of those who present them to the public as truth. What little we know about impressed slaves' service on the fortifications suggests that it is grossly misleading to characterize them as Confederate soldiers.

Way and Perry, with the assistance of archivist Earl Ijames, insist that these ten men were Confederate soldiers because they received pensions under state law. North Carolina's first pension law, enacted in 1885, contained no provisions for manual laborers who had served the Confederacy but provided an annual pension of thirty dollars to disabled Confederate soldiers or indigent widows of Confederate soldiers. In 1927, North Carolina amended its pension law, granting "to such colored servants who went with their masters to the war and can prove their service to the satisfaction of the county and State pension boards, two hundred dollars." The state's pension boards received 193 total applications from African American men or their widows; just under 20 percent listed service on the fortifications as their primary qualification. The overwhelming majority of North Carolina's black pensioners were listed simply as "servant."[10]

Virginia's first pension laws also excluded slave laborers, but in a 1924 revision, the General Assembly allowed a twenty-five dollar annual pension to body servants of Confederate soldiers, as well as to anyone who worked as a cook, hostler, teamster, or engineer laborer. In 1928, the General Assembly further expanded the act to include guards, gravediggers, and all employees of railroads, blacksmith shops, and hospitals operated by the Confederate War Department. To earn their twenty-five dollars, pensioners had to provide proof of service.[11]

Fewer than 600 black men and women applied for pensions in Virginia under this law, perhaps because very few of the qualifying workers were still alive sixty years after the war ended. Of the 512 black men who received pensions, fewer than 20 percent listed a few months' service on the fortifications as their sole qualification. Most had served as teamsters, hospital workers, cooks, or body servants, often for several years at a time; these men no doubt found it easier to locate white witnesses who could corroborate their claims to a pension than men who had been impressed for short-term work under the Engineer Department. Many of the body servants and hospital workers, however, indicated on their pension applications that they had also spent at least some time "building breastworks." Six black women also received state pensions for their work as laundresses in Confederate hospitals.[12]

So how did men granted pensions for Confederate labor in the 1920s became Confederate soldiers by 2012? Who stands to benefit from this transformation? For Greg Perry and other descendants of slaves forced to work for Confederate victory, claiming a connection to Confederate heritage puts their stories squarely inside what many still continue to treat as the defining experience of southern history and identity, thus countering the long-standing exclusion of nonwhite southerners from that identity. And it is no doubt empowering to reimagine one's ancestor as a soldier rather than as a slave or victim. Yet as Kevin Levin has persuasively demonstrated in his examination of Aaron Perry's pension record (and those of other purported "black Confederates" from North Carolina), the men awarded pensions received them precisely because they did not challenge the Lost Cause narrative of the loyal slave.[13] An annual check for two hundred dollars was their reward for not taking a visible stand against the Confederacy or its eventual successor, Jim Crow.

Meanwhile, if the online comments of their supporters are any guide, then lurking behind current SCV and United Daughters of the Confederacy attempts to commemorate black contributions to the Confederacy is the implicit suggestion that those contributions signify support of the Confederacy's goals and objectives—thus lending credence to their claim that protecting slavery was not the primary motivating factor behind secession and the formation of the Confederate States of America. "Black Confederates" thus become the newest variation of Lost Cause themes, especially since the SCV seems to have no intention of reminding anyone that state and national governments had to exercise a good deal of coercive force on both slaves and slaveholders in order to ensure that the men being commemorated were sent to the fortifications in the first place. Finally, the irony of North Carolina's SCV members fighting to commemorate something many of their qualifying ancestors insisted should never happen—black men serving as Confederate soldiers—seems lost on them.

Certainly, some aspects of impressed slaves' daily lives mirrored those of Confederate privates—inadequate rations, unpleasant living conditions, long days of mind-numbing labor. In 1936, former slave Cornelius Garner explicitly told a WPA interviewer that Virginia slaves who had helped build fortifications were "doin' soldier's wuk" during the war.[14] And we know that Confederate soldiers often spent time building fortifications because they complained about it repeatedly, usually arguing that digging ditches was the work of slaves, not soldiers. But to assume that, because Confederate soldiers were regularly expected to perform what they deemed to be slaves' work, they therefore believed that slaves doing such work for the army deserved the same status as Confederate soldiers creates a connection that many white men at the time adamantly opposed. As we have seen, North Carolina's soldiers and lawmakers were among the most vocal opponents of legislation designed to free and arm slaves in the waning months of the Confederate war, and it is interesting to imagine how those men might have viewed their descendants' efforts to honor impressed slaves as Confederate soldiers.

Slaves impressed for Confederate service straddled two worlds, as slaves always did. They were both property that the Confederate government could use to its advantage and men who performed many of the same tasks as Confederate soldiers. In "doin' soldier's wuk" they helped perpetuate their own enslavement, but their faithful performance of that work throughout the war made the decision to arm and free some black men less risky from the perspective of many Confederate officials, especially those in Virginia. And ultimately, their experiences working for the Engineer Bureau tell historians as much about the Confederacy as they do about slavery.

First, the successes of slave impressment point to a high level of cooperation between local, state, and national governments that ultimately strengthened the Confederate state. Countless state legislators and county sheriffs, as well as Governors John Letcher, William Smith, and Zebulon Baird Vance, put the Confederate Congress's legislation into action on a daily basis; slave impressment is merely one example of a legislative initiative the Confederacy would have struggled to implement without state and local participation. Even as local governments became less cooperative, moreover, the governors of Virginia and North Carolina continued to support slave impressment and eagerly approved measures that would speed its centralization under national authority. Slave impressment also led to the expansion of the Confederate bureaucracy, as the Board of Slave Claims arose to compensate slaveholders.

Epilogue / 163

Second, it is hardly surprising that slaveholders in North Carolina and Virginia raised a seemingly endless series of objections to Confederate slave impressment. After all, they had seceded from the Union primarily to prevent the national government from interfering with slavery, but their new national government proved to be even more intrusive. Yet most slaveholders in the two states complied, albeit reluctantly, with requisitions from both the state and national governments. And ironically, the men and women who protested slave impressment were instrumental in convincing the governors to support a more centralized and regulated approach to the process. Meanwhile, those who accepted slave impressment no doubt did so because they saw it as a temporary expedient for winning the war. Once the Confederacy gained its independence, it would no longer interfere with slaveholders' property rights.

Most of the complaints slaveholders raised against slave impressment point to a problematic reality echoed in nearly every other aspect of the Confederate experience—the Confederacy simply did not have sufficient labor resources to sustain an extended war effort. With almost all of the white men serving in the Confederate army, slaveholders' protests that work on the fortifications damaged slaves' health or removed them from vital agricultural or manufacturing work on the home front seem pragmatic rather than unpatriotic. Whatever their motives, of course, slaveholders' resistance to slave impressment served to hinder—but not completely preclude—its effectiveness, for the long litany of objections slaveholders raised cannot eclipse the fact that tens of thousands of slaves in Virginia and North Carolina were put to work to meet the labor demands of the Confederacy. Slaveholders' frequent objections also should not overshadow the extent to which state and local officials bore responsibility for enacting national policies—including, but not limited to, slave impressment—designed to increase the new nation's military capacity. Through slave impressment, slaves, slaveholders, and government officials all worked to defend the Confederate state, building both strong fortifications and strong lines of communication between local, state, and national governments.

APPENDIX

Tables

Table 1.1. First Call for Slaves to Work on Fortifications in Virginia, October 1862

County	October quota	Furnished	Deficit (as of November 24, 1862)
Albemarle	540	0	540
Amherst	260	145	115
Appomattox	180	109	71
Bedford	450	274	176
Buckingham	300	204	96
Campbell	400	204	196
Charlotte	230	197	33
Cumberland	210	197	13
Fluvanna	140	101	39
Halifax	350	263	87
Louisa	350	241	109
Nelson	190	109	81
Pittsylvania	580	410	170
Prince Edward	320	303	17
TOTAL	4,500	2,757	1,743

Source: Lt. Col. Jeremy F. Gilmer to George W. Randolph, October 8, 1862; Lt. Col. Jeremy F. Gilmer to Gov. John Letcher, November 24, 1862, LSEB.

Table 1.2. Second Call for Slaves to Work on Fortifications in Virginia, November 1862

County	Quota
Augusta	250
Botetourt	100
Brunswick	225
Caroline	400
Culpeper	200
Essex	150
Faquier	300
Franklin	300
Greene	75
Hanover	225
Henry	225
King and Queen	150
King William	100
Lunenburg	150
Madison	200
Mecklenburg	300
Montgomery	100
Nottoway	200
Orange	200
Page	25
Patrick	75
Prince William	50
Pulaski	50
Rappahannock	150
Roanoke	100
Rockbridge	150
Rockingham	100
Spotsylvania	350
Stafford	100
TOTAL	5,000

Source: Col. Jeremy Francis Gilmer to Maj. Gen. Gustavus W. Smith, November 20, 1862, LSEB.

Note: The majority of the counties encompassed by Virginia's first two impressment calls, shown here and in table 1.1, were from the Piedmont or Shenandoah Valley regions and thus tended to have large slave populations that were heavily engaged in the production of grain crops. The second quota also included a few counties from the more mountainous western area of the state, as well as some from the Chesapeake region; the third quota, in table 1.3, would draw heavily from these regions and the rest of Virginia's tobacco belt. The coastal counties had also sent numerous slaves under localized impressment calls prior to October 1862. Most of the deficits from the first call were eventually rectified; in fact, filling unmet quotas was one of the original purposes of the canceled March 1863 call.

Table 1.3. Third Call for Slaves to Work on Fortifications in Virginia, January 1863

County or corporation	5% of slave population	Quota
Alleghany	49	40
Amelia	383	300
Bath	47	40
Chesterfield	417	350
City of Danville	—	70
Craig	21	20
Dinwiddie	638	550
Floyd	23	20
Giles	38	30
Goochland	306	250
Grayson	27	20
Greensville	208	15
Henrico and City of Richmond	1,002	900
Nottoway	323	250
Powhatan	270	200
Russell	54	40
Smyth	51	50
Southampton	270	200
Sussex	319	250
Tazewell	60	50
Washington	127	120
Wythe	108	100
TOTAL	4,741	3,865

Source: Col. Jeremy F. Gilmer to James A. Seddon, January 13, 1863, JLEP.

Table 1.4. Call for Slaves to Work on Fortifications in North Carolina, March 1863

County	Quota	Destination
Cumberland	130	Wilmington
Davidson	60	Weldon
Guilford	80	Weldon
Iredell	85	Weldon
Johnston	160	Wilmington
Lenoir	110	Wilmington
Rowan	50	Weldon
Wake	120	Wilmington
TOTAL	795	

Source: Adjutant General's Office, Special Orders Nos. 37 and 46, March 1863, AGD.

Note: Because impressment quotas were less centralized in North Carolina than in Virginia, most of the numbers listed here are estimates and probably incomplete. It does appear, however, that quotas in North Carolina rarely exceeded 10 percent of the adult male slave population, while they were significantly higher in Virginia.

Table 3.1. Fourth Call for Slaves to Work on Fortifications in Virginia (Canceled to Protect Spring Planting Season), March 1863

County	Month called	Deficiency	New requisition	Total call
Albemarle	October	98	66	164
Amherst	October	18	36	54
Appomattox	October	15	20	35
Augusta	November	19	30	49
Bedford	October	175	58	233
Botetourt	November	3	38	41
Brunswick	November	125	97	222
Buckingham	October	94	48	142
Campbell	October	173	58	231
Charlotte	October	14	89	103
Cumberland	October	11	9	20
Fluvanna	October	25	38	63
Franklin	November	11	17	28
Greene	November	0	31	31
Halifax	October	57	185	242
Henry	November	20	37	57
Louisa	October	40	90	130
Lunenburg	November	7	83	90
Mecklenburg	November	51	38	89
Montgomery	November	20	10	30
Nelson	October	65	61	126
Orange	October	51	0	50
Patrick	November	8	16	24
Pittsylvania	October	170	137	307
Prince Edward	October	4	47	51
Pulaski	November	4	29	33
Roanoke	November	16	32	48
Rockbridge	November	11	53	64
Rockingham	November	100	0	75
TOTAL called		1,405	1,453	2,832

Source: Table for the Governor of Va., Engineer Bureau to Gov. John Letcher, March 5, 1863, JLEP.

Table 3.2. French's Report of Virginia Slaves Impressed Prior to March 1863

County	Total slaves	Males 18–45	Liable to draft	Called for	Furnished	Deficit	Expiration of last call	New call
Albemarle	12,681	2,003	400	540	442	98	January	164
Amherst	5,860	988	197	260	242	18	January	54
Appomattox	4,270	684	137	180	165	15	January	35
Augusta	4,430	708	162	250	231	19	February	49
Bedford	9,135	1,461	292	450	275	175	January	233
Botetourt	2,852	432	86	100	97	3	February	41
Brunswick	9,212	1,473	294	225	100	125	February	222
Buckingham	8,104	1,296	259	300	206	94	January	142
Campbell	8,175	1,308	261	400	227	173	January	231
Charlotte	9,245	1,479	296	230	216	14	January	103
Cumberland	6,331	1,012	203	210	199	11	January	20
Fluvanna	4,781	765	153	140	115	25	January	63
Franklin	5,887	941	188	300	289	11	February	28
Greene	1,838	294	59	75	75	0	February	31
Halifax	14,770	2,163	432	350	293	57	January	242
Henry	4,978	796	159	225	205	20	February	57
Louisa	9,169	1,467	293	350	310	40	January	130
Lunenburg	7,219	1,165	233	150	143	7	February	90
Mecklenburg	12,481	1,997	399	300	249	51	February	89
Montgomery	2,132	341	68	100	80	20	February	30
Nelson	5,356	857	171	190	129	61	January	126
Orange	5,873	939	188	200	150	50	February	50
Patrick	1,872	300	60	75	67	8	February	24
Pittsylvania	12,362	1,977	395	580	410	170	January	307
Prince Edward	6,998	1,119	224	320	316	4	January	51
Pulaski	1,636	191	38	50	46	4	February	33
Roanoke	2,763	442	88	100	84	16	February	48
Rockbridge	3,882	621	124	150	139	11	February	64
Rockingham	2,164	346	71	100	100	0	February	75
TOTAL	186,456	29,565	5,930	6,900	5,600	1,300		2,832

Source: Col. S. Bassett French to Gov. John Letcher, March 19, 1863, JLEP.

Note: Colonel S. Bassett French, an aide in the Virginia Executive Department, prepared this table to demonstrate that the counties encompassed in the March 1863 quota could afford to meet the new requisition. Secretary of War James A. Seddon disagreed, ordering the quota revoked to protect spring planting. He believed all slaves should be engaged in agricultural work after the middle of April.

Table 3.3. Calls for Slaves to Work on Fortifications in North Carolina (Estimated), March–April 1863

County	March quota	April quota
Alamance	—	30
Caswell	—	90
Chatham	—	60
Cumberland	130	—
Davidson	60	—
Guilford	80	—
Iredell	85	—
Johnston	160	—
Lenoir	110	—
Mecklenburg	—	60
Orange	—	50
Person	—	50
Rockingham	—	60
Rowan	50	40
Stokes	—	50
Wake	120	100
TOTAL	795	590

Source: Adjutant General's Office, Special Orders No. 50, April 2, 1863, AGD.

Note: Slaveholders in North Carolina, unlike those in Virginia, did have to send laborers during the spring 1863 planting season. Secretary Seddon would later intervene to ensure that those laborers were returned as quickly as possible.

Table 4.1. Fifth Call for Slaves to Work on Fortifications in Virginia, August 1863

County or corporation	Quota	Furnished	Deficit (as of December 1863)
Albemarle	200	166	34
Amelia	50	45	5
Amherst	100	45	55
Appomattox	90	90	0
Augusta	80	0	80
Bedford	200	200	0
Botetourt	60	60	0
Brunswick	130	126	4
Buckingham	180	162	18
Campbell	260	260	0
Charlotte	170	169	1
Chesterfield	150	15	135
Cumberland	80	80	0
Fluvanna	80	57	23
Franklin	70	63	7
Goochland	50	33	17
Halifax	300	300	0
Hanover	30	23	7
Henrico	140	0	140
Henry	100	88	12
Louisa	150	134	16
Lunenburg	120	111	9
Mecklenburg	200	168	32
Montgomery	50	0	50
Nelson	150	136	14
Nottoway	100	100	0
Pittsylvania	300	0	300
Powhatan	50	43	7
Prince Edward	150	147	3
City of Richmond	160	0	160
Roanoke	60	60	0
Rockbridge	90	64	26
Russell	50	0	50
Spotsylvania	30	0	30
Sussex	50	35	15
TOTAL	4,230	2,980	1,260

Source: Col. Walter H. Stevens to Gov. John Letcher, December 12, 1863, JLEP.

Note: Large (and unmet) deficiencies in this quota helped convince Virginia governor William Smith to issue another one in January 1864 and then to push for stricter legislation; Secretary Seddon would take a similar route. Both noticed that the least compliant counties were among the states' largest and wealthiest, while those with smaller slave populations usually met their quotas.

Table 4.2. Calls for Slaves to Work on Fortifications in North Carolina (Estimated), August–October 1863

County	August quota	September quota	October quota	Notes
Alamance	—	20	20	
Anson	—	70	—	
Ashe	—	—	10	
Burke	—	—	25	
Cabarrus	—	20	—	
Caldwell	—	10	—	
Catawba	—	—	20	
Chatham	—	60	60	
Cleveland	—	—	40	
Cumberland	160	—	60	
Davidson	—	30	—	
Davie	—	25	—	
Forsyth	—	30	20	
Granville	—	50	50	
Guilford	—	15	—	
Halifax	—	40	40	
Harnett	—	—	25	
Henderson	—	—	10	
Lenoir	—	—	50	
Lincoln	—	—	20	
Mecklenburg	—	—	65	
Montgomery	—	—	15	
Moore	—	—	20	
New Hanover	—	85	—	
Northampton	—	—	80	revoked
Orange	—	—	50	
Person	—	65	—	
Pitt	—	—	90	
Randolph	—	10	—	
Richmond	—	20	20	
Rockingham	—	70	70	
Rowan	—	60	30	
Sampson	—	—	60	
Surry	—	—	10	
Warren	—	120	—	
Wayne	—	—	60	
Wilkes	—	—	10	
Yadkin	—	—	10	
TOTAL	160	800	1,040	

Source: *Fayetteville Semi-Weekly Observer*, August 31, 1863; Adjutant General's Office, Special Orders No. 96, September 4, 1863; Adjutant General's Office, Special Orders No. 102, October 12, 1863, AGD.

Table 4.3. Sixth Call for Slaves to Work on Fortifications in Virginia, January 1864

County or corporation	Slave population, 1860	Slave population, 1862	Quota, January 1864	Petition
Albemarle	13,916	12,681	190	
Alleghany	990	659	10	
Amelia	7,667	7,172	120	
Amherst	6,278	5,860	110	
Appomattox	4,600	4,276	90	
Augusta	5,617	4,430	90	
Bath	946	781	10	granted
Bedford	10,176	9,135	150	
Botetourt	2,769	2,852	70	refused
Brunswick	9,148	9,212	160	
Buckingham	8,811	8,104	120	
Campbell	11,580	8,175	140	refused
Charlotte	9,236	9,245	170	
Chesterfield	8,355	7,457	130	
Craig	420	390	10	granted
Cumberland	6,705	6,331	110	
Dinwiddie and City of Petersburg	12,774 —	6,526 4,024	120 80	
Floyd	475	374	10	
Fluvanna	4,994	4,781	100	
Franklin	6,351	5,887	110	
Giles	778	708	10	granted
Goochland	6,193	5,768	100	refused
Grayson	547	551	10	
Greene	1,984	1,838	60	granted
Greensville	4,167	3,963	90	
Halifax	14,897	14,770	240	
Hanover	9,484	8,621	80	granted
Henrico and City of Richmond	20,041 —	6,557 7,915	120 140	
Henry	5,018	4,987	100	
Louisa	10,193	9,169	150	granted
Lunenburg	7,305	7,219	130	refused

County or corporation	Slave population, 1860	Slave population, 1862	Quota, January 1864	Petition
Madison	4,397	4,235	80	granted
Mecklenburg	12,419	12,481	190	
Montgomery	2,217	2,132	60	granted
Nelson	6,238	5,356	90	
Nottoway	6,468	6,342	110	
Orange	6,111	5,873	110	granted
Patrick	2,070	1,872	60	refused
Pittsylvania	14,340	12,362	190	
Powhatan	5,403	5,266	100	
Prince Edward	7,341	6,998	110	
Pulaski	1,589	1,636	60	refused
Roanoke	2,643	2,763	70	granted exemption without petition
Rockbridge	3,984	3,882	90	refused
Rockingham	2,387	2,164	60	granted
Russell	1,090	1,061	40	refused
Smyth	1,037	1,044	50	refused
Southampton	5,409	5,081	50	
Sussex	6,384	6,043	30	
Tazewell	1,202	1,124	50	granted
Washington	2,548	2,319	80	refused
Wythe	2,162	1,941	60	refused
TOTAL	309,854	282,393	5,070	

Source: Col. George W. Munford to the Clerks of the County Courts, January 22, 1864, WSEP.

Note: Governor Smith's office used both the 1860 Slaveholder Census and the 1862 state tax assessment to prepare his first impressment quota in January 1864, one of his earliest actions as governor. Approximately half of the counties included in this quota asked the governor to revoke it; he accepted only half of those petitions, granting the ones from counties that by January 1864 occupied the border between Confederate Virginia and areas under U.S. control.

Table 5.1. Virginia Slaves Impressed by Enrolling Office, September 1864

County or corporation	Quota called	Credit for recent calls	Quota due
Albemarle	253	153	100
Amelia	143	—	143
Amherst	117	17	100
Appomattox	85	—	85
Augusta	88	—	88
Town of Staunton	14	—	14
Bedford	182	—	182
Botetourt	57	—	57
Brunswick	148	—	148
Buckingham	130	147	0
Campbell	180	—	180
City of Lynchburg	30	17	13
Charlotte	178	—	178
Chesterfield	149	—	149
Cumberland	127	101	26
Dinwiddie	130	—	130
City of Petersburg	80	—	80
Fluvanna	74	86	0
Franklin	117	—	117
Goochland	115	—	115
Greensville	79	—	79
Halifax	295	—	295
Hanover	172	—	172
Henrico	131	58	73

County or corporation	Quota called	Credit for recent calls	Quota due
City of Richmond	158	344	0
Henry	85	—	85
Louisa	183	—	183
Lunenburg	118	—	118
Mecklenburg	326	—	326
Montgomery	42	—	42
Nelson	90	12	78
Nottoway	102	—	102
Pittsylvania	247	—	247
Town of Danville	20	—	20
Patrick	37	—	37
Powhatan	105	92	13
Prince Edward	120	—	120
Pulaski	32	—	32
Roanoke	54	—	54
Rockbridge	77	—	77
Russell	20	—	20
Washington	46	—	46
Wythe	38	—	38
TOTAL	4,974	1,027	4,162

Source: Special Orders No. 223, Adjutant and Inspector General's Office, September 20, 1864, *OR*, ser. I, vol. 42, part 3, 1268–69.

Table 5.2. Slaves Impressed for Fortifications at Weldon, North Carolina, October and December 1864

County	October quota
Edgecombe	120
Franklin	100
Granville	150
Halifax	150
Nash	100
Northampton	150
Warren	150
Wayne	100
Wilson	100
TOTAL	1,120

County	December quota
Alamance	30
Anson	40
Burke	20
Cabarrus	26
Caldwell	10
Caswell	48
Catawba	15
Chatham	43
Cleveland	24
Cumberland	40
Davidson	30
Davie	20
Duplin	30

County	December quota
Forsyth	15
Gaston	16
Guilford	30
Harnett	18
Iredell	30
Johnston	36
Lincoln	18
McDowell	8
Mecklenburg	40
Montgomery	14
Moore	20
Orange	40
Person	40
Randolph	26
Richmond	38
Sampson	46
Stanly	12
Stokes	20
Surry	15
Union	20
Wake	54
Yadkin	15
TOTAL	947

Source: Special Orders No. 108, October 3, 1864; Special Orders No. 175, December 23, 1864, AGD.

Table 5.3. Seventh Call for Slaves to Work on Fortifications in Virginia, December 1864

County or corporation	Quota	Revised	Furnished
Albemarle	250	125	0
Amelia	140	70	97
Amherst	120	60	62
Appomattox	80	40	0
Augusta	100	50	5
Town of Staunton	20	10	0
Bedford	180	90	2
Botetourt	50	25	0
Brunswick	150	75	0
Buckingham	130	65	85
Campbell	180	90	0
City of Lynchburg	30	15	0
Caroline	100	exempt	
Carroll	10	5	8
Charlotte	180	90	92
Chesterfield	150	75	10
Cumberland	130	65	86
Dinwiddie	130	65	0
City of Petersburg	80	40	0
Floyd	20	10	9
Fluvanna	80	40	15
Franklin	120	60	29
Goochland	120	60	0
Grayson	10	5	10
Greene	40	20	0
Greensville	80	40	0
Halifax	300	150	130
Hanover	150	exempt	
Henrico	130	65	22

County or corporation	Quota	Revised	Furnished
City of Richmond	160	80	0
Henry	80	40	0
Louisa	180	90	53
Lunenburg	100	50	56
Madison	50	exempt	
Mecklenburg	300	150	98
Montgomery	30	15	17
Nelson	80	40	21
Nottoway	90	45	87
Orange	50	25	0
Patrick	10	5	0
Pittsylvania	200	100	0
Town of Danville	10	5	0
Powhatan	90	45	61
Prince Edward	100	50	44
Pulaski	20	10	0
Roanoke	50	25	42
Rockbridge	70	exempt	
Washington	40	20	0
Wythe	30	15	21
TOTAL	5,000	2,315	1,162

Source: Gov. William Smith to County Courts, December 16, 1864, Confederate States of America Collection, Rubenstein Library, Duke University, Pamphlet #704; John B. Stanard to Gov. William Smith, March 9, 1865, WSEP.

Table 5.4. Eighth Call for Slaves to Work on Fortifications in Virginia, March 1865

County or corporation	Quota	Furnished
Albemarle	95	75
Alleghany	5	1
Amelia	50	48
Amherst	40	39
Appomattox	25	22
Bath	5	2
Bedford	70	45
Botetourt	20	18
Brunswick	74	46
Buckingham	66	59
Campbell	68	69
City of Lynchburg	12	9
Caroline	30	30
Carroll	2	2
Charlotte	80	80
Chesterfield	30	23
Cumberland	50	48
Dinwiddie	30	17
Essex	20	14
Floyd	3	1
Fluvanna	40	39
Franklin	50	49
Giles	4	4
Goochland	48	46
Grayson	4	4
Greene	10	13
Halifax	110	103
Hanover	50	37
Henrico	45	19

County or corporation	Quota	Furnished
City of Richmond	60	21
Henry	40	40
Louisa	65	55
Lunenburg	50	54
Madison	17	5
Mecklenburg	103	95
Monroe	7	6
Montgomery	13	13
Nottoway	50	50
Orange	30	15
Pittsylvania	104	104
Powhatan	30	30
Prince Edward	55	49
Pulaski	10	9
Roanoke	15	14
Rockbridge	20	23
Russell	5	3
Shenandoah	2	2
Washington	17	6
Wythe	14	12
TOTAL	1,843	1,568

Source: Capt. William H. Fry, Report of Negro Slaves received and disposed of under Circular No. 69 Conscript Office, March 28, 1865, CSA Compiled Service Records, NARA.

Table 5.5. Auditor's Statement of Black Men, 18–45, Fit for Service in Virginia, March 1865

County or corporation	Free blacks	Slaves	25% of slaves
Albemarle	102	1076	269
Alleghany	13	56	14
Amelia	51	628	159
Amherst	74	531	133
Appomattox	40	371	93
Augusta	89	439	110
Bath	17	62	15
Bedford	94	802	200
Botetourt	50	248	62
Brunswick	118	790	197
Buchanan	0	3	1
Buckingham	65	674	169
Campbell	79	854	213
Caroline	253	713	178
Charlotte	42	799	200
Chesterfield	110	639	160
Craig	6	37	9
Cumberland	85	545	136
Danville (city)	17	91	23
Dinwiddie	114	543	136
Floyd	7	41	10
Fluvanna	58	425	106
Franklin	16	522	130
Giles	16	54	13
Goochland	114	472	118
Grayson	7	48	12
Greenbrier	17	77	19
Greene	1	148	37
Halifax	132	1266	316
Hanover	34	658	165
Henrico	146	897	149
Henry	53	448	112
Highland	1	23	6
King and Queen	119	629	108
King William	67	380	95

County or corporation	Free blacks	Slaves	25% of slaves
Lee	10	93	23
Louisa	53	747	187
Lunenburg	37	612	153
Madison	13	302	75
Mecklenburg	224	1116	279
Mercer	2	45	11
Monroe	13	88	22
Montgomery	23	171	43
Nelson	26	462	115
Nottoway	29	528	132
Orange	35	457	114
Patrick	17	167	42
Petersburg (city)	794	350	87
Pittsylvania	54	1150	288
Powhatan	122	445	111
Prince Edward	82	590	147
Rappahannock	53	190	48
Richmond (city)	308	623	156
Roanoke	22	231	58
Rockbridge	85	345	86
Scott	9	43	11
Smyth	27	135	34
Spotsylvania	90	341	85
Surry	193	153	38
Sussex	131	493	123
Tazewell	10	99	25
Washington	53	231	58
TOTAL	4,722	26,196	6,424

Source: Statement of the Auditor of the Number of Slaves Fit for Service, March 25, 1865, WSEP.

Note: Governor Smith's office prepared this list of potential laborers (or even soldiers) in connection with his final impressment quota and the Confederate congressional debates on arming black men. The governor attested to its essential accuracy, so when compared to the 1860 census data for each county, it would also be useful in estimating how many Virginia slaves escaped over the course of the war.

Notes

ABBREVIATIONS

AGD   Adjutant General's Department, General Records, 1807–1950, North Carolina Department of Archives and History, Raleigh

BSC   Confederate States of America, Record Book of the Board of Slave Claims, Augusta State University Special Collections Library, Augusta, Georgia

CSW   Letters Received by the Confederate Secretary of War, 1861–1865, RG 109 M437, National Archives and Records Administration I, Washington, D.C.

HTC   Henry T. Clark Executive Papers, 1861–1862, North Carolina Department of Archives and History, Raleigh

JLEP   John Letcher Executive Papers, 1859–1863, Library of Virginia, Richmond

LSEB   Letters and Telegrams Sent by the Engineer Bureau of the Confederate War Department, 1861–1864, RG 109 M628, National Archives and Records Administration I, Washington, D.C.

LVA   Library of Virginia, Richmond

NARA   National Archives and Records Administration I, Washington, D.C.

NCAH   North Carolina Department of Archives and History, Raleigh

OR   *The War of the Rebellion: A Compilation of the Official Records of the Union and Confederate Armies* (Washington, D.C.: Government Printing Office, 1880–1901)

UVA   Albert and Shirley Small Special Collections Library, University of Virginia, Charlottesville

VED   Virginia Engineer Department, 1861–1865, Library of Virginia, Richmond

VHS   Virginia Historical Society, Richmond

WSEP   William Smith Executive Papers, 1863–1865, Library of Virginia, Richmond

ZBV   Zebulon Baird Vance Executive Papers, 1862–1865, North Carolina Department of Archives and History, Raleigh

INTRODUCTION

1. "Slavery Tested," *Richmond Whig*, February 6, 1864, p. 2, col. 3.

2. Anyone who watched Ken Burns's massively popular documentary on the Civil War heard the "died of a theory" remark, as well as a strong indictment of Governors Joseph Brown and Zebulon Baird Vance for undermining the Confederate war effort by withholding food and supplies. This interpretation suffuses many histories of the Civil War, including those intended for academic, as opposed to popular, audiences.

Owsley (*State Rights in the Confederacy*) and Beringer et al. (*Why the South Lost the Civil War*), for example, argue that strong state governors and local officials kept men out of the Confederate armies for militia duty, refused to send supplies that might reach soldiers from other states, and encouraged general discontent with the national government among their constituents.

3. McKinney, *Zeb Vance*; Mobley, "War Governor of the South."

4. Escott, *Confederacy*, 113-15. Williams makes a similar argument in (among others) *Bitterly Divided*. Robinson (*Bitter Fruits of Bondage*) and Tripp (*Yankee Town*) connect this class conflict more explicitly to nonslaveholders' perception that state and local leaders failed to fully utilize slavery in support of the war effort.

5. Faust, for example, argues that planter women deserted the Confederacy when it failed to protect their interests, foreshadowing Escott's point about the planter class as a whole (*Mothers of Invention*). Their earlier works also suggest that the planter class's weak initial attachment to the Confederacy was eventually overridden by self-interest; see Escott, *After Secession*, and Faust, *Creation of Confederate Nationalism*. My approach is more heavily influenced by those who suggest that a strong sense of Confederate identity did exist and who focus primarily on external factors when explaining Confederate defeat. See, for example, Thomas, *Confederate Nation*; Blair, *Virginia's Private War*; Gallagher, *Confederate War*; Campbell, *When Sherman Marched North from the Sea*; Rubin, *Shattered Nation*; and Sheehan-Dean, *Why Confederates Fought*.

6. Freehling, *The South vs. The South*. Bynum also explores discontented internal populations, primarily Unionists but also Quakers and Dunkers, in *Free State of Jones* and *Long Shadow*.

7. McCurry, *Confederate Reckoning*, 4-5.

8. For specific treatments of slave impressment and its relationship to insufficient Confederate nationalism among the planter class, see Trexler, "Opposition of Planters"; Nelson, "Confederate Slave Impressment Legislation"; and Robinson, *Bitter Fruits of Bondage*.

9. *Constitution of the Confederate States of America*, Preamble, Article VI, Section 3, The Avalon Project, Yale School of Law (accessed January 18, 2010).

10. Brasher, *Peninsula Campaign*.

11. Most notably, Freehling argues in his two-volume *Road to Disunion* that the decline in slaves as a percentage of state population in the Upper South signaled a declining commitment to protecting the institution, and he connects this decline to those states' slower rate of secession. Other scholars have disagreed, insisting, as Ayers and Thomas do, that "slavery was slavery to the border," remaining as intertwined in the economy, politics, and culture of the Upper South as it was in the Lower South ("Difference Slavery Made").

12. Nichols's *Confederate Engineers* contains detailed descriptions of state engineer forces, key officers in the Confederate Engineer Bureau, and key points of fortification.

13. Nelson, "Confederate Slave Impressment Legislation."

14. Warner, *Generals in Gray*, 105; Nichols, *Confederate Engineers*, 29-32.

15. Settles and Campbell, *John Bankhead Magruder*, 145-54; Gallagher, "The Undoing of an Early Confederate Hero," in *Lee and His Generals in War and Memory*, 119-21; Warner, *Generals in Gray*, 207-8; Nichols, *Confederate Engineers*, 19-20.

16. Warner, *Generals in Gray*, 334–35; Nichols, *Confederate Engineers*, 76–79.
17. See Curry, "James A. Seddon."
18. Boney, *John Letcher of Virginia*, 24–35, 74–90, 173–75.
19. See Fahrner, "William 'Extra Billy' Smith."
20. Crabtree, *North Carolina Governors*, 93–94.
21. See McKinney, *Zeb Vance*; Mobley, "War Governor of the South."
22. Extemporaneous speech of March 21, 1861, in Cleveland, *Alexander H. Stephens in Public and Private*, 721.
23. See Bancroft, *Slave-Trading in the Old South*; Dew, *Bond of Iron* and *Ironmaker to the Confederacy*; Kimball, *American City*; Takagi, *"Rearing Wolves"*; Eaton, "Slave-Hiring in the Upper South"; Barton, "'Good Cooks and Washers'"; Golland, "Industrial Intersection."
24. These observations stem from an earlier project, culminating in an essay published as Martinez, "Slave Market in Civil War Virginia."

CHAPTER ONE

1. Journal of Benjamin Fleet, September 20, 1861, *Green Mount*, ed. Fleet and Fuller, 75; Pa to Fred, September 21, 1861, ibid., 76.
2. Brig. Gen. John B. Magruder to Gen. Samuel Cooper, September 20, 1861, *OR*, ser. I, vol. 4, 654.
3. Col. Charles A. Crump to Maj. H. B. Tomlin, September 17, 1861; Maj. H. B. Tomlin to Col. J. M. Jones, September 27, 1861; Maj. H. B. Tomlin to Lt. H. T. Douglass, October 8, 1861, Tomlin's Infantry Battalion Letterbook, 1861, VHS.
4. See Brewer, *Confederate Negro*.
5. John Taylor to Gov. John Letcher, April 22, 1861, *Calendar of Virginia State Papers*, vol. 11, ed. Flournoy et al., 111.
6. Major General Commanding to Col. Andrew Talcott, April 24, 1861, VED; *Wilmington Daily Journal*, October 5, 1861.
7. Colin Shaw to wife, September 22, 1861, Williams/McEachern Papers, Lower Cape Fear Historical Society, Wilmington, N.C.
8. James R. Taylor to Lt. James Maurice, October 4, 1861, VED; Maj. Danville Leadbetter to George H. Bruce, August 28, 1861, LSEB.
9. Ely, *Israel on the Appomattox*, 404.
10. Maj. H. B. Tomlin to Gov. John Letcher, June 3, 1861; Maj. H. B. Tomlin to Col. J. M. Jones, October 10, 1861, Tomlin's Infantry Battalion Letterbook, 1861, VHS.
11. Oakley, *Keeping the Circle*, 18–19; Sider, *Lumbee Indian Histories*, 158–62; Evans, *To Die Game*, 3–18.
12. Memorandum, Capt. John J. Clarke, December 2, 1861; Capt. Alfred L. Rives to General Winder, December 2, 1861, LSEB.
13. Capt. Alfred L. Rives to Gov. John Letcher, December 3, 1861, LSEB.
14. Report of Brig. Gen. John B. Magruder, C.S. Army, August 9, 1861, *OR*, ser. I, vol. 4, 573.
15. Ibid., 569.

16. Maj. Danville Leadbetter to Maj. Gen. John B. Magruder, November 9, 1861, LSEB.

17. Capt. Alfred L. Rives to Richard M. Harrison, December 5, 1861, LSEB.

18. Pa to Fred, March 1, 1862, *Green Mount*, ed. Fleet and Fuller, 110.

19. William Roane Aylett to Alice Brockenbrough Aylett, February 26, 1862, Aylett Family Papers, VHS.

20. Catherine Ann Devereux Edmondston, August 13-14, 1862, *Journal of a Secesh Lady*, ed. Crabtree and Patton, 121.

21. Report of Maj. Gen. John B. Magruder, February 1, 1862, *OR*, ser. I, vol. 9, 42.

22. Col. H. M. Shaw to Gov. Henry T. Clark, January 10, 1862, HTC.

23. Gov. Henry T. Clark to Gen. Henry A. Wise, January 20, 1862, HTC.

24. James G. Martin to Gen. R. C. Gatlin, February 23, 1862, Adjutant General's Letterbooks, AGD.

25. Archibald McLean to Gov. Henry T. Clark, February 21, 1862, HTC.

26. Col. George A. Cunningham to Gov. Henry T. Clark, April 21, 1862, HTC.

27. Gov. Henry T. Clark to Judah P. Benjamin, February 22, 1862, Governor's Letterbooks, 1861-1862, NCAH.

28. Nichols, *Confederate Engineers*, 27, 64-65.

29. John Tyler and Col. Hill Carter to LeRoy P. Walker, August 28, 1861, in *Freedom*, ed. Berlin et al., ser. I, vol. 1, 686-87.

30. Nathaniel F. Cabell to William D. Cabell, September 5, 1862, Papers of William Daniel Cabell and the Cabell, Ellet, Hunter, etc., Families, UVA.

31. John B. Gilliam to Gov. Henry T. Clark, November 4, 1861, HTC.

32. Gov. Henry T. Clark to John B. Gilliam, November 7, 1861, Governor's Letterbooks, 1861-1862, NCAH.

33. Frank Vaughan to Gov. Henry T. Clark, November 15, 1861, HTC.

34. John E. Thomas to James Maurice, November 20, 1861; John B. Fuller to James Maurice, December 24, 1861, VED.

35. James R. Taylor to James Maurice, March 25, 1862, VED.

36. Capt. Alfred L. Rives to Christopher Gilmer, March 31, 1862, LSEB. For additional communication with and identification of impressment agents from central Virginia, see Capt. Alfred L. Rives to Nathan Enrought, March 31, 1862; Capt. Alfred L. Rives to William Turnbull, May 21, 1862; and Capt. Alfred L. Rives to Gen. John B. Magruder, April 21, 1862, LSEB; as well as Brig. Gen. Silas Casey to Capt. C. C. Suydam, June 16, 1862, *OR*, ser. I, vol. 2, 1046.

37. Capt. Alfred L. Rives to Maj. A. F. Cone [Quartermaster's Department], March 27, 1862, LSEB.

38. Capt. Alfred L. Rives to Maj. Walter H. Stevens, June 18, 1862, LSEB.

39. Capt. Alfred L. Rives to Gen. Robert E. Lee, June 21, 1862, LSEB.

40. Capt. Alfred L. Rives to Gov. John Letcher, May 12, 1862; Capt. Alfred L. Rives to Maj. Walter H. Stevens, July 11, 1862, LSEB.

41. William Daniel Cabell Journal, September 3-5, 1862; Nathaniel F. Cabell to William D. Cabell, September 5, 1862, Papers of William Daniel Cabell and the Cabell, Ellet, Hunter, etc., Families, UVA.

42. Maj. Gen. D. H. Hill to Gen. R. H. Chilton, undated 1862, *OR*, ser. I, vol. 11, 939.

43. Edmondston, *Journal of a Secesh Lady*, 233.

44. Ibid., 236.

45. John Pool to Gov. Zebulon Baird Vance, September 18, 1862, *OR*, ser. I, vol. 18, 747.

46. Brig. Gen. David Clark to Gov. Henry T. Clark, August 13, 1862, HTC.

47. Gov. Henry T. Clark to Brig. Gen. David Clark, August 17, 1862, Governor's Letterbooks, 1861–1862, NCAH.

48. Ibid.

49. Mobley, *"War Governor of the South,"* 29–32; McKinney, *Zeb Vance*, 107.

50. "Col. Vance, the Governor Elect," *Raleigh North Carolina Standard*, August 20, 1862, p. 3, col. 2.

51. *Raleigh Weekly Register*, November 19, 1862, p. 1, col. 1.

52. Brig. Gen. William H. C. Whiting to Major Gen. G. W. Smith, November 14, 1862, Maj. Gen. W. H. C. Whiting Papers, 1861–1865, NARA, RG 109.

53. Sprunt, *Tales of the Cape Fear Blockade*, 5–29; Sprunt, *Chronicles of the Cape Fear River*, 379–93; Fonvielle, *Wilmington Campaign*, 1–91; Carr, *Gray Phantoms of the Cape Fear*, 43–65; Wise, *Lifeline of the Confederacy*, 124–43.

54. Brig. Gen. William H. C. Whiting to Maj. Gen. Gustavus W. Smith, December 2, 1862, Maj. Gen. W. H. C. Whiting Papers, 1861–1865, NARA, RG 109.

55. Brig. Gen. William H. C. Whiting to Gen. Samuel Cooper, January 15, 1863, ibid.

56. *Acts of the General Assembly of the State of Virginia, 1862*, 42.

57. "An Act to Facilitate the Construction of Public Defense," *Acts and Resolutions . . . of Florida*, 55–56.

58. "An Act to Provide for the Public Safety," *Acts of the . . . General Assembly of Alabama*, 38–41.

59. "An Act to Authorize the Governor of the State of Louisiana to Press into the Service of the State, Slaves and other Property for the Public Defences of the State during the Present War," *Acts Passed by the Twenty-Seventh Legislature of the State of Louisiana*, 18–20.

60. "An Act to Authorize the Impressment of Slaves and Other Personal Property for Military Purposes," *Journal of the House of Representatives of the State of Mississippi*, 40–41.

61. Nelson, "Confederate Slave Impressment Legislation," 394–98.

62. Resolutions of November 10, 1862, *Journal of the Senate of the State of Georgia*, 69.

63. Cimprich, in *Slavery's End in Tennessee*, describes impressment by Confederate officials, as well as frequent use of recaptured runaway slaves to build fortifications, but no attempts by state officials to legislate or participate in the practice (14–17).

64. Lt. Col. Jeremy F. Gilmer to George W. Randolph, October 8, 1862, LSEB.

65. Gov. John Letcher to Pres. Jefferson Davis, October 11, 1862, JLEP.

66. George W. Munford to J. Mayo, October 21, 1862, JLEP.

67. Capt. Alfred L. Rives to Col. Walter H. Stevens, October 8, 1862, LSEB.

68. David M. Hunter to Gov. John Letcher, October 22, 1862; B. B. Woodson to P. F. Howard, Acting Secretary of the Commonwealth, October 24, 1862, JLEP; *Lynchburg Daily Virginian*, October 31, 1862, p. 3, col. 1; *Richmond Daily Dispatch*, October 17, 1862, p. 1, col. 1.

69. Albemarle County Court Minute Books, 1859–1868, November 3, November 6, November 13, and November 20, 1862, LVA.

70. John J. Bowcock [Presiding Justice, Albemarle County Court] to Gov. John Letcher, November 20, 1862, JLEP.

71. Gov. John Letcher addendum on Col. George Munford to John J. Bowcock, November 2, 1862, JLEP.

72. Albemarle County Court Minute Books, 1859–1868, December 6, 1862, and February 2, 1863, LVA.

73. Deposition before Edward M. Clark, Notary Public, February 20, 1863, Papers of Jason B. Douglass, UVA.

74. Lt. John B. Stanard to Gov. John Letcher, November 21, 1862, JLEP; Col. Jeremy F. Gilmer to Maj. Gen. Gustavus W. Smith, November 20, 1862, LSEB.

75. John G. Powell to Gov. John Letcher, December 13, 1862; Lynch A. Currin [clerk, Pulaski County Court] to Gov. John Letcher, December 16, 1862; Edmund Waddell [clerk, Charles City County Court] to Gov. John Letcher, December 23, 1862, JLEP; *Staunton Spectator*, December 23, 1862, p. 2, col. 3.

76. R. O. Dowell [clerk, Hanover County Court] to Col. George Munford, December 9, 1862; C. Chapin [clerk, Rockbridge County Court] to Gov. John Letcher, December 9, 1862; F. Mauzy [clerk, Culpeper County Court] to Gov. John Letcher, December 16, 1862, JLEP. See also Lewis A. Boggs [Presiding Justice, Spotsylvania County Court] to Gov. John Letcher, December 17, 1862; S. W. Gambill [clerk, Rockingham County Court] to Gov. John Letcher, December 18, 1862; and M. Heterick [clerk, Rappahannock County Court] to Gov. John Letcher, December 23, 1862, JLEP.

77. Historical Census Browser, University of Virginia, Geospatial and Statistical Data Center (accessed March 13, 2005).

78. William D. Tollard [clerk, King William County Court] to Gov. John Letcher, January 15, 1863, JLEP.

79. Capt. Alfred L. Rives to Gov. John Letcher, January 20, 1863, JLEP.

80. Maj. Gen. Samuel Jones to Gen. Samuel Cooper, December 29, 1862, *OR*, ser. I, vol. 21, 1081; Col. Jeremy F. Gilmer to Benjamin Wysor, January 2, 1863, LSEB.

81. Col. Jeremy F. Gilmer to James A. Seddon, January 13, 1863, JLEP.

82. Col. George W. Munford to Col. Jeremy F. Gilmer, January 22, 1863, JLEP.

83. Capt. Alfred L. Rives to Col. George W. Munford, January 28, 1863, JLEP.

84. Brig. Gen. William H. C. Whiting to Maj. Gen. Gustavus W. Smith, November 26, 1862; Maj. Gen. Gustavus W. Smith to Gen. Robert E. Lee, November 26, 1862, *OR*, ser. I, vol. 18, 786–87. Union officers made similar assessments regarding Wilmington's defensive strength; see William A. Parker to Maj. Gen. J. G. Foster, December 8, 1862, ibid., 475.

85. Gen. Robert E. Lee to Gen. Samuel Cooper, December 13, 1862, ibid., vol. 21, 1061.

86. "Wilmington," *Salisbury Carolina Watchman*, December 8, 1862, p. 1, col. 5.

87. *Governor's Message*, November 17, 1862, 3.

88. "Gov. Vance's Message—The Legislature &c," *Salisbury Carolina Watchman*, November 24, 1862, p. 2, col. 4; "Governor's Message," *Raleigh North Carolina Standard*, November 26, 1862, p. 1, col. 1.

89. *Journal of the House of Commons of North-Carolina, at its Session 1862-63*, 17; *Journal of the Senate of the General Assembly of the State of North-Carolina, at its First Session, 1862*, 28, 165.

90. "An Act to Authorize the Governor to Employ Slave Labor in Erecting Fortifications and Other Works," *Public Laws of the State of North-Carolina, 1862-1863*, 24-25; J. G. Martin to Cols. Lucas, Morrissey, Cobb, Stephens, Pemberton, and McRay, December 11, 1862, Militia Letterbook, 1862-1864, AGD.

91. "An Act to Authorize the Governor to Employ Slave Labor in Erecting Fortifications and Other Works," *Public Laws*, 24-25; "An Act to Amend the 9th and 12th Sections of Chapter 101 of the Revised Code," ibid., 25; "Resolutions to Employ Free Persons of Color on Fortifications," ibid., 48-49.

92. Brig. Gen. William H. C. Whiting to Col. W. M. McRae, December 12, 1862, Letters Sent, Gen. W. H. C. Whiting's Command, 1862-1864, NARA, RG 109; James G. Martin to Gen. David Clark, January 27, 1863; James G. Martin to Col. Thomas W. Rooker, January 29, 1863; James G. Martin to Capt. Joseph Blake, January 15, 1863; James G. Martin to Lt. E. E. Mason, January 22, 1863, Militia Letterbook, 1862-1864, AGD.

93. Brig. Gen. William H. C. Whiting to Gov. Zebulon Baird Vance, March 2, 1863, Governor's Letterbooks, 1862-1865, NCAH.

94. "Slave Labor on Fortifications," *Raleigh North Carolina Standard*, March 25, 1863, p. 1, col. 3; Adjutant General's Office, Special Orders Nos. 37 and 46, March 1863; Daniel G. Fowle to Col. Joseph Thompson, April 8, 1863, Militia Letterbook, 1862-1864, AGD.

95. "Slave Labor on Fortifications," *Raleigh North Carolina Standard*, March 25, 1863, p. 1, col. 3.

CHAPTER TWO

1. Interview with Rev. Ishrael Massie in *Weevils in the Wheat*, ed. Perdue, Barden, and Phillips, 210-11.

2. *Richmond Examiner*, January 12, 1863, p. 1, col. 1; William T. Macklin to Hon. Robert Whitfield, December 4, 1864, CSW; I. Irvin to Gov. Zebulon Baird Vance, May 6, 1864, ZBV.

3. Interviews with William I. Johnson Jr. and Robert Williams in *Weevils in the Wheat*, ed. Perdue, Barden, and Phillips, 167, 325; interview with George Rogers in *American Slave*, ed. Rawick, 15:223; interview with Cornelius Garner in *Weevils in the Wheat*, 101.

4. Mahan, *Treatise on Field Fortification*, 32-35.

5. According to modern civil engineers, one cubic foot of soil weighs from 100 to 125 pounds. Taking the lower figure, a cubic yard of soil would weigh about 2,700 pounds; six cubic yards of soil would therefore weigh 16,200 pounds, or 8.1 tons.

6. Fred to Ma, August 6, 1861, *Green Mount*, ed. Fleet and Fuller, 70.

7. Memorandum, Capt. Alfred L. Rives, May 8, 1862; Capt. Alfred L. Rives to John Hagan, May 12, 1862; Capt. Alfred L. Rives to John Hagan, May 15, 1862; Capt. Alfred L. Rives to John B. Stanard, May 21, 1862; Capt. Alfred L. Rives to John Hagan, May

24, 1862; Capt. Alfred L. Rives to Capt. John J. Clarke, May 29, 1862; memoranda written by Capt. Alfred L. Rives, June 25-26, 1862; Lt. Col. Alfred L. Rives to Maj. Gen. Jeremy F. Gilmer, October 29, 1863, LSEB; "The Slaves on the Works," *Lexington Gazette*, October 28, 1863, p. 2, col. 2; Lieutenant Oulds, in charge of Weldon Defenses, March 4, 1865, Miscellaneous Engineer Records, Reports of Operations, NARA, RG 109.

8. Capt. Alfred L. Rives to John Hagan, July 8, 1862, LSEB.

9. Claim of Benjamin Hunter, testimony of Thomas R. Peers, June 16, 1864, BSC 177; *Richmond Examiner*, January 9, 1862, p. 2, col. 5; claim of Benjamin E. Pope, testimony of Charles E. Bryant, May 16, 1864, BSC 243.

10. Capt. Alfred L. Rives to Capt. John J. Clarke, July 7, 1862, LSEB; Col. Joseph Thompson to Gov. Zebulon Vance, March 12, 1863, ZBV; R. F. Clark [clerk, Mecklenburg County Court] to Gov. William Smith, April 18, 1864; Lt. William C. Hauser to Col. Walter H. Stevens, April 21, 1864, WSEP.

11. See, for example, reference to communications with Assistant Quartermaster General in Capt. Alfred L. Rives to Thomas J. Spencer [Justice of the Peace, Charlotte County], June 27, 1862, LSEB.

12. Capt. Alfred L. Rives to Col. Larkin Smith, August 1, 1862, LSEB; claim of Benjamin E. Pope, testimony of Charles E. Bryant, May 29, 1863, BSC 244; claim of William H. Twyman, testimony of B. J. B. Ford, July 19, 1864, BSC 340.

13. Claim of Rebecca Farmer, testimony of McCajah W. Barbour, May 4, 1864, BSC 162-63; claim of Daniel B. Steger, testimony of Daniel B. Steger, April 28, 1864, BSC 217; "The Rockbridge Negroes on the Fortifications," *Lexington Gazette*, February 19, 1863, p. 2, col. 2.

14. "Augusta Slaves on Fortifications," *Staunton Spectator*, January 20, 1863, p. 2, col. 2; "The Rockbridge Negroes on the Fortifications," *Lexington Gazette*, February 19, 1863, p. 2, col. 2; "The Slaves on the Works," *Lexington Gazette*, October 28, 1863, p. 2, col. 2; *Lynchburg Daily Virginian*, February 4, 1865, p. 2, col. 1.

15. Claim of John C. Hamner, testimony of William A. Morgan, February 24, 1863, BSC 224; "Conscript Negroes," *Lexington Gazette*, February 12, 1863, p. 2, col. 2.

16. David S. Bell to Gov. John Letcher, January 12, 1863, JLEP; A. W. Johnston to Gov. Zebulon Baird Vance, April 25, 1864; Richard Y. Williams to Gov. Zebulon Baird Vance, May 10, 1864; Vance's endorsement on telegram, December 18, 1863, ZBV.

17. Col. Jeremy F. Gilmer to Gov. John Letcher, January 12, 1863, JLEP; Col. Jeremy F. Gilmer, endorsement on letter of Maj. S. Bassett French to Commissary General, December 12, 1862; Col. Jeremy F. Gilmer to Maj. William P. Smith, January 13, 1863, LSEB.

18. Col. Jeremy F. Gilmer to Maj. Gen. D. H. Hill, June 22, 1863; Lt. Col. Alfred L. Rives to Col. Walter H. Stevens, October 12, 1863; Lt. Col. Alfred L. Rives to Maj. John A. Williams, March 4, 1864; Maj. Gen. Jeremy F. Gilmer, endorsements on letters from Thomas N. Coleman and Maj. William Bassinger, August 4, 1864, and from E. G. Hudgers, August 8, 1864; Maj. Gen. Jeremy F. Gilmer to Capt. W. G. Bender, August 13, 1864, LSEB.

19. Maj. Gen. William H. C. Whiting to James A. Seddon, November 3, 1863, CSW.

20. Ibid.; Col. R. E. Whithers to John C. Breckinridge, March 29, 1865, CSW; Col. J. D. Dillard to Gov. Zebulon Vance, May 4, 1864, ZBV.

21. John B. Spiece to Attorney Gen. Wade Keyes, December 4, 1861, in *Freedom*, ed. Berlin et al., ser. I, vol. 1, 783.

22. Capt. Alfred L. Rives to Capt. Thomas M. R. Talcott, December 13, 1861, LSEB; John R. Pender to Capt. Thomas M. R. Talcott, August 14, 1861; James B. Southall to Capt. Thomas M. R. Talcott, August 18, 1861; W. D. Southall to Capt. Thomas M. R. Talcott, August 14, 1861, Correspondence of Thomas Mann Talcott, 1861-1915, Talcott Family Papers, VHS.

23. Requisitions for Medicinal and Hospital Supplies for Negroes employed on the Manchester line of fortifications near Richmond, Va., under Capt. Coleman of the Engineer Corps CSA, February 18, 1863, John M. Sawing, Assistant Surgeon; Requisitions for Medicinal and Hospital Supplies, December 17, 1862, January 6, 1863, January 26, 1863, March 10, 1863, and April 13, 1863, N. B. Tuten, Acting Assistant Surgeon, Miscellaneous Medical Records, NARA, RG 109; Cunningham, *Doctors in Gray*, 107.

24. Pharoah Richardson to Gov. Zebulon Baird Vance, January 19, 1863; N. P. Wilkins to Gov. Zebulon Baird Vance, December 5, 1863, ZBV.

25. Claim of James A. Watson, testimony of James Lysle, M.D., April 23, 1864, BSC [illeg.]; claim of Daniel Coleman, testimony of Daniel Coleman, August 20, 1863, BSC [illeg.]; claim of Jeremiah A. Earley, testimony of Jeremiah A. Earley, June 3, 1863, BSC 179.

26. Claim of Jeremiah A. Earley, testimony of Richard W. Shepperd, April 25, 1863; claim of Jeremiah A. Earley, accompanying note from H. B. Magruder, BSC 180-81.

27. Claim of D. O. Shackleford, testimony of R. W. Shepherd, date unknown, BSC [illeg.]; claim of W. C. W. Crawley, testimony of Benjamin F. Terry, M.D., February 10, 1863, BSC 198.

28. Claim of John C. Hamner, testimony of W. A. Morgan, February 24, 1863, BSC 224; claim of G. Thurmond, testimony of G. Thurmond, January 12, 1863; claim of G. Thurmond, testimony of Henry A. Alexander and Daniel R. Booth, January 12, 1863, BSC [illeg.].

29. W. S. Harris et al. to Gov. Zebulon Baird Vance, October 22, 1864, ZBV; R. C. Gatlin to Col. W. B. Richardson, October 24, 1864, Militia Letterbook, 1864-1865, AGD.

30. John B. Spiece to Attorney Gen. Wade Keyes, December 4, 1861, in *Freedom*, ser. I, vol. 1, 783; Col. Jeremy F. Gilmer to F. F. Treadway, December 18, 1862; Col. Jeremy F. Gilmer to Joseph Cloyd, December 29, 1862; Col. Jeremy F. Gilmer to Richard Epes, January 6, 1863; Col. Jeremy F. Gilmer to Gov. John Letcher, January 6, 1863; Col. Jeremy F. Gilmer to Thaddeus N. Campbell, January 9, 1863, LSEB.

31. Claim of Thomas F. Perkins, testimony of J. W. Bronaugh, M.D., January 13, 1864, BSC 160.

32. The extant records of the Board of Slave Claims consist of a single volume into which the clerks copied testimony from the successful claims. Thus, there is no way to determine why some claims were considered more valid than others, since we do not have testimony from the unsuccessful claims. It seems, from the volume, that 20-25 percent of claimants received compensation and that the board considered the cases of at least 600 claimants, mostly from Virginia.

33. Surgeon William A. Carrington, Inspector of Hospitals, to Surgeon Thomas H. Williams, Medical Director, January 9, 1863, NARA, RG 109, ch. 6, vol. 416, 27-28.

34. Cunningham, *Doctors in Gray*, reports that "each general hospital was allowed . . . one medical officer or contract physician to every seventy or eighty patients," but shortages in physicians made it difficult to maintain this ratio (75).

35. Requisitions for Medicinal and Hospital Supplies, December 10, 1862, January 5, 1863, January 13, 1863, and January 27, 1863, Richard S. Vest, Surgeon in charge, Engineer Hospital, approved W. G. Turpin, Lt. Eng. in charge, Miscellaneous Medical Records, NARA, RG 109.

36. Record of Reports Received, Inspector of Hospitals, Richmond, 1863-1864, NARA, RG 109, ch. 6, vol. 644, 133-34: "Negroe Hospital" at Smithville, N.C., Robert K. Carter, surgeon, submitted quarterly reports on April 12, 1864, and July 18, 1864; "Negroe Hospital" at Wilmington, N.C., Alexander R. Medway, assistant surgeon, submitted a quarterly report on April 12, 1864.

37. *Richmond Examiner*, December 10, 1862, p. 1, col. 4.

38. Ibid., December 11, 1862, p. 1, col. 4-5.

39. Surgeon William A. Carrington, Inspector of Hospitals, to Surgeon Thomas H. Williams, Medical Director, January 9, 1863, NARA, RG 109, ch. 6, vol. 416, 28-31.

40. Richard S. Vest to Capt. William G. Turpin, December 16, 1864, CSW; Green, *Chimborazo*, ix.

41. Claim of James H. Evans, April 27, 1864, BSC 201-3; claim of Thomas A. Osborne, April 27, 1864, BSC 204.

42. George K. Taylor [clerk, Caroline County Court], December 28, 1864, WSEP.

43. George T. Peers [clerk, Appomattox County Court] to Gov. William Smith, January 20, 1865, VED.

44. Wyatt S. Beasley [clerk, Greene County Court] to Gov. William Smith, January 9, 1865; R. A. Donwell [clerk, Hanover County Court] to Gov. William Smith, February 3, 1865, VED.

45. Mohr, *On the Threshold of Freedom*, explores the breakdown of discipline in both urban and rural settings, highlighting the greatly reduced presence of white men, the possibility of escape to the Union lines, and the deterioration of paternalism as masters struggled to provide food and supplies as key elements in undermining wartime slavery. Similar arguments appear in L. Morgan, *Emancipation in Virginia's Tobacco Belt*; Takagi, *"Rearing Wolves"*; Kerr-Ritchie, *Freedpeople in the Tobacco South*; and Cimprich, *Slavery's End in Tennessee*. Hahn characterizes wartime resistance as a form of "slaves' politics" that masters learned to take seriously (*Nation under Our Feet*); decades earlier, in *Black Reconstruction in America*, DuBois called this phenomenon "the great struggle."

46. This argument, often called the "self-emancipation thesis" as a kind of shorthand, appeared in the 1930s in the work of DuBois (*Black Reconstruction in America*) and Wiley (*Southern Negroes*) and then made its reappearance in the 1980s among scholars associated with the Freedmen and Southern Society Project (Berlin, Fields, Miller, and Reidy, *Slaves No More*). It is now part of the mainstream discussion of emancipation, although still the subject of conflict. Runaway slaves, Union soldiers, government officials, and abolitionists all contributed to the destruction of slavery, and each scholar who studies emancipation has weighted those historical actors' contributions differently. Many note that self-emancipation only really applied to areas where

the Union army had significant and long-term influence (see, for example, Kaye, *Joining Places*, 191–207). Slaves who lived hundreds of miles from Union lines were unlikely to escape, although (as discussed above) they definitely found ways to assert their autonomy without running away.

47. Brasher, *Peninsula Campaign*, reconstructs the decision to help the Union army from the slaves' point of view, demonstrating that it was not exactly a foregone conclusion. Downs, *Sick from Freedom*, explores the hardships that runaway slaves endured in the contraband camps and postwar freedom towns where epidemics raged. Glymph's forthcoming work details the heartbreaking losses that slaves following Union armies, particularly women and children, suffered during the war. In addition, some historians have looked more closely at those left out of the self-emancipation process. Fields, *Slavery and Freedom on the Middle Ground*, argues that slavery in Maryland became harsher and more firmly entrenched during the war as planters and politicians fought to avert a transition to freedom. Schwalm's *Hard Fight for We* suggests as men ran away, the women and children left behind suffered greater hardships, heavier workloads, and the wrath of their masters and mistresses.

48. McCurry criticizes historians in *Confederate Reckoning* for focusing exclusively on how runaway slaves shaped U.S. policy instead of also considering their impact on Confederate policy. Reidy, *From Slavery to Agrarian Capitalism*, suggests that Confederate impressment and hiring policies had as much impact on self-emancipation as U.S. responses to runaway slaves.

49. Interview with Rev. Ishrael Massie in *Weevils in the Wheat*, ed. Perdue, Barden, and Phillips, 211.

50. Interview with George Rogers in *American Slave*, ed. Rawick, 15:224.

51. Claim of Lavinia Shepherd, testimony of P. J. Carter, May 7, 1864, BSC 240.

52. T. Michaux et al. to Gov. John Letcher, October 17, 1863, JLEP.

53. B. B. Walker to Gov. Zebulon Baird Vance, December 21, 1864, ZBV.

54. Claim of Warren White, Norfolk County, Virginia, Allowed Case Files of the Southern Claims Commission, 1871–1879, National Archives and Records Administration II, College Park, Md.

55. Gould, *Diary of a Contraband*, 15–16.

56. *Richmond Daily Dispatch*, October 10, 1862, p. 4, col. 6.

57. "Escape of 'Contrabands'—Their Estimate of Our Strength in the Peninsula," *Richmond Daily Dispatch*, January 10, 1862, p. 2, col. 7.

58. Lt. W. T. Fentress to Appomattox County Enrolling Officer, December 21, 1864, Letters to Thomas S. Bocock, 1857–1864, Papers of Bocock Family, UVA.

59. J. P. Dillard to Gov. Zebulon Baird Vance, May 4, 1864, ZBV.

60. Payroll of Laborers on the Entrenchments at Raleigh, 1864, AGD.

61. R. C. Gatlin to Col. W. H. Knight, November 29, 1864, Militia Letterbook, 1864–1865, AGD. See also R. C. Gatlin to Eugene Grissom, January 5, 1865, ibid.

62. Claim of William and Robert Elliot, Norfolk County, Virginia, Allowed Case Files of the Southern Claims Commission, 1871–1879; claim of Joseph Atkins, Henrico County, Virginia, Disallowed Case Files of the Southern Claims Commission, 1871–1879, National Archives and Records Administration II, College Park, Md.

63. J. R. Bryan to Andrew Grinnan, July 21, 1863, Papers of the Grinnan Family, UVA.

64. Claims of Nicholas Brown, William S. Bryant, Lewis Dunn, Daniel Manuel, and Abel Payne, Cumberland County, North Carolina, Allowed Case Files of the Southern Claims Commission, National Archives and Records Administration II, College Park, Md.

65. Claim of James S. Dean, Fauquier County, Virginia, Disallowed Case Files of the Southern Claims Commission, National Archives and Records Administration II, College Park, Md.

66. William Yager et al. to Gov. William Smith, November 2, 1864, WSEP. See also John G. Kreger [clerk, Washington County Court] to Gov. John Letcher, October 26, 1863, JLEP; John R. Chambliss and Thomas H. Wrenhard to Pres. Jefferson Davis, January 27, 1863, Confederate States of America Miscellaneous Papers, VHS; Willoughby Newton to James A. Seddon, November 30, 1864, CSW; and Bailey, *Henrico Home Front*, 222–23.

67. Edmondston, February 19, 1865, *Journal of a Secesh Lady*, 668–69.

68. R. C. Gatlin to Col. D. B. Bell, February 27, 1865, Militia Letterbook, 1864–1865, AGD.

69. McCurry makes collusion between runaway slaves and masters objecting to impressment the centerpiece of the second half of *Confederate Reckoning*. "It was as much the refusal of slaves to act as property as the refusal of planters to yield that property up that thwarted Confederate attempts to make impressment work," she argues, necessitating waves of ineffective legislation at the state and national levels (281). Collusion was certainly possible, since both parties had common goals. Yet McCurry probably overestimates the importance and effectiveness of runaway slaves in the hierarchy of reasons planters gave for opposing impressment—it was one of many arguments they listed, often in rapid succession in a "throw everything at the wall and see what sticks" method of protest, and none of the others seem similarly ripe for collusion with the slaves. The most common examples of collusion were the slaveholders who sent slaves to the fortifications but then did not force their return if they ran away and came home early. This form of collusion absolutely undermined the effectiveness of slave impressment but was rarely the subject of protest letters from slaveholders to government officials.

70. James A. Seddon, endorsement on John R. Chambliss and Thomas H. Wrenhard to Pres. Jefferson Davis, January 27, 1863, Confederate States of America Miscellaneous Papers, VHS.

71. Jacob C. Bamhardt to Gov. Zebulon Baird Vance, May 7, 1864, ZBV; *Richmond Examiner*, January 12, 1863, p. 1, col. 1.

72. Wiley, in *Southern Negroes*, discusses largely unsuccessful wartime reform movements to recognize slave marriages, prevent the separation of mothers and young children, admit slave testimony in court, and allow slave literacy and preaching (166–72). Mohr's *On the Threshold of Freedom* connects wartime reform to antebellum movements and also places greater emphasis on the idea that reforming slavery would bring the Confederacy the divine favor it needed to win the war (235–71).

CHAPTER THREE

1. Diary of Francis McFarland, December 29–30, 1862, and January 2, 1863, Papers of Francis McFarland, UVA.

2. Jedediah Hotchkiss to Sara A. Hotchkiss, January 2, 1863, Hotchkiss Family Papers, *Valley of the Shadow: Two Communities in the American Civil War*, Personal Papers (accessed March 30, 2003).

3. John Herbert Claiborne to wife, December 21, 1864, Letters of John Herbert Claiborne, 1864–1865, UVA.

4. *Lynchburg Daily Republican*, January 8, 1865, p. 1, col. 3.

5. *Richmond Examiner*, January 2, 1865, p. 1, col. 4.

6. *Staunton Republican Vindicator*, March 27, 1863, 1–2.

7. *Lexington Gazette*, November 20, 1862, p. 2, col. 1.

8. General Assembly Joint Resolution, adopted January 27, 1863, JLEP.

9. Letcher's notation on William H. Trucks to Gov. John Letcher, February 11, 1863, JLEP; *Staunton Spectator*, November 3, 1863, p. 2, col. 3.

10. Petition from Rockingham County to the General Assembly of the State of Virginia, LVA, Legislative Petitions, Rockingham County, 1839–1863.

11. Col. Jeremy F. Gilmer to James A. Seddon, endorsement on petition, March 21, 1863, LSEB.

12. Col. S. Bassett French to Gov. John Letcher, March 19, 1863, JLEP.

13. Richard H. Smith to Gov. William Smith, October 13, 1864, WSEP.

14. James A. Seddon to Col. Jeremy F. Gilmer, endorsement on petition, March 30, 1863, LSEB.

15. Col. Jeremy F. Gilmer to James A. Seddon, March 31, 1863, LSEB.

16. Col. Jeremy F. Gilmer to Maj. Gen. D. H. Hill, June 27, 1863, LSEB.

17. Brewer, *Confederate Negro*, describes a call for 1,029 free blacks in March 1863 (145). Gilmer, Seddon, and Letcher also approved the impressment of Richmond's free blacks in July 1863 for immediate repairs to the Richmond defenses near Mechanicsville Road. (See Gilmer's endorsement on letter from Col. Walter H. Stevens, July 4, 1863, LSEB.)

18. Brig. Gen. William H. C. Whiting to Gov. Zebulon Baird Vance, February 20, 1863, Letters Sent, Gen. W. H. C. Whiting's Command, 1862–1864, NARA, RG 109.

19. Special Orders Nos. 37, 46, and 50, AGD.

20. Daniel G. Fowle to Col. William E. Anderson, March 17, 1863, Militia Letterbook, 1862–1864, AGD.

21. G. W. Goldston to Gov. Zebulon Baird Vance, April 15, 1863, ZBV.

22. *Lynchburg Daily Virginian*, October 30, 1862, p. 3, col. 1.

23. W. M. Scott [clerk, Alleghany County Court] to Gov. John Letcher, October 19, 1863, JLEP. Officials of the Floyd County Court made the same argument to Governor Smith in January 1865; see Henry Jenkins [Presiding Justice, Floyd County Court] to Gov. William Smith, January 7, 1865, WSEP.

24. Maj. Gen. William H. C. Whiting to Gen. Samuel Cooper, October 4, 1863, *OR*, ser. I, vol. 29, part 2, 770.

25. Gov. Zebulon Baird Vance to Maj. Gen. William H. C. Whiting, May 26, 1863, Governor's Letterbooks, 1862–1865, NCAH.

26. Maj. Gen. William H. C. Whiting to Governor Zebulon Baird Vance, May 28, 1863, ibid.

27. A. M. Fuller to Gov. Zebulon Baird Vance, June 15, 1863, ZBV.

28. William A. Lash to Gov. Zebulon Baird Vance, June 19, 1863, ZBV.

29. Vance's notation on Jordan Lyons to Gov. Zebulon Baird Vance, June 5, 1863, ZBV.

30. Maj. Gen. William H. C. Whiting to James A. Seddon, July 24, 1863, Letters Sent, Gen. W. H. C. Whiting's Command, 1862-1864, NARA, RG 109.

31. Jones, *Rebel War Clerk's Diary*, 247, July 26, 1863.

32. Stevenson talks about the unbalanced age and sex ratio of the slave communities on Virginia's Piedmont plantations when discussing the high prevalence of "broad marriages," noting the likelihood of being enslaved on a farm with a suitable marriage partner was relatively low unless one's master held at least twenty slaves (*Life in Black and White*). The North Carolina and Virginia slaveholders in my own sample fit within this pattern. In addition, among the bigger planters, between 25 and 40 percent of their slaves were children under the age of ten. Boys between the ages of twelve and eighteen usually brought the highest prices in the long-distance slave trade. For a discussion of how the local and long-distance slave trades shaped the Upper South, see Tadman, *Speculators and Slaves*.

33. Samuel Saunders to Gov. William Smith, February 17, 1864, WSEP.

34. William H. Trucks [clerk, Smyth County Court] to Gov. John Letcher, February 11, 1863, JLEP.

35. K. Raynor to Gov. Zebulon Baird Vance, July 16, 1863, ZBV.

36. Joseph Anderson was called on several times to send slaves from the Tredegar Iron Works to work on the fortifications, and he always complied, although when Richmond officials listed certain highly skilled slaves on their impressment rolls, he sought (and received) permission to send different men in their places. (See, for example, List of Negroes Sent to Work on Fortifications at Drewry's Bluff, October 7, 1864, Inspection of Ordnance and Use of Slaves, 1845-1864, Tredegar Iron Works, Records, 1801-1957, LVA.)

37. D. C. Bowman to Charles G. Talcott, October 19, 1862, JLEP.

38. Wilson Hix to Gov. John Letcher, November 3, 1862, JLEP.

39. Charles Scott to Gov. John Letcher, December 30, 1862, JLEP.

40. J. R. Anderson to Gov. John Letcher, July 1, 1863, JLEP.

41. L. B. Wetherall to Gov. John Letcher, November 8, 1862, and George W. Randolph to L. B. Wetherall, November 5, 1862, JLEP.

42. F. M. Thacker to Gov. John Letcher, November 1, 1862, and Bilhartz, Hall, & Co. to Gov. John Letcher, November 14, 1862, JLEP.

43. Col. Jeremy F. Gilmer to F. R. Deane, November 4, 1862, LSEB.

44. James G. Martin to Lt. Col. T. J. Gregory, February 3, 1863; John C. Winder to Col. J. S. Annis, February 14, 1863; R. C. Gatlin to Col. A. J. Elliot, November 2, 1863, AGD.

45. Col. Walter H. Stevens, endorsement on Col. Jeremy F. Gilmer to Charles G. Talcott, February 19, 1863, JLEP.

46. Majewski has analyzed the growth of a proslavery Confederate socialism, with particular attention to railroad subsidies and policies designed to support the Quartermaster's Department and Ordnance Bureau, in *Modernizing a Slave Economy*, especially 146-51.

47. John H. Hughson to Gov. John Letcher, October 1, 1863, JLEP.

48. Ben Bailey to Gov. Zebulon Baird Vance, May 28, 1863, ZBV.

49. Elias Bryan et al. to Gov. Zebulon Baird Vance, June 3, 1863; John H. Dillard to Gov. Zebulon Baird Vance, June 8, 1863, ZBV.

50. "Slave Labor on Fortifications," *Raleigh North Carolina Standard*, March 25, 1863, p. 1, col. 3.

51. Barton argues this convincingly in "'Good Cooks and Washers.'"

52. William D. Cabell Journal, December 1, 1864, Papers of William Daniel Cabell and the Cabell, Ellet, Hunter, etc., Families, UVA.

53. Diary of Francis McFarland, January 12–16 and 23, February 16, July 15, and November 30, 1863, Papers of Francis McFarland, UVA.

54. F. E. Shober to Gov. Zebulon Baird Vance, June 12, 1863, ZBV.

55. Margaret Ott to Enos Ott, December 6, 1864, Enos Ott Papers, *Valley of the Shadow: Two Communities in the American Civil War*, Personal Papers (accessed August 28, 2012).

56. W. Branch to Gov. John Letcher, December 10, 1862, JLEP.

57. R. V. Barksdale, endorsement on Judith C. Marr to Gov. William Smith, March 30, 1864, WSEP.

58. S. W. P. Powell to Gov. William Smith, April 21, 1864, WSEP.

59. Edith S. Hobson to Hon. John Goode Jr., February 4, 1865; W. H. DeWitt and R. A. Hale, endorsements on Hobson to Goode; J. F. Spinner to Hon. John Goode Jr., February 4, 1865; J. E. Sanderson to Hon. John Goode Jr., February 4, 1865, WSEP.

60. Lucy R. Jeter to James F. Johnson, February 4, 1865, WSEP.

61. James F. Johnson to Robert Garlick Hill Kean, February 7, 1865, CSW.

62. In *Confederate Reckoning*, McCurry presents female petitioners in two broad categories: planter women, who defined themselves as "ladies," and poor women, who embraced the idiom of "soldiers' wives." Indeed, she suggests that to slaveholding women, "soldiers' wives were the other—those 'Poor Soldiers' Wives' they claimed their overseers would charitably assist" (148). Elite women's approach to protesting impressment and conscription actually bore an interesting resemblance to that of elite and middling men, suggesting that patterns of protest may have had more to do with class than with gender. The "ladies" McCurry describes sought exemptions or details for their overseers and/or slaves who, to sweeten the deal, could also assist the less fortunate soldiers' wives in their area. Similarly, McCurry notes, "by late 1862, men seeking favors from the government knew to cite the public good and not just their own private interest" (138).

63. Petition from seven men in Franklin County to Gov. William Smith, February 18, 1864, WSEP.

64. Petition from seventeen men in Lunenburg County to Gov. William Smith, March 5, 1864, WSEP.

65. Lunenburg County resident G. T. Crutcher forwarded to the governor a list of neighbors who supported his request, but he wrote the petition himself, focusing on the help his slave could render him in planting his crop. G. T. Crutcher to Gov. William Smith, April 6, 1864, WSEP.

66. Judith C. Marr to Gov. William Smith, March 30, 1864, WSEP.

67. S. W. P. Powell to Gov. William Smith, April 21, 1864, WSEP.

68. Edith S. Hobson to Hon. John Goode Jr., February 4, 1865; J. F. Spinner to Hon. John Goode Jr., February 4, 1865, WSEP.

69. R. V. Barksdale, endorsement on Judith C. Marr to Gov. William Smith, March 30, 1864, WSEP.

70. Maria L. Bagby to Gov. William Smith, April 18, 1864, WSEP; Nancy A. Webster to Gov. Zebulon Baird Vance, n.d., ZBV; D. A. Puryear to Gov. William Smith, March 6, 1865, WSEP.

71. Irvine, *Diary of Elizabeth Ellis Robeson*; U.S. Bureau of the Census, *Eighth Census of the United States, 1860*, Slave Rolls, Bladen County, North Carolina.

72. Mary Bell to Alfred W. Bell, July 8, 1864, in Yearns and Barrett, *North Carolina Civil War Documentary*, 268.

73. Irvine, *Diary of Elizabeth Ellis Robeson*, 141.

74. M. A. Zimmerman to J. C. Zimmerman, October 19, 1862, in Yearns and Barrett, *North Carolina Civil War Documentary*, 266.

75. Caroline S. Alligood to husband, December 30, 1863, in ibid., 267.

76. Bynum, *Unruly Women*, 47–49, 55–56.

77. For example, see the *Richmond Sentinel*, December 31, 1863, p. 2, col. 2.

78. McCurry explores the connection between women's farmwork and class status, as well as the fact that white southerners were "unwilling to acknowledge" that married white women, even some slaveholders, routinely did farmwork. See *Masters of Small Worlds*, 78. Delfino further notes that while ignoring women's farmwork was a by-product of the Cult of Domesticity and thus a national problem in the mid-nineteenth century, the "close identification of field work with slavery made white women's farm work even more invisible" in slave states than in the free states. See "Invisible Woman," 285–86.

79. Sarah W. Cocke to Gov. John Letcher, October 28, 1862, JLEP.

80. Several scholars have noted the centrality of enslaved women's work to crop production on most plantations and large farms, including Ramey, *"Swing the Sickle"*; J. Morgan, *Laboring Women*; and Schwalm, *Hard Fight for We*. Ramey in particular argues that because most craft and trade occupations were open only to men, slave women bore primary responsibility for daily fieldwork and were highly productive and effective in agricultural labor (14–15).

81. Interview with Fannie Moore in *American Slave*, ed. Rawick, 15:129.

82. Interview with Charity McAllister in ibid., 15:62; interview with Essex Henry in ibid., 14:394.

83. Interview with Henrietta McCullers in ibid., 15:74.

84. For example, see James P. Sims to Gov. John Letcher, September 12, 1863, JLEP.

85. See transcripts of John C. Bectom, Charlie Crump, Lila Nichols, and Plaz Williams in *American Slave*, ed. Rawick, 14:91–98, 14:212–15, 15:147–50, 15:406–9.

86. Interview with Chana Littlejohn in ibid., 15:57.

87. John H. Hughson to Gov. John Letcher, October 1, 1863, JLEP.

88. Delfino discusses women's industrial work in the Upper South, and while mine owners and iron manufacturers did routinely hire female slaves for industrial tasks, they generally accounted for a small percentage of the total number of workers in

each establishment. Certainly, far more male slaves had experience performing industrial work in Virginia and North Carolina by the start of the Civil War. See "Invisible Woman."

89. J. W. Thompson [clerk, Tazewell County Court] to Gov. John Letcher, February 12, 1863, JLEP.

90. William H. Trucks [clerk, Smyth County Court] to Gov. John Letcher, February 11, 1863, JLEP.

91. Draft exemptions, for example, became much harder to get after the revised conscription law of May 1863 limited them to men whose farms primarily produced grain crops for sale to either the government or local families at below-market rates. Blair, *Virginia's Private War*, 83.

92. R. A. Jenkins to Gov. Zebulon Baird Vance, May 18, 1864, ZBV.

93. For a succinct overview of impressment and tax-in-kind policies, see Thomas, *Confederacy as a Revolutionary Experience*, 65–67.

94. Ellis Marlowe, M.D., to Gov. Zebulon Baird Vance, October 22, 1863, ZBV.

95. William A. Burnett [clerk, Augusta County Court] to Gov. John Letcher, October 29, 1863, JLEP.

96. Col. Jeremy F. Gilmer to James A. Seddon, February 9, 1863, LSEB.

97. Capt. Isaac W. Smith to Col. Walter H. Stevens, June 28, 1864, LSEB.

98. Diary of Francis McFarland, December 31, 1863; January 6–7 and 12, 1864, Papers of Francis McFarland, UVA.

CHAPTER FOUR

1. "A Friend of Justice" to Gov. William Smith, received February 23, 1864, WSEP.

2. Ibid.

3. "An Act to Authorize and Regulate the Impressment of Private Property for the Use of the Army and other Military Purposes," section 9, March 26, 1863, *Journals of the Congress of the Confederate States of America* 6:246–49.

4. Travis H. Epes [clerk, Nottoway County Court] to Gov. John Letcher, December 11, 1862, JLEP.

5. Thomas Bragg to Judah P. Benjamin, November 25, 1861, *Opinions of the Confederate Attorneys General*, 54–55.

6. Thomas Hill Watts to George W. Randolph, October 17, 1862, ibid., 160.

7. Thomas Hill Watts to Pres. Jefferson Davis, March 14, 1863, ibid., 247.

8. Nelson, "Confederate Slave Impressment Legislation," 394–99.

9. John A. Campbell to Col. Jeremy F. Gilmer, July 16, 1863; Lt. Col. Alfred L. Rives to Col. Walter H. Stevens, August 20, 1863; Col. Walter H. Stevens to Lt. John B. Stanard, August 20, 1863, Letters Received by the Confederate Adjutant and Inspector General, 1861–1865, NARA, RG 109.

10. Lt. John B. Stanard to Col. Walter H. Stevens, August 24, 1863, Letters Received by the Confederate Adjutant and Inspector General, 1861–1865, NARA, RG 109.

11. Nelson, "Confederate Slave Impressment Legislation," 402.

12. "An Act to Amend and Re-enact the 12th Section of an Act Passed March 13th, 1863, entitled An Act to Amend and Re-enact an Act Further to Provide for the Public

Defense, passed October 2nd, 1862," section 12, March 30, 1863, *Journals of the Congress of the Confederate States of America* 6:178-79.

13. Col. Jeremy F. Gilmer to Col. Walter H. Stevens, August 6, 1863; Col. Jeremy F. Gilmer to James A. Seddon, endorsement on letter from Col. Walter H. Stevens, August 4, 1863; James A. Seddon to Col. Jeremy F. Gilmer, endorsement on letter from Col. Walter H. Stevens, August 7, 1863, LSEB.

14. Col. Jeremy F. Gilmer to Col. Walter H. Stevens, August 13, 1863, LSEB.

15. Lt. Col. Alfred L. Rives to James A. Seddon, August 18, 1863, LSEB.

16. Col. Walter H. Stevens to Gov. John Letcher, December 12, 1863, JLEP.

17. Albemarle County Court, Minute Books, 1859-1868, September 12, 1863, LVA.

18. Nelson County Court, Order Book, 1861-1868, September 10 and 28, 1863, LVA.

19. Halifax County Court, Minutes, 1859-1866, August 18 and September 29, 1863, LVA.

20. "Draft for Slaves on Fortifications," *Staunton Spectator*, October 13, 1863, p. 2, col. 4.

21. Stevens's list from December 1863 indicates a deficit of all 300 slaves for Pittsylvania County (Col. Walter H. Stevens to Gov. John Letcher, December 12, 1863, JLEP). The minutes of the Pittsylvania County Court contain no mention of slave impressment between November 4, 1862, and February 11, 1864.

22. On July 13, 1863, the Richmond City Council authorized the mayor to arrest all nonresident free blacks and put them to work on the fortifications; it also reauthorized the hustings court to impress free blacks for work on the fortifications. Manarin, *Richmond at War*, 349.

23. "The City Fortifications," *Richmond Whig*, September 15, 1863, p. 2, col. 1.

24. Gov. John Letcher to the Virginia General Assembly, September 14, 1863, JLEP.

25. R. C. Gatlin to Col. Thomas W. Rooker, November 2, 1863, Militia Letterbook, 1862-1864, AGD.

26. R. C. Gatlin to Col. Edward Dolby, December 14, 1863, Militia Letterbook, 1862-1864, AGD.

27. Col. Jeremy F. Gilmer to Gov. Zebulon Baird Vance, August 10, 1863, *OR*, ser. I, vol. 29, part 2, 635-36.

28. R. C. Gatlin to Col. H. N. Leadbetter, September 15, 1863; R. C. Gatlin to Maj. Gen. William H. C. Whiting, September 5, 1863; R. C. Gatlin to Capt. John C. Winder, October 30, 1863, Militia Letterbook, 1862-1864, AGD.

29. R. C. Gatlin to Col. J. C. Barnhardt, January 11, 1864, ibid.

30. R. C. Gatlin to Col. H. W. Leadbetter, January 12, 1864, ibid.

31. R. C. Gatlin to Lieutenant Ossensheim, March 21, 1864; R. C. Gatlin to Col. William H. Knight, January 16, 1864, ibid.

32. Fahrner, "William 'Extra Billy' Smith," 83.

33. James A. Seddon to Gov. William Smith, February 28, 1864, WSEP.

34. Gov. William Smith to the Honorable County Courts, January 22, 1864; "An Act to Amend and Re-enact an Act further to provide for the Public Defence," passed March 13, 1863, WSEP.

35. Col. George W. Munford to the Clerks of the County Courts, January 22, 1864, WSEP.

36. The Virginia General Assembly suspended tax collection for the year 1863, so state officials never compiled lists of slave property in that year; they did not create the 1864 tax lists until well after Smith's January 1864 requisition. Thus, even the most recent information the governor's office and Engineer Bureau had was outdated, since many counties had experienced sustained contact with Union armies between the summer of 1862 and early 1864—thus losing many of their slaves.

37. Col. Walter H. Stevens to Gov. William Smith, February 26, 1864; Col. Walter H. Stevens to Gov. William Smith, February 8, 1864; Col. George W. Munford to the Clerks of the County Courts, January 22, 1864, WSEP.

38. Col. Walter H. Stevens to Gov. William Smith, January 18, 1864, WSEP.

39. Col. Walter H. Stevens to Col. George W. Munford, March 14, 1864, WSEP.

40. Lt. Col. Alfred L. Rives to Major Poor, February 24, 1864, LSEB.

41. Lt. Col. Alfred L. Rives to Col. Walter H. Stevens, February 4, 1864, LSEB.

42. James M. Garland [clerk, Amherst County Court] to Col. George W. Munford, February 9, 1864, WSEP.

43. B. B. Woodson [clerk, Cumberland County Court] to Gov. William Smith, February 10, 1864; Lynch H. Currin [clerk, Pulaski County Court] to Gov. William Smith, February 6, 1864, WSEP.

44. Col. Walter H. Stevens to Col. George W. Munford, February 9, 1864, WSEP; Col. Alfred L. Rives to Capt. Walter G. Turpin, July 26, 1864, LSEB.

45. F. Wothz [clerk, Botetourt County Court] to Gov. William Smith, February 8, 1864, WSEP.

46. Col. S. Bassett French to the County Court of Botetourt, February 12, 1864, WSEP.

47. Charles May [clerk, Lunenburg County Court] to Gov. William Smith, February 13, 1864, WSEP.

48. Smith's endorsement on May to Smith, February 16, 1864, WSEP. See also David G. Dowthal [clerk, Montgomery County Court] to Gov. John Letcher, December 12, 1862, JLEP.

49. John D. Alexander [clerk, Campbell County Court] to Gov. William Smith, February 19, 1864; James H. Gilmore et al. [Smyth County Court] to Gov. William Smith, February 29, 1864; J. K. Edmondson [clerk, Rockbridge County Court] to Gov. William Smith, February 1, 1864; Smith's endorsement on Edmondson to Smith, February 9, 1864, WSEP.

50. John Pool to Gov. Zebulon Baird Vance, September 18, 1862, *OR*, ser. I, vol. 18, 747.

51. S. W. Gambill [clerk, Rockingham County Court] to Gov. John Letcher, September 28, 1863, JLEP.

52. See, for example, John G. Kreger [clerk, Washington County Court] to Gov. John Letcher, October 26, 1863, JLEP; John R. Chambliss and Thomas H. Wrenhard to Pres. Jefferson Davis, January 27, 1863, Confederate States of America Miscellaneous Papers, VHS; and Willoughby Newton to James A. Seddon, November 30, 1864, CSW.

53. E. Johnston [clerk, Giles County Court] to Gov. William Smith, February 15, 1864, WSEP.

54. Alexander H. McClintie [Presiding Justice, Bath County Court] to Gov. William Smith, February 9, 1864; C. G. Hill [clerk, Craig County Court] to Gov. William Smith, February 24, 1864, WSEP.

55. William D. Trout to Gov. William Smith, January 31, 1864, WSEP.

56. W. P. [clerk, Tazewell County Court] to Gov. William Smith, February 26, 1864, WSEP.

57. Philip H. Fry [clerk, Orange County Court] to Gov. William Smith, February 5, 1864; John Hunter [Presiding Justice, Louisa County Court] to Gov. William Smith, February 18, 1864; F. H. Hill [clerk, Madison County Court] to Gov. William Smith, February 25, 1864, WSEP. See also Wyatt S. Beazley [clerk, Greene County Court] to Gov. William Smith, February 3, 1864, along with Smith's endorsements of February 9 and 20; and R. O. Donnell [clerk, Hanover County Court] to Gov. William Smith, February 8 and 23, 1864, with Smith's endorsement of February 26, WSEP.

58. Thomas P. Atkinson to Gov. John Letcher, November 10, 1862, JLEP.

59. Col. George W. Munford to Thomas P. Atkinson, November 12, 1862, JLEP.

60. William Walter to Gov. John Letcher, November 1, 1862, JLEP.

61. B. F. Jennings to Gov. John Letcher, November 11, 1862, JLEP.

62. C. M. Robertson to Gov. John Letcher, December 12, 1862, JLEP.

63. Albemarle County Court, Minute Books, 1859–1868, January 6, 1863, LVA.

64. D. E. Gauldin to Gov. William Smith, January 26, 1865, WSEP.

65. F. Stone to Gov. William Smith, March 11, 1865, WSEP.

66. Robert C. Davis to Gov. William Smith, February 7, 1865, VED.

67. John D. Alexander [clerk, Campbell County Court] to Gov. William Smith, February 2, 1865, VED.

68. For examples, see Nathaniel M. Mantiply to James A. Seddon, December 26, 1864, CSW; A. B. Nichols to Gov. William Smith, March 30, 1864; Philip H. Fry [clerk, Orange County Court] to Gov. William Smith, December 26, 1864; and L. Seniggs [clerk, Pittsylvania County Court] to Gov. William Smith, January 30, 1864, WSEP.

69. Col. Walter H. Stevens to Col. S. Bassett French, April 1, 1864, endorsement on Nichols to Smith, WSEP.

70. Stevens's endorsement on Lt. Col. Alfred L. Rives to Dr. R. Crockett, March 4, 1864, LSEB.

71. Lt. Col. Alfred L. Rives to Jefferson D. Turner, March 4, 1864; Lt. Col. Alfred L. Rives to the Clerk of the Court of Albemarle County, March 15, 1864, LSEB.

72. Isaac C. Carrington to Gov. William Smith, February 1864, WSEP.

73. Nathaniel Garland to Gov. William Smith, March 14, 1864, WSEP.

74. Although the 1860 census data was no longer entirely accurate in January 1864, its specificity makes it preferable to the 1862 state tax assessment lists. State tax lists recorded the total number of slaves each slaveholder owned but did not distinguish on the basis of age or sex. Only the 1860 Slaveholder Census lists the age and sex of each slave.

75. Albemarle County Court, Minute Books, 1859–1868, November 6, 1862, September 12, 1863, and March 8, 1864, LVA; U.S. Bureau of the Census, *Eighth Census of the United States, 1860*, Slave Rolls, Albemarle County.

76. Albemarle County Court, Minute Books, 1859–1868, November 6, 1862, September 12, 1863, and March 8, 1864, LVA; U.S. Bureau of the Census, *Eighth Census of the United States, 1860*, Slave Rolls, Albemarle County.

77. "Slave Draft in Bedford," *Lynchburg Daily Virginian*, November 3, 1862, p. 2, col. 1–2.

78. Bedford County Court, Order Book, 1861–1865, October 30, 1862, September 19, 1863, February 11, 1864, January 28, 1865, LVA.

79. Albemarle County Court, Minute Books, 1859–1868, November 6, 1862, September 12, 1863, March 8, 1864, LVA; U.S. Bureau of the Census, *Eighth Census of the United States, 1860*, Slave Rolls, Albemarle County; William D. Cabell Journal, February 21, 1864, Papers of William Daniel Cabell and the Cabell, Ellet, Hunter, etc., Families, UVA.

80. Albemarle County Court, Minute Books, 1859–1868, November 6, 1862, September 12, 1863, March 8, 1864, LVA.

81. Blair, *Virginia's Private War*, 84–85.

82. Andrew, "Essential Nationalism of the People," 130–31.

83. Mobley, *"War Governor of the South,"* 108–9.

84. Rable, *Confederate Republic*, 233–35.

85. Adjutant and Inspector General's Office, General Orders No. 32, March 11, 1864, *OR*, ser. IV, vol. 3, 207–8.

86. Col. Alfred L. Rives to Col. John S. Preston, April 22, 1864, LSEB.

87. Col. George H. Sharpe to Major General Humphreys, June 5, 1864, *OR*, ser. I, vol. 36, part 2, 602.

88. Captain McEntee to Major General Humphreys, August 18, 1864, ibid., vol. 42, part 3, 267.

89. Payroll of Laborers on the Entrenchments at Raleigh, AGD.

90. Gen. G. T. Beauregard to Gen. Braxton Bragg, April 22, 1864, *OR*, ser. I, vol. 51, part 2, 872.

91. Col. Alfred L. Rives to Capt. F. F. Forbes, July 5, 1864, LSEB.

92. Col. Alfred L. Rives to Capt. R. H. Fitzhugh, July 20, 1864, LSEB.

93. Col. George Munford to the Henrico County Court, October 3, 1864; John L. Marye to Gov. William Smith, October 13, 1864; Gov. William Smith to A. Deitrick, October 6, 1864, WSEP; W. C. Whickham to James A. Seddon, November 1, 1864, CSW.

94. G. Campbell Brown to W. A. Carrington, Medical Director, October 3, 1864, WSEP.

95. Col. Walter H. Stevens to Gov. William Smith, October 24, 1864, WSEP.

96. M. W. Johnston to Gov. Zebulon Baird Vance, April 25, 1864, ZBV.

97. T. T. Slade to Gov. Zebulon Baird Vance, March 21, 1864, ZBV.

98. J. M. Bullock to Gov. Zebulon Baird Vance, April 14, 1864, ZBV.

99. Gov. Zebulon Baird Vance to James A. Seddon, April 28, 1864, Governor's Letterbooks, 1862–1865, NCAH.

100. Maj. Gen. William H. C. Whiting to James A. Seddon, April 20, 1864, CSW.

101. James A. Seddon to Gov. Zebulon Baird Vance, May 3, 1864, Governor's Letterbooks, 1862–1865, NCAH.

102. Maj. Gen. William H. C. Whiting to Gen. Samuel Cooper, January 21, 1864, Maj. Gen. William H. C. Whiting Papers, 1861–1865, NARA, RG 109.

103. Rable, *Confederate Republic*, 245–48, 265–71.

104. Maj. Gen. William H. C. Whiting to James A. Seddon, June 9, 1864, Letters Sent, Gen. W. H. C. Whiting's Command, 1862–1864, NARA, RG 109. Whiting's assessment reflected a common concern. In the summer of 1863, for example, Lt. Gen. Kirby Smith, commanding the Trans-Mississippi Department, gave all his officers in Texas direct orders to delay impressments of slaves and other property until after the pending gubernatorial election. See Maj. Gen. John Bankhead Magruder to Lt. Gen. E. Kirby Smith, July 3, 1863, *OR*, ser. I, vol. 26, part 2, 102.

105. Gov. Zebulon Baird Vance to Gov. William Smith, August 25, 1864, WSEP.

106. Maj. Gen. William H. C. Whiting to Gov. Zebulon Baird Vance, September 24, 1864, *OR*, ser. I, vol. 42, part 3, 1282; Maj. Gen. William H. C. Whiting to Gov. Zebulon Baird Vance, September 25, 1864, Letters Sent, Gen. W. H. C. Whiting's Command, 1862–1864, NARA, RG 109.

107. Maj. Gen. William H. C. Whiting to Lt. Gen. Holmes, September 26, 1864, Maj. Gen. William H. C. Whiting Papers, 1861–1865, NARA, RG 109.

108. Gov. Zebulon Baird Vance to Maj. Gen. William H. C. Whiting, September 28, 1864, Maj. Gen. William H. C. Whiting Papers, 1861–1865, NARA, RG 109.

CHAPTER FIVE

1. *Journals of the Congress of the Confederate States of America*, 7:254–55.

2. John B. Baldwin to Alexander H. H. Stuart, November 18, 1864, Papers of Alexander H. H. Stuart and related Stuart and Baldwin Families, UVA.

3. "The President's Message," *Raleigh North Carolina Standard*, November 14, 1864, p. 3, col. 1.

4. George W. Behn to Jefferson Davis, November 20, 1864, CSW.

5. DuBois, *Black Reconstruction in America*, 64.

6. Nelson, "Confederate Slave Impressment Legislation," 403; Trexler, "Opposition of Planters," 224; Brewer, *Confederate Negro*, 4; Jordan, *Black Confederates*, 58; McCurry, *Confederate Reckoning*, 281.

7. Charles May [clerk, Lunenburg County Court] to Gov. William Smith, February 13, 1864, WSEP.

8. "Liability of the Confederate States for Slaves Lost," *Staunton Spectator*, February 16, 1864, p. 1, col. 7.

9. Wade Keyes to Christopher G. Memminger, November 5, 1863, *Opinions of the Confederate Attorneys General*, 345–51.

10. "The Slave Claim Board," *Richmond Examiner*, April 20, 1864, p. 1, col. 1.

11. "Claims of Slaves Impressed by the Confederate Authorities," *Richmond Whig*, February 5, 1864, p. 1, col. 1.

12. Col. Alfred L. Rives to Capt. W. H. James, April 27, 1864, LSEB.

13. Col. Alfred L. Rives to Col. John S. Preston, May 17, 1864, LSEB.

14. Col. Alfred L. Rives to Col. Walter H. Stevens, April 22, 1864, LSEB. See also R. C. Gatlin to Col. W. J. McCain, March 4, 1864, Militia Letterbook, 1862–1864, AGD.

15. Confederate States of America, Record Book of the Board of Slave Claims, Reese Library Special Collections, Augusta State University, Augusta, Georgia.

16. Edgeworth Bird to Sallie Bird, September 3, 1864, in *The Granite Farm Letters*, ed. Rozier, 194.

17. I. M. Smith et al. to John C. Breckinridge, February 20, 1865, CSW.

18. Maj. Gen. William H. C. Whiting to James A. Seddon, July 8 and 20, 1864, Letters Sent, Gen. W. H. C. Whiting's Command, 1862–1864, NARA, RG 109.

19. Maj. Gen. William H. C. Whiting to Gen. Robert E. Lee, September 24, 1864, *OR*, ser. I, vol. 42, part 3, 1280–81.

20. Maj. Gen. William H. C. Whiting to Maj. Gen. Jeremy F. Gilmer, October 5, 1864, CSW.

21. Application of Jack Ingram, Pension Files, 1927, NCAH.

22. Fonvielle, *Wilmington Campaign*, 13.

23. Lamb, "Battle of Forth Fisher," 1.

24. Gen. Robert E. Lee to James A. Seddon, September 17, 1864; James A. Seddon to Gen. Robert E. Lee, September 19, 1864; Gen. Robert E. Lee to James A. Seddon, September 20, 1864, *OR*, ser. I, vol. 42, part 3, 1256–61.

25. Special Orders No. 223, Adjutant and Inspector General's Office, September 20, 1864, ibid., 1268–69.

26. Maj. Gen. Jeremy F. Gilmer to James A. Seddon, September 14, 1864, ibid., ser. IV, vol. 3, 668.

27. A. R. Lawton to James A. Seddon, October 8, 1864, ibid., 716.

28. Jordan, *Black Confederates*, 62–63; James A. Seddon to Gen. Robert E. Lee, September 22, 1864, *OR*, ser. I, vol. 42, part 3, 1269.

29. Special Orders No. 108, October 3, 1864, AGD.

30. R. C. Gatlin to W. A. Eaton, December 23, 1864, Militia Letterbook, 1864–1865, AGD.

31. Special Orders No. 175, December 23, 1864, AGD.

32. R. C. Gatlin to Captain McDonald, January 6, 1865, Militia Letterbook, 1864–1865, AGD.

33. Special Orders No. 30, February 16, 1865, AGD.

34. R. C. Gatlin to A. K. Lane, January 7, 1865, Militia Letterbook, 1864–1865, AGD.

35. Gov. T. H. Watts to Gen. D. H. Maury, August 16, 1864, *OR*, ser. I, vol. 49, part 2, 780.

36. Mohr, *On the Threshold of Freedom*, describes Georgia's "refusal to adopt heavy-handed methods for obtaining black workers" (163).

37. "An Act to Prevent the Illegal Impressment of Property in this State," *Laws of Georgia*, 62–63; Nelson, "Confederate Slave Impressment Legislation," 408.

38. Trexler, "Opposition of Planters," 223.

39. "A Bill to Regulate the Impressment of Slaves in the State of Virginia," December 9, 1864, *Journals of the Congress of the Confederate States of America*, 6:331.

40. Maj. Gen. Jeremy F. Gilmer to James A. Seddon, December 14, 1864, *Calendar of Virginia State Papers*, ed. Flournoy et al., 254.

41. Capt. John B. Stanard to Gov. William Smith, December 14, 1864, ibid., 255–56.

42. Col. George W. Munford to County Courts, December 16, 1864, WSEP.

43. S. H. Loving [clerk, Nelson County Court] to Gov. William Smith, January 3, 1865, VED.

44. William A. Smith to George C. Hannah, January 9, 1865, Hannah Family Papers, 1760–1967, VHS.

45. Col. George W. Munford to County Courts, January 5, 1865, WSEP.

46. George T. Peers [clerk, Appomattox County Court] to Gov. William Smith, January 20, 1865, VED.

47. William A. Adams [clerk, Dinwiddie County Court] to Gov. William Smith, January 10, 1865, VED. See also William A. Smith [clerk, Charlotte County Court] to Gov. William Smith, n.d.; J. Godbey [clerk, Floyd County Court] to Gov. William Smith, January 12, 1865; Robert A. Scott [clerk, Franklin County Court] to Gov. William Smith, March 16, 1865; George D. Gravely [clerk, Henry County Court] to Gov. William Smith, January 17, 1865 (with enclosures); and R. F. Graves [clerk, Powhatan County Court] to Col. George W. Munford, January 19, 1865, VED.

48. T. Johnston [clerk, Roanoke County Court] to Gov. William Smith, January 16, 1865, VED.

49. George T. Peers [clerk, Appomattox County Court] to Gov. William Smith, January 21, 1865, VED.

50. William A. Adams [clerk, Dinwiddie County Court] to Gov. William Smith, January 10, 1865, VED.

51. William M. Lackland [clerk, Botetourt County Court] to Gov. William Smith, January 25, 1865, VED.

52. J. C. Didlake [clerk, Lynchburg Hustings Court] to Gov. William Smith, January 18, 1865, VED.

53. Gov. William Smith to the Clerk of the Hustings Court of the City of Lynchburg, January 23, 1865, WSEP.

54. Col. George W. Munford to The Honorable County Court of Greene County, January 28, 1865, WSEP.

55. "Impressment of Slaves," *Lynchburg Daily Virginian*, February 1, 1865, p. 2, col. 1.

56. Richard B. Shaw [Presiding Justice, Buckingham County Court] to Gov. William Smith, February 1, 1865, VED.

57. Robert A. Scott [clerk, Franklin County Court] to Gov. William Smith, January 23, 1865, VED.

58. B. B. Woodson [clerk, Cumberland County Court] to Gov. William Smith, January 26, 1865, VED.

59. Robert W. Snead [Sheriff, Amherst County] to Gov. William Smith, February 6, 1865, VED.

60. Gen. Robert E. Lee to Gov. William Smith, February 9, 1865, WSEP.

61. Capt. John B. Stanard to Gov. William Smith, March 9, 1865, WSEP.

62. Gov. William Smith to the General Assembly of Virginia, February 10 and 28, 1865, WSEP.

63. Virginia General Assembly, "An Act Prescribing the Mode of Apportioning Slaves to Work on Fortifications and Other Public Works, and Regulating the Impressment of Slaves therefor by the Confederate Government," March 4, 1865, section 1, WSEP.

64. Ibid., sections 4–5.

65. Gov. William Smith to The Honorable Courts of the Counties, Cities, &c, March 14, 1865, *OR*, ser. IV, vol. 3, 1138–39.

66. Capt. W. G. Bender to Col. Alfred L. Rives, March 22, 1865, Miscellaneous Engineer Records, Letters Received Engineer Bureau Rives, NARA, RG 109.

67. Col. Walter H. Stevens's endorsement on Bender to Rives, March 25, 1865, ibid.

68. Capt. William H. Fry, Report of Negro Slaves received and disposed of under Circular No. 69 Conscript Office, March 28, 1865, C.S.A. Compiled Service Records, NARA, RG 109.

69. John D. Alexander [clerk, Campbell County Court] to Col. George W. Munford, March 23, 1865, WSEP.

70. Richard B. Shaw, Jr. [Presiding Justice, Buckingham County Court] to Gov. William Smith, March 26, 1865, WSEP.

71. H. Clay Graves [clerk, Powhatan County Court] to Gov. William Smith, March 27, 1865, VED.

72. Bailey, *Henrico Home Front*, 234.

73. Gov. William Smith to Gen. Robert E. Lee, March 25, 1865, WSEP.

74. Gov. William Smith to the General Assembly, February 20, 1865, WSEP.

75. *Journals of the Congress of the Confederate States of America*, 7:254.

76. Resolutions Against the Policy of Arming the Slaves, February 3, 1865, *Public Laws of the State of North Carolina*, 33.

77. Jordan, *Black Confederates*, 242.

78. Gen. Robert E. Lee to Hon. Ethelbert Barksdale, February 18, 1865, in McCabe, *Life and Campaigns of General Robert E. Lee*, 574.

79. Durden, *Gray and the Black*, 287.

80. Dillard, "'What Price Must we Pay for Victory?,'" 316–28.

81. *Raleigh North Carolina Standard*, April 4, 1864, p. 1, col. 6.

82. T. O. Chestney to Maj. I. H. Carrington, October 5, 1864; Maj. Thomas P. Turner to Capt. W. H. Hatch, October 14, 1864; James A. Seddon to Gen. Robert E. Lee, October 15, 1864, *OR*, ser. II, vol. 7, 988, 991.

83. Gen. Robert E. Lee to Lieut. Gen. Ulysses S. Grant, October 19, 1864, ibid., 1011–12.

84. "From Richmond," *Charlottesville Daily Chronicle*, October 18, 1864, p. 2, col. 2.

85. "The Voice of the Army," *Richmond Enquirer*, February 18, 1865, Accessible Archives, The Civil War Collection, Part I: A Newspaper Perspective (accessed April 1, 2004).

86. "Resolutions from the Army," *Richmond Daily Examiner*, January 6, 1865, p. 1, col. 3.

87. "The *Enquirer's* Programme," *Richmond Whig*, January 10, 1865, p. 2, col. 2.

88. *Richmond Whig*, February 17, 1865, p. 2, col. 1.

89. *Richmond Enquirer*, February 3, 1865, Accessible Archives, The Civil War Collection, Part I: A Newspaper Perspective (accessed April 1, 2004).

90. Benning's speech to Virginia State Convention, February 19, 1861, quoted in Dew, *Apostles of Disunion*, 66.

91. Levine, *Confederate Emancipation*, 109.

92. "From the *Richmond Enquirer*," *Lexington Gazette*, January 4, 1865, p. 1, col. 2.

93. M. G. Harman to Pres. Jefferson Davis, January 12, 1865, CSW.

94. Alexander F. Thitch to Thomas S. Bocock, February 19, 1865, Letters to Thomas S. Bocock, 1857–1865, Papers of Bocock and of the Bocock, etc. Families, UVA.

95. John A. McKinney to Lt. W. T. Fentress, December 21, 1864; Lt. W. T. Fentress to Lt. Col. J. C. Shields, December 21, 1864, ibid.

96. Statement of the Auditor of the Number of Slaves Fit for Service, March 25, 1865, WSEP.

97. Historical Census Browser, University of Virginia, Geospatial and Statistical Data Center (accessed March 13, 2005).

98. John C. Meeks to Pres. Jefferson Davis, January 23, 1865, CSW.

99. Sheehan-Dean, *Why Confederates Fought*, 198; Hilderman, *They Went into the Fight Cheering*, xv.

EPILOGUE

1. Bellamy, *Memoirs of an Octogenarian*, 7.

2. Adam Bell, "Marker Rejected for Slaves in South's Army," *Charlotte Observer*, February 16, 2011; Poland, "Union Countys, NC."

3. Adam Bell, "Marker Honoring Black Confederate Army Veterans Coming to Union County," *Charlotte Observer*, August 3, 2012; Adam Bell, "Monroe Ceremony Honors Slaves Who Served in Confederate Army," *Charlotte Observer*, December 8, 2012.

4. Adam Bell, "New Marker Honors Service by Union County Slave in Confederate Army," *Charlotte Observer*, February 16, 2012.

5. Bell, "Marker Rejected for Slaves in South's Army."

6. Bell, "Marker Honoring Black Confederate Army Veterans Coming to Union County."

7. Kevin Levin, "Honoring a False Past in Union County, North Carolina," *Civil War Memory*, December 10, 2012 (accessed December 29, 2012).

8. Reader comments on Bell, "Marker Honoring Black Confederate Army Veterans Coming to Union County" (accessed August 28, 2012).

9. Bell, "Marker Rejected for Slaves in South's Army."

10. North Carolina General Assembly, "An Act to Amend Chapter 92, Third Volume Consolidated Statutes Relative to Confederate Pensions," March 4, 1927, section 2, *Public Laws of the State of North Carolina*; Pension Files, 1927, NCAH.

11. Virginia General Assembly, "An Act to amend and re-enact an act approved February 28, 1918, . . . relating to Confederate pensions," March 14, 1924, section 6; Virginia General Assembly, "An Act to amend and re-enact section 6 of an act . . . relating to Confederate pensions, approved March 14, 1924," March 10, 1928, section 6, *Acts of the General Assembly of the State of Virginia*.

12. Military Resources and Records, Confederate Pension Rolls, Veterans and Widows, LVA, digitized applications (accessed May 16, 2008).

13. Kevin Levin, "SCV Butchers Another Slave's History," *Civil War Memory*, February 16, 2012 (accessed August 28, 2012).

14. Interview with Cornelius Garner in *Weevils in the Wheat*, ed. Perdue, Barden, and Phillips, 101.

Bibliography

MANUSCRIPT COLLECTIONS

Albert and Shirley Small Special Collections Library, University of Virginia, Charlottesville
    Bedford County Slave Appraisal List, 1863
    Folly Farm Papers of the Smith, Lewis, and Cochran Families, 1774–1891
    Letters of John Herbert Claiborne, 1864–1865
    List of Slaves and Slave Owners, Bedford County, 1865
    Papers of Bocock and of the Bocock, etc., Families
    Papers of William Daniel Cabell and the Cabell, Ellet, Hunter, etc., Families
    Papers of the Caperton Family, 1839–1896
    Papers of Robert Coleman, 1801–1905
    Papers of Jason B. Douglass
    Papers of the Grinnan Family
    Papers of the Hunter and Garnett Families, 1704–1940
    Papers of Francis McFarland
    Papers of the Minor and Wilson Families, 1764–1936
    Papers of the related Morton and Dickinson Families, 1727–1978
    Papers of the Noland Family, 1814–1948
    Papers of Alexander H. H. Stuart and the related Stuart and Baldwin Families
    Papers of Samuel Pannill Wilson
    Papers Relative to the Recent Call for Slaves to Work on Fortifications, 1863
Augusta State University Special Collections Library, Augusta, Georgia
    Confederate States of America, Record Book of the Board of Slave Claims, 1863–1864
Library of Virginia, Richmond
    Albemarle County Court, Minute Books, 1859–1868
    Bedford County Court, Order Book, 1861–1865
    Caroline County Court, Minute Books, 1861–1866
    Confederate Pension Rolls, Veterans and Widows
    David S. Baker Journal, 1860–1869
    Fluvanna County Court Records
    Halifax County Court, Minutes, 1859–1866
    Jerdone Family Slave Record Book, 1761–1865
    John Hart Collection of Confederate Letters and Receipts
    John Letcher Executive Papers, 1859–1863
    Legislative Petitions, Rockingham County, 1839–1863
    Nelson County Court, Order Book, 1861–1868

Papers of Joseph R. Anderson, 1846–1896
Pittsylvania County Court, Records, 1861–1865
Robert E. Lee Papers, 1854–1865
Secretary of the Commonwealth, Records, 1853–1884
Spotsylvania County Court, Order Book, 1858–1871
Tredegar Iron Works, Records, 1801–1957
Virginia Engineer Department, 1861–1865
William Massie Slave Record Book, 1762–1865
William Smith Executive Papers, 1863–1865
Lower Cape Fear Historical Society, Wilmington, North Carolina
  Williams/McEachern Papers
National Archives and Records Administration I, Washington, D.C.: War Department Collection of Confederate Records, Record Group 109
  Confederate States of America, Compiled Service Records
  Gen. John Bankhead Magruder Papers, 1852–1864
  Letters and Telegrams Sent by the Engineer Bureau of the Confederate War Department, 1861–1864
  Letters Received by the Confederate Adjutant and Inspector General, 1861–1865
  Letters Received by the Confederate Engineer Bureau, 1865
  Letters Received by the Confederate Secretary of War, 1861–1865
  Letters Sent, Gen. W. H. C. Whiting's Command, 1862–1864
  Letters Sent and Received, Medical Director's Office, Richmond, 1862–1865
  Lists of Patients and Employees, Smallpox Hospital
  Maj. Gen. William H. C. Whiting Papers, 1861–1865
  Miscellaneous Engineer Records
  Miscellaneous Medical Records
  Record Book, General Hospital No. 9, Richmond, 1863–1865
  Record Book, General Hospital No. 10, Richmond, 1863–1865
  Record of Clothing Issued Slaves, 1863–1864, Records Relating to Supplies and Accounts
  Record of Reports Received, Inspector of Hospitals, Richmond, 1863–1864
  Register of Patients—Union and Negro
  Register of Slaves Impressed, 1865, Records Relating to Conscription, Exemption, and Details
  Slave Payrolls, 1861–1865
  Statistical Reports of Patients and Attendants, Office of the Medical Director of Hospitals in North Carolina, 1863–1865
National Archives and Records Administration II, College Park, Maryland
  Allowed Case Files of the Southern Claims Commission, 1871–1879
  Disallowed Case Files of the Southern Claims Commission, 1871–1879
North Carolina Department of Archives and History, Raleigh
  Adjutant General's Department, General Records, 1807–1950
  Bertie County Court, Minute Books, 1853–1867
  Cumberland County Court, Minute Books, 1860–1865
  Governor's Letterbooks, 1861–1865

Henry T. Clark Executive Papers, 1861–1862
　　　Iredell County Court, Minute Books, 1857–1868
　　　Military Collection, Miscellaneous Civil War Records
　　　New Hanover County Court, Minute Books, 1861–1865
　　　Papers of David Clark, 1861–1863
　　　Pension Files, 1927
　　　Robeson County Court, Minute Books, 1860–1865
　　　Sampson County Court, Minute Docket, 1858–1865
　　　Stokes County Court, Minute Books, 1857–1865
　　　Wake County Court, Minute Books, 1859–1865
　　　Zebulon Baird Vance Executive Papers, 1862–1865
Rubenstein Library, Duke University, Durham, North Carolina
　　　Adeline Hester Bowling Letters
　　　Alfred Landon Rives Papers
　　　Confederate States of America Collection
　　　James Shreckhise Letters
　　　Winn Family Papers
Southern Historical Collection, University of North Carolina, Chapel Hill
　　　Anita Dwyer Withers Diary
　　　Jeremy Francis Gilmer Papers
　　　Lafayette McLaws Papers
　　　Macay and McNeely Family Papers
　　　Mary Jeffreys Bethell Diary
　　　William Alexander Graham Papers
Valley of the Shadow: Two Communities in the American Civil War (digital archive,
　　　University of Virginia)
　　　Personal Papers
　　　　　Enos Ott Papers
　　　　　Hotchkiss Family Papers
Virginia Historical Society, Richmond
　　　Aylett Family Papers
　　　Charles Tayloe Mason Papers
　　　Confederate States of America Engineer Office Letterbook
　　　Confederate States of America Miscellaneous Papers
　　　Enrolling Office, Caroline County, Certificate issued John R. Baylor
　　　Hannah Family Papers
　　　James H. Evans Papers
　　　Talcott Family Papers
　　　Tomlin's Infantry Battalion Letterbook, 1861

NEWSPAPERS

Asheville (N.C.) News
Bristol (Tenn.) Southern Advocate
Charlotte (N.C.) Observer
Charlottesville (Va.) Daily Chronicle
Fayetteville (N.C.) Semi-Weekly Observer
Lexington (Va.) Gazette

Raleigh Weekly Register
Richmond Daily Dispatch
Richmond Enquirer
Lynchburg (Va.) Daily Republican
Lynchburg (Va.) Daily Virginian
Marion (Va.) Ensign
Petersburg (Va.) Daily Express
Raleigh North Carolina Standard
Richmond Examiner
Richmond Sentinel
Richmond Whig
Salisbury (N.C.) Carolina Watchman
Staunton (Va.) Republican Vindicator
Staunton (Va.) Spectator
Wilmington (N.C.) Daily Journal

GOVERNMENT DOCUMENTS

Acts and Resolutions Adopted at the First Session 12th General Assembly of Florida. Tallahassee: Dyke and Carlisle, 1863.

Acts of the Called Session, 1862, and or the Second Regular Annual Session General Assembly of Alabama, Held in the City of Montgomery, Commencing on the 27th Day of October and Second Monday in November, 1862. Montgomery: Montgomery Advertiser Book and Job Office, 1862.

Acts of the General Assembly of the State of South Carolina, Passed in September and December 1863. Columbia: Charles P. Pelham, State Printer, 1864.

Acts of the General Assembly of the State of Virginia. Richmond: William F. Ritchie, Public Printer, 1862–1865, 1924, 1928.

Acts Passed by the Twenty-Seventh Legislature of the State of Louisiana: In Extra Session at Opelousas, December 1862 and January 1863. Natchitoches: Louis Dupleix, 1864.

Bailey, James H., ed. *Henrico Home Front, 1861–1865: A Picture of Life in Henrico County, Virginia, from May 1861 through April 1865.* Richmond: Whittet and Shepperson, 1963.

Berlin, Ira, et al., eds. *Freedom: A Documentary History of Emancipation, 1861–1867.* Series 1: The Destruction of Slavery. Cambridge: Cambridge University Press, 1985.

Confederate States of America, House of Representatives. *Estimate of Five Hundred Thousand Dollars Needed to Meet Claims against the Engineer Department.* February 1, 1864.

The Constitution of the Confederate States of America. The Avalon Project, Yale School of Law. http://avalon.law.yale.edu/19th_century/csa_csa.asp.

Flournoy, H. W., et al., eds. *Calendar of Virginia State Papers and Other Manuscripts from January 1, 1836 to April 15, 1869.* Volume 11. Richmond: Commonwealth of Virginia, 1893.

Ingram, E. Renée, ed. *In View of the Great Want of Labor: A Legislative History of African American Conscription in the Confederacy.* Westminster, Md.: Willow Bend Books, 1999.

Johnston, Frontis W., ed. *The Papers of Zebulon Baird Vance.* Volume 1, 1843–1862. Raleigh: State Department of Archives and History, 1963.

Journal of the House of Representatives of the State of Mississippi, December Session of 1862, and November Session of 1863. Jackson: Cooper and Kimball, 1864.

Journal of the Senate of the State of Georgia, at the Annual Session of the General Assembly, Begun and Held in Milledgeville, the Seat of Government, in 1862. Milledgeville: Boughton, Nisbet, and Barnes, State Printers, 1862.

Journals of the Congress of the Confederate States of America. Washington, D.C.: Government Printing Office, 1904–1905.

Journals of the House of Commons and Senate of the General Assembly of the State of North Carolina. Raleigh: W. W. Holden, 1862–1865.

Laws and Resolutions of the State of North Carolina, Passed by the General Assembly at Its Session of 1885. Raleigh: P. M. Hale, 1885.

Laws of Georgia: Acts of the General Assembly of the State of Georgia Passed in Milledgeville at an Annual Session in November and December 1863; also, Extra Session of 1864. Milledgeville: Boughton, Nisbet, Barnes, and Moore, State Printers, 1864.

Mahan, Dennis Hart. *A Treatise on Field Fortification.* New York: Wiley and Putman, 1846.

Manarin, Louis, ed. *Richmond at War: The Minutes of the City Council, 1861–1865.* Chapel Hill: University of North Carolina Press, 1966.

Mobley, Joe A., ed. *The Papers of Zebulon Baird Vance.* Volume 2, 1863. Raleigh: Division of Archives and History, North Carolina Department of Cultural Resources, 1995.

North Carolina, Executive Department, Adjutant General's Office. *Special Orders No. 50 to North Carolina Militia.* April 2, 1863.

Patrick, Rembert W., ed. *The Opinions of the Confederate Attorneys General, 1861–1865.* Buffalo, N.Y.: Dennis & Co., 1950.

Public Laws of the State of North Carolina, Passed by the General Assembly. Raleigh: W. W. Holden, 1862–1865, 1924–1927.

Ramsdell, Charles W., ed. *Laws and Joint Resolutions of the Last Session of the Confederate Congress (November 7, 1864–March 18, 1865) Together with the Secret Acts of the Previous Congresses.* Durham: Duke University Press, 1941.

U.S. Bureau of the Census. *Eighth Census of the United States, 1860.* Washington, D.C.: Government Printing Office, 1865.

U.S. War Department. *Official Records of the Union and Confederate Navies in the War of the Rebellion.* Washington, D.C.: Government Printing Office, 1894–1922. http://ebooks.library.cornell.edu/m/moawar/ofre.html.

———. *The War of the Rebellion: A Compilation of the Official Records of the Union and Confederate Armies.* Washington, D.C.: Government Printing Office, 1880–1901. http://ebooks.library.cornell.edu/m/moawar/waro.html.

Vance, Zebulon Baird. *Governor's Message,* Doc. No. 1 Ses. 1862–63. Raleigh: W. W. Holden, 1862.

Virginia, Executive Department. *Call for Slaves from Virginia Counties.* December 16, 1864.

———. *Papers Relative to the Recent Call for Slaves to Work on Fortifications.* September 10, 1863.

Virginia, Office of the Secretary of the Commonwealth. *Circular to Virginia County Courts.* December 14, 1864.

———. *Circular to Virginia County Courts.* January 5, 1865.

Virginia General Assembly. *Acts of the General Assembly of the State of Virginia, 1861-1864.* Richmond: William F. Ritchie, 1862-1864.

PUBLISHED DIARIES, JOURNALS, AND MEMOIRS

Baer, Elizabeth R., ed. *Shadows on My Heart: The Civil War Diary of Lucy Rebecca Buck of Virginia.* Athens: University of Georgia Press, 1997.

Bell, John W., ed. *Memoirs of Governor William Smith of Virginia.* New York: Moss Engraving Company, 1891.

Bellamy, John. *Memoirs of an Octogenarian.* Charlotte: Observer Printing House, 1942.

Buck, William P., ed. *Sad Earth, Sweet Heaven: The Diary of Lucy Rebecca Buck during the War Between the States, 1861-1865.* Birmingham: Cornerstone Press, 1973.

Cleveland, Henry, ed. *Alexander H. Stephens in Public and Private: With Letters and Speeches, Before, During, and Since the War.* Philadelphia: National Publishing Co., 1866.

Crabtree, Beth G., and James W. Patton, eds. *Journal of a Secesh Lady: The Diary of Catherine Ann Devereux Edmondston, 1860-1866.* Raleigh: Division of Archives and History, Department of Cultural Resources, 1979.

Fleet, Betsy, and John D. P. Fuller, eds. *Green Mount: A Virginia Plantation Family during the Civil War: Being the Journal of Benjamin Robert Fleet and Letters of His Family.* Charlottesville: University Press of Virginia, 1962.

Gould, William B. *Diary of a Contraband: The Civil War Passage of a Black Sailor.* Palo Alto: Stanford University Press, 2002.

Grimes, Bryan. *Extracts of Letters of Major-Gen'l Bryan Grimes to His Wife.* Raleigh: Edwards, Broughton and Co., 1883.

Hassler, William W., ed. *One of Lee's Best Men: The Civil War Letters of General William Dorsey Pender.* Chapel Hill: University of North Carolina Press, 1999 (reprint).

Irvine, Ida Robeson, ed. *The Diary of Elizabeth Ellis Robeson, Bladen County, North Carolina, from 1847 to 1866.* Elizabethtown, N.C.: Bladen County Historical Society, 1975.

Jones, John B. *A Rebel War Clerk's Diary at the Confederate States Capital.* Philadelphia: Lippincott, 1866.

Kean, Robert Garlick Hill. *Inside the Confederate Government.* Edited by Edward Younger. Baton Rouge: Louisiana State University Press, 1985.

Lamb, William. "The Battle of Forth Fisher, North Carolina." Reprinted from *Battles and Leaders of the Civil War.* Wilmington, N.C.: Harriss Printing and Advertising Co.

McGuire, Judith W. *Diary of a Southern Refugee During the War.* New York: E. J. Hale and Son, 1867.

Paxton, Elisha Franklin. *Memoir and Memorials: Elisha Franklin Paxton, Brigadier-General, C.S.A.* New York: Neale Publishing Co., 1907.

Perdue, Charles L., Jr., Thomas E. Barden, and Robert K. Phillips, eds. *Weevils in the Wheat: Interviews with Virginia Ex-Slaves.* Charlottesville: University Press of Virginia, 1976.

Rawick, George P., ed. *The American Slave: A Composite Autobiography.* 18 vols. Westport, Conn.: Greenwood, 1972–79.

Robertson, Mary D., ed. *Lucy Breckinridge of Grove Hill: The Journal of a Virginia Girl, 1862–1864.* Kent, Ohio: Kent State University Press, 1979.

Ross, Fitzgerald. *Cities and Camps of the Confederate States.* Edited by Richard Barksdale Harwell. Champaign: University of Illinois Press, 1958.

Rozier, John, ed. *The Granite Farm Letters: The Civil War Correspondence of Edgeworth & Sallie Bird.* Athens: University of Georgia Press, 1988.

Sprunt, James. *Tales of the Cape Fear Blockade: Being a Turn of the Century Account of Blockade-Running Told by the Hon. James Sprunt.* Edited by Cornelius M. D. Thomas. Wilmington, N.C.: J. E. Hicks, 1960.

Wright, Louise Wigfall. *A Southern Girl in '61: The War-Time Memories of a Confederate Senator's Daughter.* New York: Doubleday, Page, 1905.

Yearns, W. Buck, and John G. Barrett, ed. *North Carolina Civil War Documentary.* Chapel Hill: University of North Carolina Press, 1980.

BOOKS

Bancroft, Frederic. *Slave-Trading in the Old South.* Baltimore: J. H. Furst, 1931.

Beringer, Richard E., Herman Hattaway, Archer Jones, and William N. Still Jr. *Why the South Lost the Civil War.* Athens: University of Georgia Press, 1986.

Berlin, Ira, Barbara J. Fields, Steven F. Miller, and Joseph P. Reidy. *Slaves No More: Three Essays on Emancipation and the Civil War.* Cambridge: Cambridge University Press, 1992.

Blair, William A. *Virginia's Private War: Feeding Body and Soul in the Confederacy.* New York: Oxford University Press, 1998.

Boney, F. N. *John Letcher of Virginia: The Story of Virginia's Civil War Governor.* Tuscaloosa: University of Alabama Press, 1966.

Boritt, Gabor S., ed. *Why the Confederacy Lost.* New York: Oxford University Press, 1992.

Brasher, Glenn David. *The Peninsula Campaign and the Necessity of Emancipation: African Americans and the Fight for Freedom.* Chapel Hill: University of North Carolina Press, 2012.

Brewer, James H. *The Confederate Negro: Virginia's Craftsmen and Military Laborers, 1861–1865.* Durham: Duke University Press, 1969.

Bynum, Victoria E. *The Free State of Jones: Mississippi's Longest Civil War.* Chapel Hill: University of North Carolina Press, 2001.

———. *The Long Shadow of the Civil War: Dissent and Its Legacies.* Chapel Hill: University of North Carolina Press, 2010.

———. *Unruly Women: The Politics of Social and Sexual Control in the Old South.* Chapel Hill: University of North Carolina Press, 1992.

Campbell, Jacqueline Glass. *When Sherman Marched North from the Sea: Resistance on the Confederate Home Front.* Chapel Hill: University of North Carolina Press, 2003.

Carr, Dawson. *Gray Phantoms of the Cape Fear: Running the Civil War Blockade.* Winston-Salem: John F. Blair, 1998.

Cimprich, John. *Slavery's End in Tennessee, 1861–1865.* Tuscaloosa: University of Alabama Press, 1985.

Click, Patricia C. *Time Full of Trial: The Roanoke Island Freedmen's Colony, 1862–1867.* Chapel Hill: University of North Carolina Press, 2001.

Crabtree, Beth G. *North Carolina Governors, 1585–1974.* Raleigh: North Carolina Division of Archives and History, 1974.

Cunningham, Horace H. *Doctors in Gray: The Confederate Medical Service.* Baton Rouge: Louisiana State University Press, 1958.

Delfino, Susanna, and Michele Gillespie, eds. *Neither Lady nor Slave: Working Women of the Old South.* Chapel Hill: University of North Carolina Press, 2002.

Dew, Charles B. *Apostles of Disunion: Southern Secession Commissioners and the Causes of the Civil War.* Charlottesville: University Press of Virginia, 2001.

———. *Bond of Iron: Master and Slave at Buffalo Forge.* New York: W. W. Norton, 1994.

———. *Ironmaker to the Confederacy: Joseph R. Anderson and the Tredegar Iron Works.* New Haven: Yale University Press, 1966.

Donald, David, ed. *Why the North Won the Civil War.* Baton Rouge: Louisiana State University Press, 1960.

Downs, Jim. *Sick from Freedom: African American Illness and Suffering during the Civil War and Reconstruction.* New York: Oxford University Press, 2012.

DuBois, W. E. B. *Black Reconstruction in America.* New York: Oxford University Press, 2007 (reprint).

Durden, Robert F. *The Gray and the Black: The Confederate Debate on Emancipation.* Baton Rouge: Louisiana State University Press, 1972.

Ely, Melvin Patrick. *Israel on the Appomattox: A Southern Experiment in Black Freedom from the 1790s through the Civil War.* New York: Alfred A. Knopf, 2004.

Escott, Paul D. *After Secession: Jefferson Davis and the Failure of Confederate Nationalism.* Baton Rouge: Louisiana State University Press, 1978.

———. *The Confederacy: The Slaveholders' Failed Venture.* Santa Barbara: Praeger, 2010.

———, ed. *North Carolinians in the Era of the Civil War and Reconstruction.* Chapel Hill: University of North Carolina Press, 2008.

Evans, William McKee. *To Die Game: The Story of the Lowry Band, Indian Guerillas of Reconstruction.* Baton Rouge: Louisiana State University Press, 1971.

Faust, Drew Gilpin. *The Creation of Confederate Nationalism: Ideology and Identity in the Civil War South.* Baton Rouge: Louisiana State University Press, 1988.

———. *Mothers of Invention: Women of the Slaveholding South in the American Civil War.* Chapel Hill: University of North Carolina Press, 1996.

Fields, Barbara Jeanne. *Slavery and Freedom on the Middle Ground: Maryland in the Nineteenth Century.* New Haven: Yale University Press, 1984.

Fonvielle, Christopher E., Jr. *The Wilmington Campaign: Last Rays of Departing Hope.* Campbell, Calif.: Savas, 1997.

Freehling, William W. *The Road to Disunion: Secessionists at Bay, 1776–1854.* New York: Oxford University Press, 1990.

———. *The Road to Disunion: Secessionists Triumphant, 1854–1861.* New York: Oxford University Press, 2006.

———. *The South vs. The South: How Anti-Confederate Southerners Shaped the Course of the Civil War.* New York: Oxford University Press, 2001.

Gallagher, Gary W. *The Confederate War.* Cambridge, Mass.: Harvard University Press, 1997.

———. *Lee and His Generals in War and Memory.* Baton Rouge: Louisiana State University Press, 1998.

Glymph, Thavolia. *Out of the House of Bondage: The Transformation of the Plantation Household.* New York: Cambridge University Press, 2008.

Gordon, Lesley J., and John C. Inscoe, eds. *Inside the Confederate Nation: Essays in Honor of Emory M. Thomas.* Baton Rouge: Louisiana State University Press, 2005.

Green, Carol C. *Chimborazo: The Confederacy's Largest Hospital.* Knoxville: University of Tennessee Press, 2004.

Greenberg, Kenneth S. *Masters and Statesmen: The Political Culture of American Slavery.* Baltimore: Johns Hopkins University Press, 1985.

Hahn, Steven. *A Nation under Our Feet: Black Political Struggles from Slavery to the Great Migration.* Cambridge, Mass.: Belknap of Harvard University Press, 2003.

Hilderman, Walter C. *They Went into the Fight Cheering: Confederate Conscription in North Carolina.* Boone, N.C.: Parkway Publishers, 2005.

Inscoe, John C. *Race, War, and Remembrance in the Appalachian South.* Lexington: University Press of Kentucky, 2008.

Inscoe, John C., and Gordon B. McKinney. *The Heart of Confederate Appalachia: Western North Carolina in the Civil War.* Chapel Hill: University of North Carolina Press, 2000.

Jordan, Ervin L., Jr. *Black Confederates and Afro-Yankees in Civil War Virginia.* Charlottesville: University Press of Virginia, 1995.

Kaye, Anthony. *Joining Places: Slave Neighborhoods in the Old South.* Chapel Hill: University of North Carolina Press, 2007.

Kerr-Ritchie, Jeffrey R. *Freedpeople in the Tobacco South: Virginia, 1860–1900.* Chapel Hill: University of North Carolina Press, 1999.

Kimball, Gregg D. *American City, Southern Place: A Cultural History of Antebellum Richmond.* Athens: University of Georgia Press, 2000.

Knight, H. Jackson. *Confederate Invention: The Story of the Confederate States Patent Office and Its Inventors.* Baton Rouge: Louisiana State University Press, 2011.

Levine, Bruce. *Confederate Emancipation: Southern Plans to Free and Arm Slaves during the Civil War.* New York: Oxford University Press, 2006.

Litwack, Leon F. *Been in the Storm So Long: The Aftermath of Slavery.* New York: Alfred A. Knopf, 1979.

Majewski, John. *Modernizing a Slave Economy: The Economic Vision of the Confederate Nation.* Chapel Hill: University of North Carolina Press, 2009.

McCabe, James D., Jr. *Life and Campaigns of General Robert E. Lee.* Atlanta: National Publishing Company, 1866.

McCurry, Stephanie. *Confederate Reckoning: Power and Politics in the Civil War South.* Cambridge, Mass.: Harvard University Press, 2010.

———. *Masters of Small Worlds: Yeoman Households, Gender Relations, and the Political Culture of the Antebellum South Carolina Low Country*. New York: Oxford University Press, 1995.

McKinney, Gordon. *Zeb Vance: North Carolina's Civil War Governor and Gilded Age Political Leader*. Chapel Hill: University of North Carolina Press, 2004.

Mobley, Joe A. *"War Governor of the South": North Carolina's Zeb Vance in the Confederacy*. Gainesville: University Press of Florida, 2005.

Mohr, Clarence L. *On the Threshold of Freedom: Masters and Slaves in Civil War Georgia*. Athens: University of Georgia Press, 1986.

Morgan, Jennifer L. *Laboring Women: Gender and Reproduction in the Making of New World Slavery*. Philadelphia: University of Pennsylvania Press, 2004.

Morgan, Lynda J. *Emancipation in Virginia's Tobacco Belt, 1850-1870*. Athens: University of Georgia Press, 1992.

Morris, Thomas D. *Southern Slavery and the Law, 1619-1860*. Chapel Hill: University of North Carolina Press, 1996.

Nichols, James L. *Confederate Engineers*. Tuscaloosa: Confederate Publishing, 1957.

Oakley, Christopher Arris. *Keeping the Circle: American Indian Identity in Eastern North Carolina, 1885-2004*. Lincoln: University of Nebraska Press, 2005.

Owsley, Frank L. *State Rights in the Confederacy*. Chicago: University of Chicago Press, 1925.

Quarles, Benjamin. *The Negro in the Civil War*. Boston: Little, Brown, 1953.

Rable, George C. *The Confederate Republic: A Revolution against Politics*. Chapel Hill: University of North Carolina Press, 1994.

Ramey, Daina Berry. *"Swing the Sickle for the Harvest Is Ripe": Gender and Slavery in Antebellum Georgia*. Urbana: University of Illinois Press, 2010.

Reidy, Joseph P. *From Slavery to Agrarian Capitalism: Central Georgia, 1800-1880*. Chapel Hill: University of North Carolina Press, 1992.

Roark, James L. *Masters without Slaves: Southern Planters in the Civil War and Reconstruction*. New York: W. W. Norton, 1977.

Robinson, Armstead L. *Bitter Fruits of Bondage: The Demise of Slavery and the Collapse of the Confederacy, 1861-1865*. Charlottesville: University of Virginia Press, 2005.

Rose, Willie Lee. *Rehearsal for Reconstruction: The Port Royal Experiment*. New York: Bobbs-Merrill, 1964.

Rubin, Anne Sarah. *A Shattered Nation: The Rise and Fall of the Confederacy, 1861-1868*. Chapel Hill: University of North Carolina Press, 2005.

Schwalm, Leslie. *A Hard Fight for We: Women's Transition from Slavery to Freedom in South Carolina*. Urbana: University of Illinois Press, 1997.

Settles, Thomas A., and Kimberly C. Campbell. *John Bankhead Magruder: A Military Reappraisal*. Baton Rouge: Louisiana State University Press, 2009.

Sheehan-Dean, Aaron. *Why Confederates Fought: Family and Nation in Civil War Virginia*. Chapel Hill: University of North Carolina Press, 2007.

Sider, Gerald M. *Lumbee Indian Histories: Race, Ethnicity, and Indian Identity in the Southern United States*. New York: Cambridge University Press, 1993.

Sprunt, James. *Chronicles of the Cape Fear River, 1660-1916*. Wilmington, N.C.: Dram Tree Books, 2005 (reprint).

Stevenson, Brenda. *Life in Black and White: Family and Community in the Slave South*. New York: Oxford University Press, 1996.

Tadman, Michael. *Speculators and Slaves: Masters, Traders, and Slaves in the Old South*. Madison: University of Wisconsin Press, 1989.

Takagi, Midori. *"Rearing Wolves to Our Own Destruction": Slavery in Richmond, Virginia, 1782–1865*. Charlottesville: University Press of Virginia, 1999.

Thomas, Emory. *The Confederacy as a Revolutionary Experience*. Columbia: University of South Carolina Press, 1991 (reprint).

———. *The Confederate Nation: 1861–1865*. New York: Harper and Row, 1979.

———. *The Confederate State of Richmond: A Biography of the Capital*. Baton Rouge: Louisiana State University Press, 1998 (reprint).

Tripp, Steven Elliot. *Yankee Town, Southern City: Race and Class Relations in Civil War Lynchburg*. New York: New York University Press, 1997.

Vandiver, Frank E. *Ploughshares into Swords: Josiah Gorgas and Confederate Ordnance*. Austin: University of Texas Press, 1952.

Warner, Ezra W. *Generals in Gray: Lives of the Confederate Commanders*. Baton Rouge: Louisiana State University Press, 1959.

Wiley, Bell Irvin. *Southern Negroes, 1861–1865*. Baton Rouge: Louisiana State University Press, 1965.

Williams, David. *Bitterly Divided: The South's Inner Civil War*. New York: New Press, 2008.

Wills, Brian Steel. *The War Hits Home: The Civil War in Southeastern Virginia*. Charlottesville: University Press of Virginia, 2001.

Wise, Stephen R. *Lifeline of the Confederacy: Blockade Running during the Civil War*. Columbia: University of South Carolina Press, 1988.

Zaborney, John J. *Slaves For Hire: Renting Enslaved Laborers in Antebellum Virginia*. Baton Rouge: Louisiana State University Press, 2012.

ARTICLES AND ESSAYS

Andrew, Rod, Jr. "The Essential Nationalism of the People: Georgia's Confederate Congressional Election of 1863." In *Inside the Confederate Nation: Essays in Honor of Emory M. Thomas*, edited by Lesley J. Gordon and John C. Inscoe, 128–46. Baton Rouge: Louisiana State University Press, 2005.

Ayers, Edward L., and William G. Thomas III. "The Difference Slavery Made: A Close Analysis of Two American Communities." *American Historical Review* 108, no. 5 (December 2003), http://www2.vcdh.virginia.edu/AHR/.

Barton, Keith C. "'Good Cooks and Washers': Slave Hiring, Domestic Labor, and the Market in Bourbon County, Kentucky." *Journal of American History* 84, no. 2 (September 1997): 436–60.

Berlin, Ira. "Emancipation and Its Meaning in American Life." *Reconstruction* 2, no. 3 (1994): 35–44.

———. "Who Freed the Slaves?: Emancipation and Its Meaning." In *Union and Emancipation: Essays on Politics and Race in the Civil War Era*, edited by David W. Blight and Brooks D. Simpson, 105–21. Kent, Ohio: Kent State University Press, 1997.

Campbell, Randolph B. "Slave Hiring in Texas." *American Historical Review* 93, no. 1 (February 1988): 107-14.

Curry, Roy Watson. "James A. Seddon, a Southern Prototype," *Virginia Magazine of History and Biography* 63, no. 2 (April 1955): 123-50.

Delfino, Susanna. "Invisible Woman: Female Labor in the Upper South's Iron and Mining Industries." In *Neither Lady nor Slave: Working Women of the Old South*, edited by Susanne Delfino and Michele Gillespie, 285-307. Chapel Hill: University of North Carolina Press, 2002.

Dillard, Phillip D. "'What Price Must we Pay for Victory?' Views on Arming Slaves from Lynchburg, Virginia, to Galveston, Texas." In *Inside the Confederate Nation: Essays in Honor of Emory M. Thomas*, edited by Lesley J. Gordon and John C. Inscoe, 316-34. Baton Rouge: Louisiana State University Press, 2005.

Dirck, Brian R. "Posterity's Blush: Civil Liberties, Property Rights, and Property Confiscation in the Confederacy." *Civil War History* 48, no. 3 (September 2002): 237-56.

Eaton, Clement. "Slave-Hiring in the Upper South: A Step toward Freedom." *Mississippi Valley Historical Review* 46, no. 4 (March 1960): 663-78.

Fahrner, Alvin A. "William 'Extra Billy' Smith, Governor of Virginia 1864-1865: A Pillar of the Confederacy." *Virginia Magazine of History and Biography* 74, no. 1 (January 1966): 68-87.

Gallagher, Gary W. "Disaffection, Persistence, and Nation: Some Directions in Recent Scholarship on the Confederacy." *Civil War History* 55, no. 3. (September 2009): 329-53.

Martinez, Jaime Amanda. "The Slave Market in Civil War Virginia." In *Crucible of the Civil War: Virginia from Secession to Commemoration*, edited by Edward L. Ayers, Gary W. Gallagher, and Andrew J. Torget, 106-35. Charlottesville: University of Virginia Press, 2006.

McPherson, James M. "Who Freed the Slaves?" In *Drawn with the Sword: Reflections on the American Civil War*, 192-207. New York: Oxford University Press, 1996.

Mohr, Clarence L. "Southern Blacks in the Civil War: A Century of Historiography." *Journal of Negro History* 59, no. 2 (April 1974): 177-95.

Nelson, Bernard H. "Confederate Slave Impressment Legislation, 1861-1865." *Journal of Negro History* 31, no. 4 (October 1946): 392-410.

Trexler, Harrison A. "The Opposition of Planters to the Employment of Slaves as Laborers by the Confederacy." *Mississippi Valley Historical Review* 27, no. 2 (September 1940): 211-24.

Wesley, Charles H. "The Employment of Negroes as Soldiers in the Confederate Army." *Journal of Negro History* 4, no. 3 (July 1919): 239-53.

UNPUBLISHED PAPERS AND BLOG POSTS

Golland, David Hamilton. "Industrial Intersection: Slavery and Industry in Late Antebellum Virginia." M.A. thesis, University of Virginia, 2002.

Levin, Kevin. "Honoring a False Past in Union County, North Carolina." *Civil War Memory*, December 10, 2012, http://cwmemory.com (accessed December 29, 2012).

———. "SCV Butchers Another Slave's History." *Civil War Memory*, February 16, 2012, http://cwmemory.com (accessed August 28, 2012).

Nicoletti, Cynthia. "The Law of Slavery in the Southern Confederacy." Seminar paper, University of Virginia, 2005.

Poland, Patricia. "Union County, NC: Confederate Pensioners of Color." Pamphlet, Union County Public Library, 2012.

Acknowledgments

As I approached the finish line with this book, I looked forward to writing the acknowledgments. It is wonderful to have an opportunity to offer some small measure of gratitude to the many people who helped me get to this point, although it is far less than they deserve. It is also a little nerve-wracking, as I've no doubt lost track of some of the people who contributed to a project that began ten years, three homes, and four laptops ago. So, if I left somebody out, I apologize, and please know that you are included in this blanket "thank you."

First, special thanks are due to the brave souls who read complete drafts of my manuscript at various points in time and stages of development. Gary Gallagher, Peter Onuf, Maurie McInnis, and Scot French reviewed the very first full draft, and their comments helped me to refine my arguments and clarify how I wanted to interact with other scholars as I made further revisions. Two anonymous readers for the University of North Carolina Press each read two additional drafts, always providing detailed and constructive feedback for which I am deeply grateful. Ryan Anderson and Rose Stremlau have read bits and pieces of every chapter, often more than once, over the last two years, and it is fair to say that I absolutely could not have completed this book without their help. In addition to being excellent scholars, writers, and readers, they are wonderful friends, and our weekly writing group meetings have provided invaluable moral support for both the writing process and the demands of our day-to-day teaching responsibilities.

I am also thankful for the many people who read smaller sections of the manuscript. Ed Ayers, Stephen Ash, Joan Waugh, Andrew Torget, Calvin Schermerhorn, and Aaron Sheehan-Dean made valuable suggestions on proposals and early conference papers. George Rable, Paul Escott, and William Barney read more recent conference papers, and their support for the project was especially encouraging. Charles Beem, Tamika Carey, Jan Davidson, Anita Guynn, Fran Fuller, and José Rivera all helped me refine individual chapters and sections.

Many other people provided crucial support along the way. The numerous scholars who sent me research suggestions over the years demonstrate just how supportive the community of historians can be. Of these, Cynthia Nicoletti and Susanna Michelle Lee deserve special recognition. Cynthia alerted me to the presence of the Board of Slave Claims record book at the Augusta State Library at a time when I had just realized the board even existed. While I'm sure I would have eventually found these records (which are a crucial part of chapter 2) on my own, her tip saved me a great deal of time. Susanna sent me notes on Southern Claims Commission cases whenever she encountered something I could use, greatly streamlining my work with those documents. Their help allowed me to make more effective use of my time in libraries and archives, as did the work of Interlibrary Loan staff at the University of Virginia's Alderman Library and

UNC Pembroke's Mary Livermore Library. I am also grateful to collections specialists at UVA's Small Special Collections Library, the Library of Virginia, and the North Carolina State Archives. I was fortunate that many of the resources I needed for this project were within easy reach, and so very few of my research trips involved overnight stays. I do have two excellent hosts to thank, however: Norma Reyes let me use her guest room (and cooked me tostones!) during a week-long sojourn in the Raleigh–Durham–Chapel Hill area in 2006, while my sister Leigh repeatedly let me sleep on her couch or air mattress when I visited the National Archives in Washington, D.C., or College Park (payback, perhaps, for her childhood tendency to invade my bedroom). Kristen Anderson converted maps and images into publication-ready formats, patiently enduring my numerous emails and last-minute changes.

I would also like to thank the many people who attempted to keep me sane while I finished writing and revising this book. Caitlin Bell-Butterfield and Paul Betz at UNC Press reduced my anxiety by answering my questions quickly and thoroughly. David Perry and all four Civil War America series editors gave me frequent encouragement. Julie Bush and Jessica Ryan did excellent work copyediting and proofreading, respectively. My colleagues at UNC Pembroke, especially Janet Gentes, Rose Stremlau, Ryan Anderson, and Jeff Frederick, provided both moral and practical support on a regular basis. I am fortunate to teach in a history department where I am surrounded by role models—the women and men I work with on a daily basis are dedicated teachers, talented scholars, and genuinely kind people who represent some of the best of what our profession has to offer.

In reviewing not only the time I spent writing this book but also my entire life as a student, I am struck by the huge debt of gratitude I owe to both the teachers who knew me well and the unknown men and women who chose to support my education. I had the blessing of an outstanding K–12 public education and am especially indebted to the English teachers who helped me become a better writer. The writing skills they honed allowed me to make a good impression on Gary Gallagher during my freshman year at Penn State; he then facilitated my entrance to the University of Virginia for graduate school. In between, Bill Blair taught me how to critique other scholars' arguments and to present my own more effectively. Both have been extraordinary mentors, and I am humbled by and grateful for their support and encouragement. In terms of financial support, I would like to thank the men and women who established the two academic scholarships I received during my tenure at Penn State, as well as John L. Nau III for endowing the Jefferson Scholars Foundation graduate fellowship and research fund I was fortunate to receive. Thanks are also due to Jimmy Wright, Byron Hulsey, Julie Innes Caruccio, and the other members of the JSF staff, all of whom understand so well that their responsibility for supporting education extends well beyond handing out checks (although the checks, of course, were quite nice). Whatever success I have achieved rests on a foundation provided by dozens of great teachers and the many people who supported their work.

This book is dedicated to my first and most important teacher: my mother, Linda Christman Martinez, who has always been a cheerleader, a critic, and a role model. She taught me to read but then forced me to put my books down to engage with actual people, encouraged me to value the full range of my peers' abilities, expected me to respond to both compliments and criticism with grace, and never accepted anything less than my best work. I am a better scholar for her many lessons.

Index

African Americans: free, impressment of, 16–17, 23, 25, 65–66, 111, 122, 138, 160, 199 (n. 17), 204 (n. 22); enslaved women, 92–94, 202 (n. 80), 202–3 (n. 88); as Confederate soldiers, 133, 152–56, 159–63; as Union soldiers, 153–54; and state pensions, 161–62. *See also* Impressed slaves; Slave hiring
American Indians. *See* Native Americans
Army of Northern Virginia, 13, 140
Attorney general, C.S.A., 100–101

Benjamin, Sec. of War Judah P., 13, 22–23
Bird, Edgeworth, 137
Board of Slave Claims, 10, 12, 47, 59, 65, 99, 133–38, 165, 195 (n. 2)
Bragg, Atty. Gen. Thomas, 100–101
Bread riots, 73, 105
Brockenbrough, Maj. J. B., 136–37
Bureau of Conscription, C.S.A. *See* Conscript Bureau, C.S.A.
Bureau of Engineers, C.S.A. *See* Engineer Bureau, C.S.A.

Campbell, Asst. Sec. of War John A., 102
Clark, Gov. Henry T., 15, 23–25, 29–30
Class conflict, 3, 81–84, 88–89, 118–20, 188 (nn. 4–5, 8), 201 (n. 62)
Commissary Department, C.S.A., 25, 33
Confiscation Acts, U.S.A., 17, 28, 197 (n. 48)
Congress, C.S.A., 7, 70, 129, 132–36; and 1863 elections, 121
Conscript Bureau, C.S.A., 6, 10–11, 120; and control of slave impressment process, 133–52 passim
Conscription: and 1862 Conscription Act, 20, 43; and slave impressment, 73, 80, 94; and 20-slave exemption, 87, 203 (n. 91)
Constitution, C.S.A., 4; and slave impressment, 29. *See also* Federalism
Cooper, Adj. and Insp. Gen. Samuel, 78, 141
County courts, Virginia. *See* Virginia county courts

Davis, Jefferson, 8, 11, 37, 105, 113, 120; November 1864 message to Congress, 132–33; and proposals to arm slaves, 133, 152, 155–56
Dimmock, Capt. Charles H., 53

Engineer Bureau, C.S.A.: personnel, 12–13, 23, 47; and hired labor, 21–22; and impressed labor, 22–24, 26–28, 33, 37, 45, 103–6, 136, 139, 150, 159; and cooperation with state and local governments, 33, 37, 43, 74–75, 96, 105–6, 109–10, 116–17, 128–31, 144–45, 148, 158; and care provided to workers, 49–63, 69–70; and exemptions from slave impressment, 115–16, 147; and centralization of slave impressment, 120, 132–33
Engineer Department, Virginia, 24–26
Engineer Hospital, 56, 59–62. *See also* Impressed slaves: and medical care; Medical Department, C.S.A.

Fayetteville, N.C., 7, 24, 105, 108
Federalism: and theories of states' rights,

2–3, 125–26, 129–30, 158, 163–64, 187–88 (n. 2); and Confederate Constitution, 4–5; and slave impressment laws, 5, 9, 17, 99, 102; and strength of state governments, 9–10, 99–100, 103, 105–10, 127–31, 142, 149–52, 156, 163; and growth of Confederate government, 10–11, 130–31, 137–38, 143–44, 152, 156, 164; and cooperation between Engineer Bureau and Commonwealth of Virginia, 123, 129, 144–45

Fort Caswell, 7, 64

Fort Fisher, 7, 13, 139

Fort Monroe, 13, 22, 26, 64

French, Col. S. Bassett, 75, 112

Gatlin, Adj. Gen. Richard C., 58, 65–66, 107–8, 142–43

General Assembly, Virginia. *See* Virginia General Assembly

Gilmer, Maj. Gen. Jeremy Francis, 102, 139; biographical sketch, 12–13; direct involvement in slave impressment, 33–35, 38, 52–54, 75–76, 85–86, 105, 107, 123, 141, 145; actions taken to protect agriculture, 95–96

Goldsboro, N.C., 7, 41, 128, 139

Gould, William Benjamin (escaped slave), 64

Hill, Maj. Gen. Daniel Harvey, 28–29, 76

Holden, William W.: support for slave impressment, 40–43, 87; campaign for governor of North Carolina, 126

Home front, economic activities of, 6–7, 29, 79, 127, 157–58, 164, 188 (n. 11), 200 (n. 46); railroads, 5, 15, 84, 140, 147; agriculture, 15, 28, 72–73, 94–97, 141; industry, 15, 83–85, 147; blockade-runners, 139. *See also* Class conflict; Slave hiring; Women

Impressed slaves: testimony of, 12, 45–47, 56–58, 64, 66–67, 159, 163; work performed, 47–50, 193 (n. 5); and punishment, 49–50; and shelter, 51; and rations, 51–55; and medical care, 55–61, 196 (n. 34); and opportunities for escape, 65–66, 156; and memory, 159–63. *See also* African Americans; Runaway slaves

Impressment, food and supplies, 73, 95, 203 (n. 93)

Impressment, slaveholders' objections to, 2, 7, 10–11, 19, 38, 44, 98–99, 134–35, 143–46, 164; and law, 28–29; and agriculture, 42–43, 72–97 passim; and health of slaves, 46–47, 54–55, 68–70; and runaway slaves, 66–68, 113; and compensation for lost slaves, 135. *See also* Home front, economic activities of; Runaway slaves

Impressment agents, 11, 25–28

Impressment laws, national, 3–4, 9, 99, 151; of March 1863, 102, 105; of February 1864, 121–23, 133; of September 1864, 127

Impressment laws, state, 9, 31–32, 151; Florida, 32, 101; Louisiana, 32, 101; Mississippi, 32–33, 101; Alabama, 33, 101, 143; Georgia, 33, 101, 143; South Carolina, 33, 143; Tennessee, 191 (n. 63)

—North Carolina, 9, 20, 101; of December 1862, 38–41

—Virginia, 9, 20, 28, 101; of October 1862, 32, 46, 105; resolutions to protect agriculture, 74, 144; resolutions related to national law, 103, 135, 143; of March 1865, 149–52

Impressment quotas

—North Carolina: March–April 1863, 76–77, 168, 171; September 1863, 105–8, 173; October 1863, 108, 173; December 1863, 108; September 1864, 138, 145; December 1864, 142, 178–79; January 1865, 142–43

—Virginia: October 1862, 33–35, 72, 75, 165, 170; November 1862, 35–37, 72,

75, 166, 170; January 1863, 37–38, 72, 167; March 1863, 74–76, 169–70; August 1863, 105–6, 172; January 1864, 109–14, 135, 174–75; December 1864, 133, 144–50, 180–81; March 1865, 133, 149–52, 182–83; September 1864, 138, 141, 145, 176–77; October 1864, 141, 145

Johnston, Gen. Albert Sidney, 12
Johnston, Maj. Gen. Joseph E., 27
Jones, Maj. Gen. Samuel, 37

Keyes, Atty. Gen. Wade, 55, 136

Lamb, Col. William, 12, 140
Lawton, Quartermaster Gen. A. R., 141
Leadbetter, Maj. Danville, 12, 22
Lee, Gen. Robert E.: and slave impressment in Virginia, 11, 13, 27, 39, 140–41, 148; and Wilmington fortifications, 138–40; and proposals to arm slaves, 153
Letcher, Gov. John, 8, 20–21, 27, 42; biographical sketch, 14; and actions taken to enforce slave impressment, 33–34, 36–38, 43–44, 97, 105–7, 113, 115; and statements of support for slave impressment, 52, 163; and exemptions from impressment, 74, 84–85
Longstreet, Lt. Gen. James A., 152
Lower South, 6, 155
Lynchburg, Va., 5, 7, 21, 37, 105, 111, 150; and resisting impressment, 147–48

Magruder, Gen. John Bankhead, 6, 142, 147; biographical sketch, 13; and slave impressment, 18–19, 22–23, 27, 37–38
McClellan, Maj. Gen. George B., 26–27
Medical Department, C.S.A.: and hired slave labor, 5, 15, 85, 123, 132, 147; personnel, 55, 59–62, 69; and medical care for impressed slaves, 55–56, 58–60; and investigation of Engineer Hospital, 60–62
Munford, Sec. of the Commonwealth George, 33–34, 110, 115, 145–48, 150

Native Americans, 16–17, 21; Lumbee, 21; Pamunkey, 21
Negro Labor Battalions, 10–11, 141, 152–53
Newspapers, support for slave impressment by, 39–70 passim, 106
North Carolina militia, 11, 82, 107–9, 130, 142–44
North Carolina State Legislature, 7, 19, 153

Peninsula (Virginia), 6–7, 18–19, 22–23, 27, 37–38
Perry, Aaron (impressed slave), 160–62
Petersburg, Va., 7, 20, 28, 58, 64, 105, 140–58 passim
Piedmont, 81; Virginia, 34–35, 38, 81–82, 200 (n. 32); North Carolina, 76–77, 108

Quartermaster's Department, C.S.A., 141; and hired slave labor, 85, 116, 147

Randolph, Sec. of War George W., 33, 84
Richmond, Va.: and fortifications, 7, 20–21, 26–27, 33–34, 105, 123, 140–58 passim; as Confederate capital, 25; and city government, 37–38, 106–7, 204 (n. 22); and smallpox, 58
Rives, Capt. Alfred Landon, 12, 13, 21, 37; as Acting Chief of Engineer Bureau, 23, 26, 27, 105, 107, 117, 136, 150
Roanoke Island, N.C., 24–25
Runaway slaves, 63–65, 68, 95–96, 113–14, 134, 156–57; and "self-emancipation," 1, 6, 38, 63, 196 (n. 45), 196–97 (n. 46), 197 (n. 47); impressment as cause of, 17, 65–68, 122, 197 (n. 48), 198 (n. 69); recaptured, 22,

Index / 231

122–23; and "ameliorative" reform, 69–70, 198 (n. 72); and Virginia, 144, 146, 157, 184–85, 205 (n. 36)
Ryland, Charles H., 60

Saltville, Va., 7, 37, 105, 111, 158
Secretary of War, C.S.A., 8, 14, 30
Seddon, Sec. of War James A., 8, 37, 68, 70, 154; biographical sketch, 14; and direct participation in slave impressment, 52–54, 110, 113, 122, 133, 138, 140–41; and actions taken to protect agriculture, 74, 76, 79, 96, 105, 122, 126, 138; and cooperation with state leaders, 125–26, 129
Slave Claims Board. *See* Board of Slave Claims
Slave hiring, 16, 22, 96, 111, 122, 156–58, 161, 202–3 (n. 88); and agriculture, 71–72; and exemptions from impressment, 115–16. *See also* Engineer Bureau, C.S.A.; Medical Department, C.S.A.; Quartermaster's Department, C.S.A.; War Department, C.S.A.
Smith, Maj. Gen. Gustavus, 39
Smith, Gov. William "Extra Billy," 8, 10, 11, 66, 98; biographical sketch, 14; and statements of support for slave impressment, 52, 109, 133, 149, 163; and actions taken to enforce slave impressment, 97, 100, 109–14, 123, 135, 144–52; and revoking or reducing quotas, 112–14, 148; and centralization of slave impressment, 114–15, 120, 130–44 passim; and complaints from slaveholders, 117, 121–22; and plan to enlist slaves as soldiers, 152–53
Sons of Confederate Veterans, 160, 162
Southern Claims Commission, 12, 66
Spence, W. A., 136–37
Stanard, Lt. John B., 12, 27, 34–35, 60, 85, 136, 145, 148; and recommendations for impressment laws, 102–3
State legislatures. *See* General Assembly, Virginia; North Carolina State Legislature
States' rights. *See* Federalism
Stevens, Col. Walter H., 12, 27, 34, 85–86, 102–23 passim, 140, 149–50

Talcott, Capt. Thomas M., 12, 55
Tax-in-kind, 73, 95, 203 (n. 93)
Tidewater Virginia, 36–38, 82
Tomlin, Maj. H. B., 18, 21
Tredegar Iron Works, 15, 84, 200 (n. 36)

Vance, Gov. Zebulon Baird, 3, 8, 10, 19, 42, 46, 70, 187 (n. 2); biographical sketch, 15; and election campaigns, 29–30, 125–26, 208 (n. 104); and statements of support for slave impressment, 30, 39–40, 52, 146, 152, 163; and actions taken to enforce slave impressment, 43–44, 76, 97, 100, 107–9, 113, 123, 142–44; and actions taken to protect agriculture, 77–78, 96, 109, 126; and dispute with General Whiting, 123–27; and centralization of slave impressment, 127–43 passim
Vest, Richard S., 59–62
Virginia county courts, 8–11, 34, 79, 81–82, 85–86, 135, 149, 204 (n. 21); Albemarle County, 34–35, 117–20; Henrico County, 37–38, 66, 106–7, 151; and declining support for slave impressment, 106–20 passim; and December 1864 impressment quotas, 144–48
Virginia General Assembly, 7, 19–20, 74–75, 106, 135, 149, 152–53, 205 (n. 36)

Waddell, Col. James D., 136–37
War Department, C.S.A.: and hired slave labor, 5, 15–16, 84, 116, 120, 161; and cooperation with state governments, 17, 35, 107, 121, 144–45; and centralization of slave impressment, 130–31, 138

232 / Index

Watts, Atty. Gen. Thomas Hill, 100, 143
Weldon, N.C., 7, 41, 65, 108, 128, 139, 142
Whiting, Maj. Gen. William H. C., 12, 43, 103, 130, 142; biographical sketch, 13–14; takes command at Wilmington, 30; and requests for slave labor, 30–31, 39, 41, 76–78, 100, 107–9, 126–27, 138–40; and failure to return slaves, 73, 78–79, 82, 123, 125, 143; and dispute with Governor Vance, 123–27

Wilmington, N.C.: and fortifications, 4, 7, 13–14, 21, 24, 38–39, 67, 128, 136, 143, 158; value to Confederacy, 31, 139–40; and demand for labor, 39, 41, 78, 105, 107–8, 123–25, 138–39, 160; and yellow fever, 58, 64
Women: and agricultural work, 73, 90–93, 157, 202 (n. 78); and petitions about slave impressment, 80, 88–90, 119, 201 (n. 62); enslaved, 92–94, 202 (n. 80), 202–3 (n. 88)

CPSIA information can be obtained at www.ICGtesting.com
Printed in the USA
LVOW08s2248290615

444314LV00005B/6/P